Praise for *The Power of Money*

"In *The Power of Money*, economist and long-time World Economic Forum contributor Paul Sheard masterfully unpacks one of the most foundational yet confounding aspects of the modern economy—money—and shows that its creation rests on a true public-private partnership. Policymakers, business people, members of civil society, and anyone looking to better understand complex and often vexing policy issues should read this book."

—Klaus Schwab, Founder and Executive Chairman
of the World Economic Forum

"The consequences of monetary and fiscal policy are now felt more directly than at any time in decades, and there could not be a more timely exploration of the issue—essential as it is to understanding not only economics but also politics and even international affairs today—than *The Power of Money*. Paul Sheard cuts through the confusion and jargon that too often surrounds the topic and explains the real power of money in the world today."

—The Hon. Dr. Kevin Rudd, 26th Prime Minister of
Australia and Global President of the Asia Society

"In many ways, money makes the world go round, never more than now. Paul Sheard's *The Power of Money* provides provocative and interesting perspectives for anyone concerned with our monetary future."

—Lawrence H. Summers, Charles W. Eliot University Professor at
Harvard University and 71st Secretary of the United States Treasury

"Paul Sheard has done a brilliant job explaining money. He skillfully sets *The Power of Money* apart from other books on the topic by taking often misunderstood issues and clarifying them in a thoughtful and approachable way. Whether you're an economist or someone who simply is interested in financial and economic affairs, this book is for you."

—Douglas L. Peterson, President and CEO of S&P Global

"An unusual, lucid explanation of what money really is and how it works, which can be easily grasped by the lay reader. This is highly useful reading at a time when innovations such as bitcoin and policy experiments like quantitative easing have made it more important than ever to understand how money does—and does not—really work."

—Gillian Tett, Chair of the US Editorial Board and
Editor-at-Large of the *Financial Times*

"Paul Sheard treats critical topics that no one else touches. If you care about the economy and the future, and your portfolio, you must read this book."

—Robert L. Dilenschneider, Founder and CEO of the Dilenschneider Group

"In this must-read book, Paul Sheard pulls back the veil, showing how governments, commercial banks, central banks, and financial markets all play a part in the creation of money. His book sheds light on such topics as inequality, financial crises, the future of the euro, and cryptocurrencies. Read it to learn and to gain an edge in the investing world."
—Stephanie Kelton, Professor of Economics and Public Policy at Stony Brook University and Author of *The Deficit Myth*

"Paul Sheard deftly brings clarity to one of the most abstract concepts ever created by humanity—money. Learn how the world creates, enables, measures, and rewards value exchange and understand the *Power of Money*."
—R. "Ray" Wang, Founder and CEO of Constellation Research, Inc. and two-time Bestselling Author

"*The Power of Money* is uniquely valuable in at least three dimensions: it explains eloquently the role of money in the workings of a modern economy, it dispels convincingly many popular misconceptions about money, and it reflects thoughtfully on such big issues as the independence of central banks and the reserve currency status of the US dollar. I highly recommend it to scholars, industry professionals, policymakers, and the general public."
—Yiping Huang, Professor of Economics and Director of the Institute of Digital Finance at Peking University

"Business leaders, policymakers, and money managers will find this book indispensable in challenging and reshaping their current assumptions about economic and monetary matters. Japanese policymakers in particular will be well served by giving it close study. It is high time for economic experts to refocus, relearn, and reconsider what money is and what it can do, lest economic mismanagement and inefficiency result. I highly recommend this book."
—Yoshihiko Miyauchi, Senior Chairman of ORIX Corporation

"Paul Sheard explains some complex concepts—how money is created, the role of government debt, what the Federal Reserve does—in a very plain English manner. He also explains why some common assumptions about how money works are wrong or at least not the full story. No prior background in finance or economics is required. This is a very lucid book about a very important and complicated subject."
—Timothy Massad, Research Fellow at Harvard Kennedy School and 12th Chairman of the Commodity Futures Trading Commission

"*The Power of Money* is a wide-ranging, lucidly written assessment of the future of money and how it is interwoven in the fabric of economic life. Particularly noteworthy are the author's timely policy recommendations on such critical issues as the interplay of monetary and fiscal policy and the impact of financial sanctions on the reserve currency status of the US dollar. This important and accessible contribution to scholarship concludes with a trenchant discussion of cryptocurrencies—the latest innovation in the history of money."
—Noel V. Lateef, President and CEO of the Foreign Policy Association

THE
POWER
OF
MONEY

Also by Paul Sheard

International Adjustment and the Japanese Firm (editor)
Japanese Firms, Finance, and Markets (editor)
The Crisis of Main Bank Capitalism (in Japanese)
Corporate Mega Restructuring (in Japanese)

THE POWER OF MONEY

How Governments and Banks Create Money and Help Us All Prosper

PAUL SHEARD

Matt Holt Books
An Imprint of BenBella Books, Inc.
Dallas, TX

Matt Holt is an imprint of BenBella Books, Inc.
10440 N. Central Expressway
Suite 800
Dallas, TX 75231
benbellabooks.com
Send feedback to feedback@benbellabooks.com

BenBella and *Matt Holt* are federally registered trademarks.

Printed in the United States of America
10 9 8 7 6 5 4 3 2 1

Library of Congress Control Number: 2022046868
ISBN 9781637743157 (hardcover)
ISBN 9781637743164 (electronic)

Editing by Katie Dickman
Copyediting by James Fraleigh
Proofreading by Kellie Doherty and Isabelle Rubio
Indexing by Amy Murphy
Text design and composition by PerfecType, Nashville, TN
Author photo courtesy of S&P Global
Cover design by Brigid Pearson
Cover image © Shutterstock / Andrei Kuzmik
Printed by Lake Book Manufacturing

For curious kindred spirits—and for my family.

CONTENTS

INTRODUCTION

Money makes the world go 'round.
John Kander and Fred Ebb, Cabaret

M oney really does make the world spin—at least the *economic* world. Without money the economy as we know it would not exist, and, to borrow from Thomas Hobbes, life would likely be "solitary, poor, nasty, brutish, and short."[1] Imagine if the only way to obtain the things you needed from others was to offer things you have or the services you could provide in exchange. That's called bartering, and it is a recipe for not much getting done in the world; economic activity would be highly localized and inefficient. Money is so intrinsic to the economy that barter economies likely never really existed, other than in the primordial mists of time and the pages of economics textbooks. Money allows everyone in the global economy to trade with one another *indirectly*, over space and through time.

This is a book about money, but it is not a book about how to *make* money: there are plenty of those around and better people to write them than me. Rather, I *explain* money—what it is, how it comes

1

into existence, and how governments, commercial banks, and central banks create it and influence its creation.[2] Understanding money better might help you make money, but I'll leave that to you.

Why does the world need another book about money? Because, for all of its importance—or perhaps because of it—misunderstandings, confusion, and controversies about money abound. I'm willing to bet that most of what you think you know about money is suspect, needs serious qualification, or is flat-out wrong. Here are a few misconceptions many people have:

- *Money is a simple, unambiguous concept.* In fact, it is a surprisingly slippery concept. There is no easy way to define and measure it, and it means different things to different people.
- *It is central banks like the Federal Reserve in the United States, the European Central Bank, and the Bank of Japan that "print" money.* They can and do in a narrow sense, but it's governments and commercial banks that really "print," or create, money, in the first place.
- *Central banks have created trillions of dollars, euros, pounds, yen, and other currencies since the Global Financial Crisis, and again in response to the economic impact of the COVID-19 pandemic.* They have not so much *created* money as they have *converted* it from one form (government bonds) into another (deposits of banks at the central bank).
- *By racking up such a mountain of debt, the US government is imposing a huge burden on our grandchildren and mortgaging their future.* In fact, government debt is an asset for those who hold it and helps society transfer purchasing power (money) into the future. While the government may need to withdraw money from circulation through taxation, it doesn't really need to repay its debt as such.
- *The unequal distribution of money in the world—income and wealth inequality—is an abhorrent and avoidable aspect of market economies.* In fact, it is more a feature than a bug of

a prosperity-generating system, and has more going for it than much of the usual hand-wringing would suggest.

- *The newest monetary kids on the block—Bitcoin and other cryptocurrencies—are set to displace money as we know it.* More likely, when they grow up, most of them will be out of a job.

WHAT IS MONEY?

Given the many misconceptions about money, that question turns out to be trickier to answer than it seems. To the ordinary person, "money" is often synonymous with "financial wealth": if someone is very rich, they have "a lot of money." But much of that "money" would not be money as economists define it. Financial wealth, particularly of the very wealthy, typically comprises a range of financial assets such as bank deposits, money market funds, mutual funds, portfolios of individual stocks and bonds, and such "alternative investments" as hedge funds and private equity funds.

Economists, on the other hand, have two ways of defining money: one conceptual, the other empirical. Following the nineteenth-century economist William Stanley Jevons, virtually every economic textbook defines money in terms of the three functions it performs: as a *unit of account*, a *medium of exchange*, and a *store of value*.[3] This functional definition does not identify what money *is* but rather what it has to be able to *do* in order to be considered money. Economists empirically classify money into various categories according to who issues it (the government or commercial banks), how easy it is to use (think a checking account versus a time deposit or a certificate of deposit), and how it functions as a store of value (more on that in the next chapter).

Money being a *unit of account* means that prices are quoted in that unit: dollars and cents in the US, yen (and, in the old days, sen) in Japan, euros and cents in much of Europe, pounds and pence in the United Kingdom, and so on, depending on the country. Unit of account status also makes a currency a common benchmark for comparing the value and facilitating the exchange of the myriad goods, services, and assets in an economy. The price of something is just the number of units of money you need to buy it. The unit of account aspect of money extends to all the prices of goods, services, and financial instruments (assets and liabilities) in the economy.[4] In the US, virtually everything is quoted in US dollars.

We use money as a *medium of exchange* when we buy things. I give Starbucks five dollars, and Starbucks gives me a cup of coffee; now I have coffee, and Starbucks has five dollars. Money being a medium of exchange is what allows an advanced, dispersed market economy to operate and prosper. As long as I have enough money, I can obtain anything that is for sale: the person selling me the item doesn't have to worry about where I got the money, nor do I have to worry about what that person is going to do with it. Money breaks those nexuses on both sides.

The economy produces an amazing array of goods and services, thanks to millennia of civilizational progress and associated scientific discovery and technological and social innovation. All of these goods and services are transacted and tallied in a simple common denominator: money. The US economy produced $25 trillion worth of goods and services in the most recent year (to third quarter 2022). Think about it: we are able to summarize virtually the entire economic activity of the giant US economy with one simple number in an agreed-upon common unit.[5]

Money is also a means of transferring purchasing power from the present into the future. If I have twenty dollars in my pocket, I can spend it today or tomorrow. Money—or financial assets more broadly—allows people to save, by transferring some of the purchasing power they receive today to a later date; and also to borrow, by bringing forward some of the purchasing power they expect to acquire in the future, to enjoy today. Money connects the economic past, present, and future.

Money being a good *store of value* means that it holds its value, reasonably well at least, over time. If I have a hundred dollars today,

I can spend it on a fancy meal now or put it away and have that nice meal in a year's time. If I decide to wait, it would be nice if that hundred dollars still fetches me the fancy meal I was looking forward to having, rather than just a club sandwich at the local diner. That's where inflation comes in.

The hundred-dollar-meal exemplifies stored value but is a little inaccurate because of inflation. In a market economy, prices of individual goods and services rise and fall in response to changes in supply and demand. That's a good thing because it helps scarce resources to be allocated efficiently in a society. What matters for money holding its value over time is not that prices of *individual* goods and services remain stable but that the *overall* price level does. The overall price level refers to the value of a "representative" basket of goods and services that a typical consumer might be expected to buy. Changes in this "cost of living" are what the consumer price index (CPI) and other, similar price indices aim to capture. In the modern world, society assigns central banks the primary responsibility for maintaining the purchasing power of money over time or at least not letting it erode too rapidly. Most central banks do this by targeting a CPI inflation rate of about 2 percent.[6] More on all of this in chapter three.

The store of value aspect of money is very broad: all financial assets serve as stores of value in that they allow purchasing power to be transferred across time. But the riskiness of financial assets varies, and with it their reliability. If a financial asset has to be a stable or very stable store of value to be considered money, that narrows down the range of acceptable candidates. But where to draw the line? The real value of banknotes and other fixed nominal claims can be eroded by inflation (or increased by deflation). Banks can default on their deposits, often calling their stability as a store of value into question. Governments counter that risk by insuring bank deposits (up to certain per depositor, per bank limits, currently $250,000 in the US). US Treasury securities are widely considered "risk free" (in terms of coupon payments and the repayment of principal), but despite being a highly stable store of value, they are not conventionally classified as being money (I take issue with this). Over the long run, stocks, particularly a well-diversified portfolio, have proven quite good stores of value, in addition to increasing their value handsomely.[7]

THE TWO ECONOMIES: REAL AND MONETARY

The economy actually comprises two different but intricately related economies: a *real* economy and a *monetary* economy. The real economy is what Gross Domestic Product (GDP) tries to measure: the economy of goods and services that businesses produce using capital equipment and human labor and that consumers buy and consume either now ("perishables" or "nondurable goods," such as fresh food and taxi rides) or over time ("consumer durables," such as personal computers and automobiles).

The monetary economy is the financial mirror of the real economy. It keeps tabs on the real economy and oils its wheels. The monetary economy is part of the real economy in that the financial and monetary system consumes and employs real resources: computers, telecommunications networks, managers and workers in the financial sector, and the buildings and other capital equipment they use; the financial sector and its output are part of what is measured as GDP. But the monetary economy is also largely virtual and imagined, a world full of symbols, conventions, and beliefs.

It is tempting to think of money as a thing, as something real and tangible. And while it is certainly used to obtain real, tangible things, money is really a "social construct"—one or more conventions that society adopts and agrees to follow. As historian Yuval Noah Harari has put it, money "involved the creation of a new inter-subjective reality that exists solely in people's shared imaginations."[8]

Money in the modern world is "fiat" money, or money by decree: a twenty-dollar bill has twice the value of a ten-dollar bill because society deems that to be so, even though the cost of producing the different bills is the same (even more so for monetary entries in banks' computer ledgers). True, banknotes and coins are real things you can see and hold in your hand. But the value or cost of the paper, metal, and labor that goes into making currency is just a fraction of what that physical money can buy (the difference accrues to the government as what is called "seigniorage," one of the trickier monetary words to spell). And physical money is just a small fraction of the total amount of money that we recognize as existing. Most money is digital—numbers in electronic ledgers. If you have a thousand dollars "in the bank," the bank has an electronic record in its computer system containing such information as your name, your account number, and the number of dollars: one thousand. The bank invests in a bunch of assets—loans, corporate bonds, other risk assets, and government bonds—but, other than some vault cash and reserves at the country's central bank, there is really no money "in the bank."[9] Some people rail against the purported fraudulent nature of this "fractional reserve banking system," but it is really a feature of the modern economic system, by and large, a desirable one—not a bug.

Money is society's way of tallying who has a claim to the output of the economy and the economic machinery (literal and figurative) that produces it. We can think of money as points that represent purchasing power, now and into the future.

Money exhibits very strong network effects; there is a big advantage to everyone being on the same "platform." It also solves a coordination problem: as long as I know that other people in society will accept the money I have as payment for the goods, services, or assets they will transfer to me, I will be prepared to receive it in the first place. Money doesn't have to have any intrinsic value, but it will have value if everyone agrees to use it. But how does everybody in society agree to use the same thing as their unit of account, medium of exchange, and store of value? Involving the government in producing and regulating money helps solve that coordination challenge and ensures that the network effects of money are fully captured. A key part of the "fiat" in fiat money is the government's ability to decree which money it will accept in payment for taxes— that is, what it will accept from me that will extinguish my debt to it.

MONEY AS DEBT

This underscores another key aspect of money: money thought of as debt.[10] Take a look at a twenty-dollar bill. It is a Federal Reserve Note, a liability of the country's central bank, the Federal Reserve, and has printed on it: "This note is legal tender for all debts, public and private." Not all countries make this clear on their banknotes, but the US puts it in black and white (or should I say green and white?): this banknote is an asset that its holder can use to extinguish debts.

The bill also has "The United States of America" printed on it, as well as the seal of the United States Treasury, and is signed by the Treasurer of the United States and the Secretary of the Treasury, two distinct positions and people within the US government.[11] The Federal Reserve is an agency of the US government, and banknotes are a form of US government debt.

Because banknotes are technically debts of the central bank, they appear on the liability side of a central bank's balance sheet. But what exactly does the central bank owe? In a modern fiat-money system, nothing except the banknote itself. A banknote, such as a Federal Reserve Note, may be debt, but it is a special kind of debt: one that never has to be repaid. The days are long gone when you could present a banknote to its issuer and demand and receive the gold or silver backing it. If, hypothetically, you were to present that twenty-dollar bill at the Federal Reserve and demand that the Fed repay the debt it owes you, the only way it could do so would be to turn around and give you back the twenty-dollar bill, or maybe two ten-dollar bills or twenty one-dollar bills. However, if you owe the government twenty dollars in taxes, you can extinguish that debt by presenting the twenty-dollar bill (after depositing it in a bank account). The government's liability is an asset to you and can be used to wipe out the debt you owe the government by way of your tax obligation.

There is a funny thing about what we normally think of as money: some of it is a debt of the central bank, which means the government, and some of it—in fact most of it—is a debt of commercial banks. And it is a feature of our monetary system, one we largely take for granted, that money in the form of banknotes (and coins) and as commercial bank deposits are exchangeable at par—that is, one for one.[12] If you have one hundred dollars in the bank, the bank owes you one hundred dollars; if you withdraw that hundred dollars from the bank, the central bank (the government) now owes you a hundred dollars instead. By the same token, when you deposit a hundred-dollar banknote into your bank account, you are changing your asset from a government debt into a commercial bank debt. This is a manifestation of a broader point and theme of this book: governments, central banks, and commercial banks are joined at the hip in the creation of money, and fiscal policy and monetary policy are not as distinct and separate as commonly supposed.

WHAT'S AHEAD IN THE BOOK

In **chapter one**, I explore how money in today's world comes into existence—or "into circulation," as the jargon goes. Who actually *creates* the money that we earn when we work, borrow from a bank, or receive when we sell something—or that the government hands out to us? It turns out that commercial banks, the government, and the central bank are all involved in creating money, conceived in the narrow sense of banknotes and bank deposits. Think of all that money (about $20 trillion in the US at the time of writing) sitting in a huge bucket. Banks, the government, and the central bank all have hoses for pouring money in and scoops for taking it out. But, as we will see, those hoses are intertwined in a complex way. If we conceive of money in the broadest sense of financial wealth, we see another hose and scoop, one connected to financial markets, particularly the stock market.

In **chapter two**, I debunk much of the misunderstanding and alarm that surround government debt levels (about $31 trillion in the US at the time of writing). Running a budget deficit is one way the government gets money into circulation—in principle, a good thing. The government usually turns that money into a different form, that of government bonds (Treasuries in the US). Government bonds allow households, businesses, and investors to accumulate wealth and transfer purchasing power into the future. Too much government spending and too high a stock of government debt can create problems for the economy now and in the future, but not because the debt has to be repaid or because it is a burden on future generations. The government, as part of its fiscal policy, may have to raise taxes to drain consumer purchasing power and tamp down inflation, but it never has to tax in order to raise the money to pay down its debt.

In **chapter three** (and in the Technical Handout), I explain how central banks and commercial banks fit into the money-creation process and how the "monetary policy" implemented by central banks works. Much of the money in the economy is created when commercial banks extend loans. Banks don't "lend out" the deposits they "take in"; rather, they create deposits when they lend. Central banks use their control over interest rates to stimulate or restrain bank lending, as needed, doing so to keep inflation in check and the economy humming along.

In response to the Great Recession of 2007–2009, as triggered by the Global Financial Crisis, and more recently in response to the even sharper February–April 2020 recession triggered by the COVID-19 pandemic, major central banks eased monetary policy by pumping up their balance sheets, in a policy known as quantitative easing (QE).[13] In **chapter four**, I explain what QE is and how it works. QE is commonly described, and often decried, as massive "money printing" by central banks, but this is misleading. When QE involves the central bank buying its own government's bonds, as it usually does, it is better viewed as changing the form of the "money" created by prior and ongoing budget deficits. QE can only "pump" money (liquidity) into the system by "sucking" assets (usually government bonds) out.

In **chapter five**, I zoom out and look at money through a wider lens. The real economy and the monetary economy together produce an enormous amount of wealth and prosperity, but that wealth is very unevenly distributed within and across societies. Reducing inequality has become one of the clarion calls of our times. Here I look at some of the economic forces behind these wealth disparities, particularly in relation to the emergence of a relatively tiny cohort of the über-rich. I argue that extreme wealth inequality is, to a significant extent, a by-product of prosperity-generating market processes and that, in purely economic terms, the über-rich do much less harm than is often claimed or assumed. If the government, acting for society, deems it desirable to improve the plight of the poor, it can do so (or at least try to) independently of whether and how it "taxes the rich."

In **chapter six**, I consider the flip side: money can also wreak havoc on an economy and society. Financial crises come in many shapes and sizes, and are a recurrent theme in modern economic history. The monetary economy helps the real economy do its job of generating prosperity, but the former occasionally goes off the rails and takes the latter with it. There is an inherent mismatch between the *liquidity* of the financial claims that the monetary economy generates and the *illiquidity* of the productive assets that comprise the real economy. This mismatch creates the risk of "runs" on the banking system and, in turn, financial crises. The central bank's role as the "lender of last resort" empowers it to prevent financial crises and quell those that occur. I argue in this chapter that the Federal Reserve erred in not acting as lender of last resort to Lehman Brothers in September 2008.

In Europe, the Global Financial Crisis of 2007–2009 morphed into the euro area sovereign debt crisis, which was bookended by a more localized sovereign debt crisis that erupted in Greece in early 2010 and subsided when Greece received a major rescue package from the European Union and the International Monetary Fund in mid-2015. In **chapter seven**, I argue that the euro area sovereign debt crisis manifested a deep structural flaw in the economic architecture of the euro area: member states have to pool their monetary sovereignty (by forming a single currency and monetary union), but do not also pool their fiscal sovereignty (by centralizing budgetary matters and forming a fiscal union). They cede their monetary sovereignty to the European Central Bank while retaining responsibility for their fiscal affairs. The situation that results is tantamount to member nations having to borrow in a foreign currency, one they cannot produce at will. Worse, members of the euro area have to accept stringent fiscal restraints.

The book to this point examines single-currency systems, those of individual countries or, in the case of the euro, of multiple countries sharing the same currency. In **chapter eight**, I zoom out in a different way and look at how the myriad currencies or monetary systems of the world fit together and interact with one another. Floating exchange rates, reserve currencies, and the outsized role of the Federal Reserve all play important roles in this process.

In **chapter nine**, I switch digital gears and look at the latest innovation—a truly remarkable one—in the millennia-spanning history of money: Bitcoin and other cryptocurrencies. Cryptocurrencies are a product of disruptive twenty-first-century technological innovation and break new monetary ground. Developed out of dissatisfaction with, and as an insurgent challenge to, sovereign-centered monetary systems, cryptocurrencies eschew central authority and gatekeeping intermediaries by using novel "blockchain" technology to operate a decentralized peer-to-peer currency and payments system.

As audacious and technologically impressive as Bitcoin and other cryptocurrencies are, they are not as detached from the legacy monetary system as they appear, and are likely to struggle to compete with it when it comes to fulfilling the three canonical roles of money: unit of account, medium of exchange, and store of value. Cryptocurrencies are likely to find a permanent niche in the monetary ecosystem, however, and may still be early in their innovation cycle, making definitive predictions treacherous.

At the very least, the advent of cryptocurrencies is shaking up the existing sovereign-based monetary system: every major central bank is now actively exploring the feasibility and desirability of introducing its own central bank digital currency. Rather than seriously challenge (let alone displace) the traditional monetary system, it seems more likely that cryptocurrencies and their foundational technologies, by spurring innovation, will help to reshape it.

Last, I offer **concluding thoughts** to tie these threads together with an eye to the future of money.

1

MONEY CREATION: A POWERFUL PARTNERSHIP

We thus have side by side State-Money or Money-
Proper and Bank-Money or Acknowledgments-of-
Debt . . . But the tendency is towards a preponderant
importance for Bank-Money . . . and towards State-
Money occupying a definitely subsidiary position.

John Maynard Keynes, 1930[1]

Where does money come from? That is, how does money
spring into existence or enter circulation in the modern
economy? The answer is crucial to understanding how the
economy operates and is influenced by the economic policies of governments and **central banks**.[2] When it comes to dissecting today's
economic controversies, the dynamics of money creation hold the
key to separating fact from fiction.

The question of how money is created today differs from that of how the institution of money came into existence in the first place and developed through history. There are many fascinating histories of money.[3] They tell a story of money coming into existence and slowly evolving over the centuries into one of the key institutional underpinnings of the modern market economy. Money is a testament to the power of human ingenuity.

The typical account emphasizes the idea that moneys of various forms evolved to eliminate the manifest inefficiencies associated with trade in a barter economy, solving the "double coincidence of wants" problem. Let's say I have shoes and you have bread, and I want your bread, but you want vegetables, not my shoes. Then I have to find someone with vegetables who wants my shoes so that I can get them as payment for the bread I want from you. How much more convenient and efficient it would be if there were one common unit and medium of exchange in which we could all transact. Money coming into existence as a solution to the double coincidence of wants problem, and thereby unlocking the gains from trade and propelling economic prosperity, is a compelling story.[4] It probably didn't take our ancestors long, however, to figure out how to ditch barter in favor of some form of money or a system for keeping tabs on who owes what to whom; there is even some evidence that monkeys can be taught to use money.[5] Barter likely gave way to some form of money very early in human civilizational development.

Metal coins issued by kings and emperors feature prominently in the early part of money's history, as the abundant museum collections of coins from the ages attest. Histories of money then usually describe how paper money was adopted and helped birth the modern banking system. When owners of precious metals and other valuable items such as grain deposited them with warehouse operators, they received receipts, and these receipts started to circulate as "money," an I-owe-you (IOU) of the issuer but a claim on something valuable for the holder, that is, **"purchasing power."** Commodity-backed money was born.

There typically follows an account of how money backed by something evolved into money backed by nothing at all besides the full faith and credit of a sovereign government: **fiat money**. "Fiat" means that such money has value because the government says it has, but the actual reason it has value is because lots of people use it.

In my exploration of money, however, I probe a different set of questions: where does money come from, and how does it get into existence and circulation in the modern-day economy and monetary system? These might strike you as strange or obvious. Most people work for a living, at least at some stage in their life. They earn money for labor and sometimes make more by investing some of it. That's where it seems like money comes from: your job and from saving and investing.

But that doesn't really answer the question; it just moves it around one space. Your employer deposited your pay into your bank account, where it became your money, but that just means they transferred it from their account. How did the money get into *their* bank account? Your employer, if it is a business, has customers and sales revenue, and the money in its bank account came from the bank accounts of those customers. But where did *those* folks get it from?

Now we are going around in circles, like a dog chasing its tail. Money moves around the economy from one person or business to another, but it has to originate somewhere. We need to step back and ask how money first enters circulation. It wasn't always there. Economies are expanding all the time and new money is constantly coming into existence, as the **monetary economy** mirrors and supports the **real economy**. The US is now (according to the latest data available as of December 2022) a $25 trillion economy with $2.2 trillion in banknotes and $17.8 trillion in commercial bank deposits; twenty years ago, it was a $10.7 trillion economy with $625 billion in banknotes and $4.2 trillion in bank deposits. Where did all that money come from?

One answer would be: bank deposits arise or increase when people put money—banknotes—in the bank. That is true, as far as it goes. If I take a wad of hundred-dollar bills to my bank—say a hundred of them—and deposit them in my bank account, my deposit balance, and bank deposits in the overall economy, will go up by ten thousand dollars. But that doesn't say very much. First of all, banknotes make up only a small percentage of the **money supply** in most economies: even if everyone deposited all their banknotes in banks, bank deposit money would go up by only 12 percent—hardly a gamechanger in a $25 trillion economy.

The Federal Reserve does not dispense banknotes directly; rather, they come out of bank deposit accounts. Every dollar of banknotes in circulation started life in a bank account. So, we are going around in circles again! Where do bank deposits come from?

Enough suspense. Every dollar in a bank account started life in one of three ways: a bank created it when it made a loan; the government created it when it spent and didn't withdraw it by taxing (i.e., when it ran a **budget deficit**); or the central bank created it when it bought a government debt security (or other asset) from the public at large. Banks, the government, and the central bank are all involved in the creation of money, in their own ways, as part of an interconnected system. In every case, the money was conjured up out of thin air, or more accurately with the tap of a computer key. That is the mystery of modern money. But before we get more into that, a brief detour on measuring money is in order.

TAKING THE MEASURE OF MONEY

Economists have developed a method of classifying money in terms of increasingly broader, and less liquid, forms of "money supply"—liabilities issued by central banks and **commercial banks** (or other financial intermediaries). Termed "**monetary aggregates**," these are typically denoted by ascending levels of M, as in MB (monetary base), M0 (M zero), **M1**, **M2**, and M3, corresponding to ever wider sets of money-like financial instruments or assets (the classification differs slightly depending on the country). This is sometimes likened to an inverted monetary pyramid. It is a useful pedagogical device, but can invite confusion.

At the base of the monetary pyramid—actually the *tip*, because it is inverted—are **"bank reserves,"** or just "reserves": the deposits of banks at the central bank. These reserves, which are not to be confused with **foreign exchange reserves**,[6] play a critical role in the monetary system: it is in these accounts that the ultimate settlement (or "netting out") of financial transactions in the economy occurs, and they play a pivotal role in the central bank's conduct of **monetary policy**.

Banknotes and coins in circulation—that is, "cash" held by the public, expressed as M0—and reserves make up the "monetary base" or "base money" (MB). The monetary base largely corresponds to the liability side of a central bank's **balance sheet**.[7] Roughly speaking, M1 adds checking accounts and demand deposits to M0; M2 adds savings accounts, small-denomination time deposits, and retail money market funds to that; and M3 adds large-denomination time deposits, institutional money market funds, and short-term repurchase agreements. In this conventional classification, government debt securities (Treasury bills and bonds) are not regarded as money, something I take issue with in this book. Further, reserves, the key part of the monetary base, are (somewhat confusingly) not considered part of the M0 and higher monetary "aggregates."

The key idea behind this classification, and the distinction between "narrow" and "broad" money, is that the closer money is to the base, the more it is used to make payments; the further away it is, the more it serves as a store of value. But there is no bright line between when money stops being money and starts becoming a (nonmonetary) financial asset from the holder's point of view. And what characteristics the various categories of money have depends considerably on financial innovation and regulation. The different categories of money reflect what kind of liability (including the kinds of services attached to it) the bank chooses and is allowed, by regulation, to issue. This menu has shifted over time with financial deregulation and innovation.

It is the medium of exchange aspect of money that maps most closely to economists' monetary-aggregates classification of money. Reserves, banknotes and coins, checking accounts, and demand deposits are the forms of money most commonly and readily used to make the payments associated with purchasing goods, services, and assets. But, again, there is no bright line: financial innovation and regulation have shifted the border, and will do so again.

In this way, money, rather than being a clearly and unambiguously identifiable thing, like water or gold, is multifaceted and varies along a spectrum. The unit of account aspect of money pertains to all assets and transactions in the economy. Similarly, the store of value aspect of money pertains to all assets, whether financial, such as stocks and bonds, or real, such as automobiles and houses; they all serve to translate current into future purchasing power or command over the services that assets provide. What shifts across a spectrum here is how "good" the respective assets are as stores of value, notably how risky they are. How much shares in a company will sell for in the future is highly uncertain, the more so the further into the future one looks. The price may go up, but in principle (and less pleasant) it could go to zero. Stocks are a store of value, but they are a risky one.

Money as a medium of exchange is more circumscribed. Banks settle transactions among themselves using their accounts at the central bank, known as reserve accounts, the money in those accounts being known as reserves. Banknotes and coins are used as a medium of exchange (mainly by individuals) in many small-lot transactions. Individuals and businesses mainly use checking and demand deposit accounts to settle their transactions, which they typically engage in by using credit and debit cards or electronic wallets and similar payment services. But other forms of money that cannot be directly used as a medium of exchange, more by via virtue of custom and convention (that is, self-imposed rules) than technological feasibility, such as savings and term deposits or government bonds, are readily convertible into forms that can.

Now, back to how money comes into existence.

BANKS CREATE MONEY

Most existing money in deposits was created by commercial banks. Banks create money when they make loans: the act of a bank making a loan is the act of it simultaneously crediting the deposit account of the loan's recipient, the borrower.

That banks create money when they make loans surprises many people because we are so used to hearing the opposite: banks collect or "take in" deposits and use those deposits to make or "fund" new loans. Deposits would seem to come before loans, rather than being a necessary consequence of them. Banks lend out their deposits, which in turn "fund" loans, correct? Not so. This way of describing things is so ingrained it even has a name: the "loanable funds" theory. It dominates the popular imagination, even the academic one, but it is flat-out wrong. It is actually the other way around: deposits do not (allow banks to) create loans; loans create deposits, in the sense that the act of a bank making a loan is one of it crediting the borrower with a deposit. Deposits "fund" loans only in the sense that the two sides of a bank's balance sheet must balance.

Part of the confusion stems from the standard financial language used, particularly the words "fund" and "finance." If a company wants to buy some new equipment or significantly expand its business, it likely won't have enough cash on hand and will need to borrow money from a bank. It makes sense to say that the company finances or funds its business expansion by taking out a loan from its bank. Without the loan, the business expansion wouldn't happen. The new loan by the bank creates the money that the company needs and uses to finance its business expansion.

However, banks don't function that way: they don't attract deposits and then use those deposits to fund the loans they make. It may look that way, but that is an optical illusion.

To understand this better, it's useful to look at a simplified bank balance sheet (which in this case omits equity, for simplicity). A balance sheet, as the name suggests, has two sides that need to balance. By convention, assets are recorded on the left-hand side and liabilities and equity on the right-hand side: what you have and what you owe, or how you financed the purchase of the assets, respectively.

Assets	Liabilities
Reserves	Central bank loans
Interbank loans	Interbank loans
Loans	Deposits

Reserves are a bank's deposits with the central bank, which the central bank can supply by buying assets from the bank or from someone with a deposit account with the bank, or by directly lending them (central bank loans). Banks can lend these reserves to one another, but not to anyone else, so interbank loans can be an asset or a liability, depending on which bank is lending and which is borrowing them.

Imagine that the bank wants to make a new loan of $10. Does it need to find $10 in deposits from somewhere and then lend that $10 to the borrower? No. The bank just creates the $10 loan and the $10 deposit out of thin air. It just marks up its loans by $10 and credits $10 to the deposit account of the borrower (with a bit of legal paperwork thrown in).

Now, the borrower wants to borrow that $10 for a reason, and the first thing they will likely do is spend or use the money for whatever purpose they decided to borrow it. There are a couple of cases to consider. Let's assume that whoever received the $10 from the borrower has an account at the same bank and keeps it on deposit there. Then, although the deposit changes hands, the bank does not have to attract any new deposits: the loan in effect is self-financing.

But assume the deposit leaves the bank in question and becomes a deposit of another bank, that of whoever received the $10 from the borrower. The borrower's bank will accommodate the $10 deposit outflow by running down its reserves (deposits) at the central bank by $10. The receiving bank's deposits will increase by $10, matched by an increase of $10 in its reserves at the central bank. For the banking system as a whole, deposits and reserves will be unchanged; they will just have moved between banks. The new loan is not self-financing for the initiating bank anymore, but it is for the banking system as a whole.

The individual banks won't see or feel it that way, however. Suddenly, as a result of making a $10 loan, the first bank is short of reserves by $10, and the other bank has $10 too much in reserves. Banks cannot lend their reserves to anyone that doesn't have an account at the central bank, but they can lend them to one another. They do this in what is called the "interbank money market" or "overnight call market," applying the interest rate set by the central bank (more on why and the mechanics of that in chapter three). So, most likely, the bank with the $10 in surplus reserves will lend it to the bank that is $10 short of reserves, and Bob's your uncle.

Yet, it is not quite that simple. Banks need three things in order to make loans. The most important is a willing borrower, on the terms that the bank finds it profitable for it to want to extend a loan. Without a willing borrower that is attractive to the bank, bank credit creation doesn't get to first base.

The second is sufficient capital, since banks face capital adequacy requirements set by their regulators.[8] Suppose that the lending bank was just meeting its capital adequacy requirements before making the new loan; now it is short of capital and will need to raise more (or shrink some of its other assets, including possibly securitizing the loan it just made—that is, making it part of a security that it can sell to investors). A healthy bank that is making profitable loans (i.e., loans likely to be repaid with an amount of net interest more than compensating for the risk of default) should have no trouble raising the necessary capital to support the expansion of its loan book.

The third thing a bank needs is sufficient reserves, because central banks impose on commercial banks minimum reserve requirements, linked to the amount of deposits they have. These have taken a backseat after years of central bank **quantitative easing** (QE), the act of central banks pumping up their balance sheets in an attempt to stimulate the economy. This is because QE floods banks with reserves, making minimum reserve requirements moot (more on QE in chapter four). The idea of minimum reserve requirements is to ensure that banks have sufficient liquid funds (money) on hand to meet the withdrawal demands of their customers without having to call on the central bank to provide those funds in a scramble. Banks have to maintain an amount of reserves (on the asset or left-hand side of the balance sheet) corresponding to a certain percentage of the deposits they have (on the liability or right-hand side).[9] Because more loans create more deposits, and assuming that the bank was just meeting its minimum reserve requirements before it made the new loan, it will need to hold more reserves now.

Not to worry—the central bank will always provide the necessary reserves to the banking system. To understand why minimum reserve requirements are never a constraint, consider a simplified central bank balance sheet:

Assets	Liabilities
Government bonds	Reserves
	Government deposits
	Banknotes

Being a balance sheet, one side must equal the other. Rearranging the balance sheet's identity and expressing it in change terms, we can see that an increase (decrease) in reserves occurs when one or more of the following happens: the central bank buys (sells) government bonds, the government decreases (increases) its deposits at the central bank, or the public decreases (increases) its holdings of banknotes.

If there are too many reserves, the central bank can extinguish the excess by selling government bonds to banks or the public; if there are not enough, it can make up the shortfall by buying bonds. Often central banks don't buy and sell government bonds outright but do so under short-term repurchase agreements or "repos." Under a repo, the central bank buys a security from a bank with an agreement to sell it back again after a short, specified period (usually the next day). Buying the security increases the central bank's reserves by that amount; selling it back extinguishes them. Under a reverse repurchase or "reverse repo" operation, the central bank sells a security to a bank with an agreement to buy it back again after a short, specified period (usually the next day). Selling the security drains or extinguishes the central bank's reserves by that amount; buying it back restores them.

Since the **Global Financial Crisis**, and then again with the COVID-19 pandemic, central banks have often been operating in or near zero interest rate territory and doing QE. In normal times, however, central banks seek to keep the aggregate amount of reserves roughly in line with the amount corresponding to total minimum reserve requirements; in fact, because central banks historically did not pay any interest on reserves before these crises, they had to operate this way in order to keep short-term interest rates in line with their target. Because flows in and out of reserve accounts are subject to fairly predictable daily and seasonal patterns, central banks often prefer to offset them using repos rather than outright purchases or sales.

A useful analogy for understanding how central banks operate is a leaky bucket into which water is flowing from a tap. Water flows in and leaks out, respectively, in an irregular if somewhat predictable way. Imagine that the bucket has a waterline marking the amount of water that needs to be maintained in the bucket at all times. It is the central bank's job to make sure the amount of water stays at the waterline. To do this, it has a scoop and a hose: if the flow of water in and out of the bucket is such that the water level is above the waterline, the central bank scoops enough water out to bring it down; if the water level falls below the waterline, the bank uses its hose to top it up.

Because banks, in aggregate, have to maintain at least the amount mandated by the central bank–imposed minimum reserve requirements, the central bank has to supply at least that amount. Failure to do so would leave some banks short of reserves even when all other banks had just secured enough; the resulting scramble for reserves by those banks would push the interbank interest rate (in the US, the federal funds rate) above the interest rate targeted by the central bank.

But why does the central bank have to ensure that there are not too many reserves—that is, scoop water out of the bucket when it rises above the waterline? For an analogous reason. Until fairly recently, the Fed and other major central banks did not pay interest on the reserves held by banks.[10] That meant that banks, having secured their needed amount of reserves, generally did not want to hold any more. So, if they ended up holding too many reserves due to the flows in and out of their little buckets (which in aggregate make up the big bucket that the central bank manages), they would want to lend them at the prevailing interbank interest rate, which the central bank will adjust (using its scoop and hose) to keep in line with its interest rate target.

If the aggregate amount of reserves exceeds the amount corresponding to the total of the individual banks' minimum reserve requirements, some banks will have excess reserves after all the other banks have secured just enough, but none in excess. These banks will then try, in vain, to offload these reserves to other banks, putting downward pressure on the interbank interest rate in the process and forcing it below the central bank's target. So, if the central bank wants to do its job of hitting its interest rate target, it has to make sure there are neither too many nor too few reserves—the water level has to be just at the line.

We see here again the importance of the distinction between the reserves level of an individual bank and that of the banking system as a whole (all banks). The central bank can, and generally does, control the level of reserves in the entire banking system. How it does so is intricately related to how it conducts monetary policy—in particular, whether it is operating a normal interest rate regime, is doing quantitative easing, or is operating with the legacy of a QE-bloated balance sheet (more on QE in chapter four).

But if one bank is short of reserves because it increased its lending, the central bank doesn't need to provide reserves to that bank; it can just make sure that the banking system as a whole has enough reserves and rely on the fact that banks that end up with more reserves than they need will lend those reserves, in the interbank market, to banks that are short.

The individual bank–banking system reserves distinction is also useful when considering how loans are "financed." I put "financed" in quotes because, in an important sense—that of the system as a whole—loans are self-financing, because a corollary of lending is the act of creating deposits. But it doesn't feel that way for an individual bank—loans typically being quite illiquid, deposits inherently being fleet of foot. After all, the first thing a borrower usually does with the money it receives from the bank is to spend it! But, even if the entirety of the deposit created by the loan immediately leaves the individual bank in question, for the system as a whole the deposit can go to only one of two places: deposits at other banks or into banknotes. The part that "leaks" into banknotes is likely to be relatively small, given that the public tends to hold most of its money as bank deposits. On the central bank's balance sheet, any such leakage will cause reserves to go down (by the same amount), and the central bank, because it needs to supply sufficient reserves to the banking system, will top up the reserves by buying bonds or lending reserves.

Because banking systems usually have a few dominant megabanks, as deposit money newly created by one of them circulates, some of it will likely flow back into that bank. But if, as is likely, the bank in question sees some net loss in deposits to other banks, the necessary "funding" will happen naturally, as those banks find themselves with too many reserves and lend them to the bank that is short.

At the level of individual banks, it may feel like they are competing with one another to attract the necessary deposits to "fund" their loans, and this is how they tend to describe things. For the banking system as a whole, however, assisted by the central bank's role in adjusting reserves as necessary to satisfy the public's demand for banknotes, banks' loan books always will be funded.

But what happens, one might ask, if depositors lose faith in the banking system and try to move their deposits offshore, into another currency? Such financial panics involving "capital flight" can and do occur, when the value of the assets held by banks collapses, causing depositors and investors to fear they won't get their money back (more on that in chapter six). The economic consequences can be dire. But we need to carefully understand what is going on in such situations. When domestic depositors try to convert their deposits into foreign currency, they are essentially trying to find someone who is willing to swap their foreign-currency deposits for their domestic-currency ones. Given that something has occurred to cause investors in general to lose confidence in the country in question, the exchange rate will have to fall sufficiently for holders of foreign deposits to find it attractive to swap them with the domestic deposits of those trying to "flee." And all the while, as the exchange rate falls, the attraction of the increasingly expensive-looking foreign deposits to the domestic depositors dwindles. In turn, the collapse in the exchange rate will unleash all kinds of financial and economic damage.

As crops up in many economic contexts, a "fallacy of composition" effect is in play: what may be true for part of a system is not true for the whole. Deposits, once created, are essentially trapped in the system, but it will not feel like that to individual depositors. Their attempts to act on their perceived individual degrees of freedom, amid a financial panic, can wreak havoc on the system as a whole.

BUDGET DEFICITS CREATE DEPOSITS

The second way in which bank deposits are created is when the government runs a budget deficit. When the government runs a budget deficit, it injects more money into the economy via its spending on goods and services and its transfers (such as subsidies and social welfare payments) than it withdraws via its taxing. This budget deficit—and it usually is a deficit—shows up as increased bank deposits and reserves (i.e., money) in the banking system and economy.

Budget deficits create money. This may sound counterintuitive—don't governments run deficits when they are spending too much? Yes, but that is the point: spending too much is what creates money, money (or at least the part created by the government) being a government IOU. Remember what it says on that twenty-dollar bill.

It is often hard for us to get our heads around the idea that governments create money by running a deficit because we are so used to thinking about government finances in the same way that we think about our personal finances. If we spend more than we earn in a given period, we have to borrow or run down our savings to make up the difference. Why isn't that true of the government, which, after all, is just a giant collection of us?

The reason is that one of the functions of the government is to *supply* money. Remember, money is not something real, or something that exists in fixed or short supply; it is something conceptual and collectively imagined that helps the economy to produce real things. It is something that helps us tally who has a claim to the current and future output of the economy and, via the "price system," helps that economy function now and in the future in an efficient, decentralized way. Producing money (but, as we will see in chapter three, and as the inflationary lessons of history have taught us, not producing too much) is a large part of the role of the government, acting on behalf of all of us.

Another reason why it seems hard to accept the idea that the government *produces* money when it runs a budget deficit, rather than *needing* it in order to run one, is that we are used to thinking that the government has to issue bonds or debt securities (Treasuries in the US) to finance its budget deficit.[11] When the government runs a deficit, it issues a corresponding amount of bonds to investors, who draw on cash they have to buy those bonds. It looks like the government has to borrow in order to spend, but the government is "borrowing" money that it has already produced! Or, depending on the order in which the two things (the issuing of bonds and the spending) happen, money that it *will* produce once it has spent the money it has borrowed.

The Monetary Garden of Eden

The simplest way to grasp the fact that the government creates money when it runs a budget deficit is to imagine that the central bank is just a department of the government and that there is no government bond market—that there is no separation of monetary and **fiscal policy**. Think of the treasury doubling as the central bank.

Betraying my Catholic upbringing, I liken this situation to being in a "Monetary Garden of Eden," a primitive state of nature before monetary and fiscal policy existed as separate and qualitatively different functions.[12] The government routinely runs a budget deficit, injecting more purchasing power into the economy via its GDP-based spending than it withdraws via its net taxes (taxes net of transfers). Banks have accounts with the government and accumulate monetary credits equivalent to accumulated budget deficits minus banknotes in circulation. In this world, there is no distinction between the central bank and the treasury or between monetary policy and fiscal policy.

Suppose the government runs a budget deficit in a certain period of $100, by writing checks totaling $200 to social security program recipients, government contractors, and government employees, and taking in taxes of $100. The net effect of those checks being received and cleared and the taxes being collected will be to increase deposits and reserves in the banking system by $100. A hundred dollars of new money will have been created.

However, there is a danger in this Monetary Garden of Eden of the government "abusing" its unbridled ability to create money by running too large a budget deficit, such that too much money, created with the tap of computer keystrokes, ends up chasing too few goods, whose production requires sacrificial toil in the real economy. Yielding to such temptation no doubt would lead to runaway inflation.

The analog to Adam and Eve being banished from the Garden of Eden for eating the forbidden fruit is for separate monetary and fiscal functions to be established and, as much as possible, to be hived off from each other. When this is done, the government cannot just create however much money it wants by running arbitrarily large budget deficits; rather, it has to issue bonds (debt securities) to the private sector (the market) to "finance" the gap between its expenditures and its tax revenues. Recall from the earlier central bank balance sheet that the government issuing bonds increases its deposits at the central bank, which dollar for dollar (or euro for euro, or yen for yen) decreases reserves. In this **Modern Monetary Theory (MMT)** way of looking at things, the government does not issue bonds to raise money but rather to shackle itself against creating too much of it in the first place.[13] The fiscal functions aim to facilitate monetary control.[14]

Assume for the moment that the central bank allowed the government's account to go into overdraft automatically and without limit. Then government spending would create deposits and reserves in the banking system, and the accumulation of reserves on the liability side of the central bank's balance sheet would be matched one for one by the overdraft in the government's account (also on the liability side). There would be no reason for anybody to be concerned about the government's large and (as long as the government was running a budget deficit) ever-accumulating overdraft at the central bank per se, as this would just be a book entry in an electronic ledger, and it cancels out on the **consolidated government**'s balance sheet. (The consolidated government is the government plus government-owned entities like the central bank.[15])

The operational separation of the central bank from the treasury, or the "independence" of monetary from fiscal policy, means that in modern practice things usually don't work this way. Legislation normally prohibits the government from running an overdraft in its account with the central bank. Instead, if the government is running a budget deficit, it has to issue bonds to "finance" it. Doing so extinguishes the reserves and, depending on who buys the bonds, may extinguish the deposits, too.[16]

If the law or operational practice allows the government to temporarily go into overdraft in its central bank account, then the order in which these operations take place doesn't matter. Assume for simplicity that the government starts with a zero balance in its account at the central bank. If the government issued bonds *after* running a deficit in a given period, that deficit would create reserves equal to the amount of its resulting overdraft, and issuing the associated bonds would then extinguish those reserves and return its account to a zero balance. If the government issued bonds *before* running a deficit, it would drain an amount of reserves equal to its expected deficit to stockpile that amount in its account; then, as it ran the deficit, it would run down its account balance to zero, replenishing those reserves as it did. Either way, the net effect will be no change in the central bank's balance sheet, and an amount of government bonds in the hands of the private sector equal to that of the deficit.

Government bonds are not usually counted as part of the stock of money (that is, any of the Ms), but this is more a convention than a matter of substance. The excess of government spending over taxing creates net nominal purchasing power whether it is held in the form of bank deposits, banknotes, or government bonds. *Fiscal* policy is a very *monetary* affair.

CENTRAL BANKS CREATE MONEY

The third way in which bank deposits are created is when the central bank buys bonds (or other assets) from non–banking-system private sector agents. The central bank pays for these assets by creating reserves, which have deposits as their counterpart on the other side (the liability side) of the banking system's balance sheet. This is normally the least important way in which money (i.e., bank deposits) is created, because, as explained earlier, in normal times a central bank operates monetary policy so as to keep excess reserves in the banking system around zero. Before the 2008 financial crisis, reserves totaled only about $46 billion; as of the time of writing, they total about $3.17 trillion (having peaked at $4.27 trillion).

If the central bank is doing quantitative easing, and is buying government bonds (or other assets) from the non–banking-system private sector, deposits will be created in the banking system.

The usual textbook explanation for how money comes into existence focuses on this third channel: the central bank expanding the money supply by "open market operations"—that is, by buying government bonds (or, if it wants to reduce the money supply, selling them). This "money multiplier model" subsumes the active role of banks as creators of money by assuming that banks want to hold an amount of reserves equal to a fixed percentage of their deposits. All the central bank then needs to do to increase the money supply is to increase the amount of reserves, and banks will start increasing their lending and deposit base until that fixed percentage is restored. Meanwhile, textbooks do not treat government bonds as money, so that channel is downplayed or ignored.

But the monetary system does not work like this. It is normally the central bank, not banks, that operates mechanically.

Any deposit in the banking system, traced to its birth, will have been created because the bank made a loan, the government ran a budget deficit, or the central bank bought an asset.[17] Banks, the government, and the central bank are joined at the hip in creating money and in the operation of what we call "monetary policy" and "fiscal policy."

MONEY BEGETS MONEY

This discussion has focused on the question of how the basic feedstock money—deposits in banks—comes into existence in a modern economy. That story is complicated enough. But where does all the other money come from? The basic **money stock** (M2) in the US totaled about $21 trillion at the time of writing, but this is only a fraction of total "money" in the form of financial assets. US stock market capitalization—the value of all publicly listed companies—was about $46 trillion; the value of household (and nonprofit organizations) financial assets (as of the second quarter of 2022) was about $109 trillion. What is this other money's source? It turns out that the bank deposit money created by commercial banks, governments, and central banks plays a pivotal role. Without it, the economic world, and the stock markets that help drive it, would not go around.

Let's focus on that $46 trillion of "money" in the stock market. What happens when a company issues shares? Let's say a company issues you ten dollars' worth of new shares. You pay for the shares with ten dollars from your bank account and the company now has an extra ten dollars in its bank account. Ten dollars of new shares came into existence (on the liability, or right-hand, side of the company's balance sheet and on the asset, or left-hand, side of yours) and the bank deposit asset shifted from your (notional) balance sheet to the company's (official) one. So far this just describes a process of money in the form of bank deposits being shuffled from one balance sheet to another.

A share in a company represents a claim to its future profits, either profits the company is expected to retain when they are earned or those paid out as dividends. The stock market capitalization of a company is the current stock price times the number of shares issued. This is the value that the stock market, or investors in aggregate, is said to "put on" the company or the amount at which the stock market "values it." For example, Amazon's stock market capitalization as of the time of writing was $960.28 billion; its annual net profit (for the twelve months ending in September 2022) was $11.32 billion, implying a price-to-earnings ratio of about eighty-five times.[18] A company could be posting losses today, yet have a healthy stock market valuation, because investors are "looking through" today's losses and discounting an uncertain flow of expected future profits to the present. The stock market links the future to the present and puts numbers on it, linking future money to current.

Stock prices go up and down according to supply and demand. At any given time, the potential supply of shares is fixed, but the actual supply—the number of shares offered to potential buyers—depends on the prevailing price. If the stock price is ten dollars at a certain time, it is because the marginal seller (the owner of shares who is the next most likely to sell) will sell if offered a little bit more than ten dollars and because the marginal buyer (the investor who is the next most likely to buy and who already might own shares in the company) will buy if offered a little bit less than ten dollars. The share price is ten dollars because that is the price, at that instant in time, that matches supply with demand. This supply and demand is a little different from the kind encountered in introductory economics textbooks because what is being traded is a claim on something that doesn't even exist yet: future profits from future economic activity, driven by future consumers, some of whom may not even have been born!

Stock prices are notoriously volatile: they move up or down randomly from second to second as new information about the world arrives and traders and investors revise their views about myriad stocks and other financial assets available. A company's stock price rises when someone in the world who is contemplating buying that stock feels more strongly about doing so than the people who currently own the stock, specifically the person who is already on the verge of selling but hasn't pulled the trigger. Likewise, a company's stock price falls when the people who currently own the stock, specifically the person who is on the verge of selling, feels more strongly about doing so than someone out there who is on the verge of buying.

To continue with the simple illustrative example, imagine that the next day, investors wake up and for whatever reason feel more optimistic on average about the future prospects of this company. The stock price will go up, because the person who was on the verge of buying at ten dollars a share yesterday will be happy to pay more today, and the person who was on the verge of selling at ten dollars a share yesterday will now want to hold on. The price will keep going up until the balance of supply and demand is restored. Let's say the price at which that happens is eleven dollars a share. At that stock price, someone who didn't want to sell at any price below eleven dollars is now on the verge of doing so, and the last person out there who wanted to buy has been deterred from doing so because the price has gotten too high for them.

Notice what has happened. No bank deposit money was created in this example; it just moved around the system. I transferred my ten-dollar deposit to the company, which transferred it to someone else (such as its employees or suppliers) as it put the money to work in the production process. As the movement of bank deposit money helped drive economic activity, it created "money" in the wider sense of financial wealth.

TWO MONEY SPIGOTS

Think of money flowing into the economy primarily via two spigots: one emanating from the credit creation of the banking system, but modulated by the central bank's monetary policy (more on that in chapter three); the other driven by the fiscal red ink of the government. The output of the economy tends to grow over time, as the population grows (usually),[19] as the capital stock increases thanks to prior **investment**, and as technological innovation allows more to be produced from the same amount of capital and labor. The economy needs more money to support it as it expands, so the spigots need to remain open but must be adjusted continually to ensure that there is enough money but not too much (figure 1.1). The premise of the money supplied by the banking system is that it will be repaid eventually, but because the economy and the capital stock supporting it is expanding, new bank loans tend to be created at a faster rate than old ones are repaid, so the stock of money created by bank loans tends to increase over time. The government usually runs a budget deficit, so the amount of money it supplies also tends to increase over time.

When the government runs a budget deficit, it creates money. Money is purchasing power, which the government may destroy by taxing some of those who have it, but it is not debt in the sense of a financial obligation that *has* to be repaid. The money that the government creates is usually converted into another form called "government bonds" (Treasuries in the US) and viewed as "debt." Why it is misleading to view government bonds as "debt," and why doing so causes unnecessary confusion and angst, are the subject of the next chapter.

FIGURE 1.1 US NOMINAL GDP AND M2 MONEY STOCK, 1980–2022

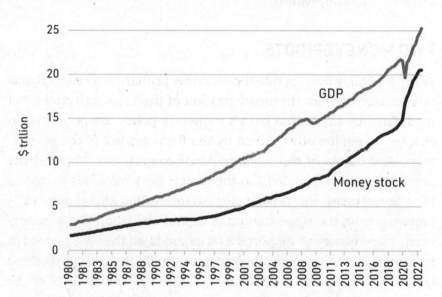

US Bureau of Economic Analysis (GDP) and Board of Governors of the Federal Reserve System (money stock), retrieved from FRED, Federal Reserve Bank of St. Louis; seasonally adjusted.

2

THE POWER OF GOVERNMENT DEBT

> Treasury bonds represent the rights to share in the future production of the United States of America.
>
> *Frank Newman, former US deputy secretary of the treasury, 2013*[1]

The US government publishes a Monthly Statement of the Public Debt of the United States. As of the time of writing, this statement recorded that the government had a total public debt outstanding of $31.24 trillion.

Here are some of the things that many people believe about this debt:

- This is a truly daunting amount of money.
- This debt represents money that the government *owes* and at some point in the future will have to pay back.

- This debt is a burden on future generations: we are mortgaging the future of our grandchildren—and possibly their grandchildren.
- The government is being irresponsible when it piles up so much debt by running big budget deficits year in, year out; it should aim for a balanced budget.
- The associated mountain of debt and ongoing big deficits may not be a problem now, but it will be as soon as the "bond vigilantes" hit town.
- Foreigners own a big chunk of the federal debt ($7.30 trillion, as of third quarter 2022); there will be a day of reckoning when they call it in.

They are all wrong, or at the very least misleading. The following points are closer to the truth:

- The amount of government debt is not particularly high relative to the size of the US economy, which produced $25.00 trillion of output in the past year (to third quarter 2022). If I had a job paying $25,000 a year and I owed $31,240, I could probably handle things—and I'm not even the government!
- The $31 trillion of debt represents money that the government has *created*. It never has to repay its debt, any more than it has to repay a twenty-dollar bill it has issued.
- Government debt is an asset for those holding it: for the generation inheriting it, the debt and the asset cancel out. Future generations inherit a hugely productive capital stock and an accumulated stock of scientific, technological, and societal knowhow.
- The budget deficit should be viewed as a policy *tool*, not as a policy *target*. The government is not a household and should not be likened to one; it is a vehicle for societal collective action. Its job is to serve the people, not balance its books.
- The public has to hold the money (debt) created by government deficits: the money has nowhere else to go.

- Foreigners can only spend their dollars in the US economy on US goods and services, which will provide employment and income for the future workers who supply those. Foreigners who hold dollars and want to offload them can only do so to other foreigners. Future workers probably do not much care whether the output they get paid to help produce is consumed by other Americans or by foreigners.

None of this is to suggest that government deficits or debt "don't matter" or that governments can spend willy-nilly without having to worry about the consequences. One likely consequence if the government did so would be **inflation**. This would particularly be the case if the central bank did not have the independence to counter high inflation by tightening monetary policy.

In trying to understand fiscal policy debates, it is important to distinguish between two levels of analysis we might call the fundamental level and the institutional level. By "fundamental level" I mean how things work in principle or in the abstract; by "institutional level" I mean how things work in practice, in the real world, given the institutional rules (including laws and regulations) in place. Depending on the level being presumed, what is true and what is not true can differ. It is easy for different people to talk past one another or, worse, be at loggerheads over their assertions, conclusions, or policy recommendations simply because they are considering them at different levels. To complicate matters, it is precisely because certain things are true at the fundamental level that institutional mechanisms have been developed to make them untrue at the institutional level!

At the fundamental level, governments create money when they run a budget deficit. At the institutional level, it appears that they have to borrow money in order to run a budget deficit. At the fundamental level, government debt never has to be repaid. At the institutional level, debt securities have set maturities, such as two, five, ten, or thirty years, making it appear that the government has to repay its debt when it matures. At the fundamental level, the treasury and the central bank are just two parts of the same entity. At the institutional level, barriers are erected between them. At the fundamental level, the government can set the interest rate on the money it issues because it can control the amount of money it creates. At the institutional level, it allows most of these interest rates to be set by trading in money and bond markets.

THE "GOVERNMENT AS A HOUSEHOLD" FALLACY

Most of the misunderstandings and myths surrounding government debt stem from the fallacy of thinking of the government as if it functioned like a household or a company. It does not; rather, it is the vehicle for collective action of the whole society. That makes a heck of a difference.

An individual has to balance their budget; they cannot spend more than they earn, not indefinitely at least. Of course, an individual can borrow against future expected income, but the debt so incurred has to be repaid; they cannot run up the balance on their credit card without limit. An economy runs on self-interest, not charity.

A company functions similarly. A business borrows in order to invest, the premise being that it will repay the money borrowed with interest and make a profit to boot. A company cannot borrow without limit or regard for whether it will ever be able to repay its debt; if nothing else, lenders will make sure of that.

A national government is different. Governments don't "borrow" money; rather, they "create" it. They create money when they spend and they destroy money when they tax. Because governments can create money at will, they can't run out of it and they don't need to pay it back. Money is not a promise to pay something back; it is a vehicle for facilitating economic exchange in the present and transferring purchasing power and claims on assets into the future.

The government "destroying" money when it taxes may sound odd, but effectively that is what it does.[2] Suppose you earn $100 and the government takes $20 in income tax. Where does that $20 go? You might think that the government uses it to finance $20 of its spending. But the government creates money by the act of spending; it doesn't need your $20 to do that. Here's what happens: $20 from your bank account disappears as the check you wrote to the government clears. This causes $20 of reserves to disappear on both the asset side of the banking system's balance sheet and on the liability side of the central bank's balance sheet. At the same time, the government's deposit at the central bank increases by $20. This simultaneous increase of $20 on the liability side of the central bank's balance sheet and on the asset side of the government's balance sheet cancel out within the overall or consolidated government's balance sheet. The net effect on balance sheets in the economy of the government taxing you $20 is that bank deposits and reserves—that is, money—fall by $20. "Destroy" is not too harsh a word for that.

We shouldn't be worrying about the government racking up too much debt because it might overwhelm the ability of the government to repay it or because future generations will inherit too large a debt burden. Rather, we should be worried about, or debating, other things: What is the right size and role of the government? Is it too big or not big enough? How actively should it seek to manage the macroeconomy and how? How proactive a role should the government play in steering economic activity and seeking to redistribute income? Is it creating too much money relative to the capacity of the economy now and in the future to absorb the associated purchasing power without causing excess inflation? Is the right institutional framework in place to ensure that inflation is neither too high nor too low? Is the productive potential of the economy on track to grow fast enough to sustain the viability of the promises society makes to itself?

Understanding what role the budget deficit plays in the economy, and what drives how big it is, is central to sorting through issues relating to the debt. The stock of government debt is nothing other than the cumulative sum of prior budget deficits and budget surpluses. The amount of debt increases each year by the amount of the prior year's deficit; if the government happens to run a budget surplus, it decreases by that amount. The stock of government debt represents the net amount of money that it has created to date. Money is nominal (not real) purchasing power, which can be used in the present or held over into the future. The relevant question from a macroeconomic policy perspective is not "Has the government borrowed too much?" but rather "Has the government created too much purchasing power?" The first question is a non sequitur, because the government does not really borrow money—it just looks like it does. The answer to the second question hinges on how much of that purchasing power is being released into the economy at any point in time relative to the capacity of the economy to absorb it without causing inflation to take off.

Just because governments can create money doesn't mean that they *should*. In fact, it is precisely because governments can create money merely by wishing it into existence—that's what "fiat money" means—that society has developed institutional mechanisms to restrain its ability to do so. These center on separating "monetary" and "fiscal" functions within the government and granting the central bank the independence from the fiscal authorities to conduct monetary policy, one of the effects of which is to constrain fiscal policy.

I put "monetary" and "fiscal" in quote marks because these are not primitive, God-given categories; rather, they reflect particular institutional arrangements that have evolved over time to constrain the government's ability to create money. These arrangements serve a useful purpose, but their very success in doing so tends to obscure the fact that, deep down, they are two aspects of the same thing: government money creation.

Let's unpack a bit the notion that the government creates money when it runs a budget deficit and destroys money when it runs a budget surplus. The budget deficit is equal to the government's spending on goods and services minus the net taxes it collects, net taxes being taxes minus transfer payments. Take a simple example. Let's say: (1) that the government spends $100 building or buying things, like bridges and missiles, and employing public sector workers; (2) that it receives $80 in income, corporate, and other taxes; and (3) that it pays out $20 in social welfare and other income transfers. That means it runs a budget deficit of $40. That's $40 more in someone's bank account and $40 more in reserves in the banking system.

So far, we haven't mentioned debt. Money is debt, so in a sense we have mentioned it, but I mean debt as usually understood: government debt securities such as Treasury bills, notes, and bonds in the US. (The convention in the US is to call Treasury securities of one year's maturity or less "Treasury bills," those of two- to ten-year maturity "Treasury notes," and those of twenty- or thirty-year maturity "Treasury bonds." For simplicity I will refer to them all as "Treasury bonds," "Treasuries," or just "bonds.")

Where and how do Treasuries enter the picture? The simplest way to understand these questions is to imagine that, after the government creates the $40 of new money in the form of reserves, it issues $40 of Treasuries. This action's effect on balance sheets in the economy will depend on whether the bonds are bought by banks or the nonbank public (which could be individuals or, more likely, professional investors, such as mutual funds and **hedge funds**). In either case, the effect of the government issuing $40 of Treasuries is to reduce reserves by $40: the reserves the budget deficit created are expunged. What happens to the bank deposits depends on who buys the bonds. If banks buy them, the deposits remain; if the nonbank public buys them, the deposits disappear, and the depositors now have bonds instead of deposits.

Another way to understand how Treasuries enter the picture would be to assume that the government starts by issuing Treasuries, $40 worth in this case, and then runs a $40 deficit as a result of its spending, transfer, and taxing actions. Let's trace that through. What happens when the government issues $40 of Treasuries again depends on who buys them: banks or nonbanks. In both cases, reserves are reduced by $40. If banks buy the Treasuries, the bonds just replace the reserves on the asset side of the banking system's balance sheet; if nonbanks buy them, $40 of deposits (on the liability side of the banking system's balance sheet) are expunged along with the reserves. In the nonbank case, the net effect of the government running a deficit and its issuing the same amount of bonds would be to leave the amount of reserves and bank deposits unchanged, and therefore the amount of money, as conventionally defined (whether narrowly as the monetary base or more broadly as **M2 money supply**), unchanged as well.

Unfortunately, the right language doesn't exist to describe all of this in a way that doesn't obscure the underlying reality and lead people up the garden path. The normal language would be to say that the government "financed" its deficit by issuing bonds. That would imply that the government needed the money it raised in order to run the deficit it did. But this would be misleading: running a deficit creates money, not the other way around.

In the case where nonbanks rather than banks buy the bonds, no deposit money is created. This is misleading, too. Economists do not traditionally consider government bonds to be money because bonds are not used as a medium of exchange. Also, in their simple macro models, economists historically have drawn a sharp distinction between money and bonds, the latter being seen as an asset (store of value), not as money (medium of exchange). It is more logical and intuitive to regard government bonds as one *form* of money, albeit one for which a small step has to be taken for it to serve as a medium of exchange, namely selling the bond.

By law, the government's deposit account at the central bank usually is not allowed to go into overdraft. In the modern world, the central bank is part of the government; it is also the bank *of* the government (the bank the government does its banking with). From an economic point of view, the government's deposit account at the central bank "disappears" or cancels out within the overall (or consolidated) government, being simultaneously an asset of the treasury and a liability of the central bank. From that perspective, you would think there would be no problem with the government's account balance at the central bank going into negative territory as it deficit-spent, each dollar of overdraft just generating a dollar of reserves and bank deposits. When the government issued its bonds (to banks or nonbanks), its deposit balance would increase; that is, its overdraft balance would decrease, and reserves would decrease dollar for dollar, too.

THE PURPOSE OF BONDS

If the government does not need to issue bonds to raise money to pay for its deficit spending, and bonds are best thought of as just another form of money, what purpose do they serve? The answer is, there are two related ones: bonds help the central bank conduct its monetary policy in the way that it does; and they help secure the operational independence of the central bank—that is, they help the government commit credibly to not creating too much money.

The government running a deficit increases reserves by the same amount; the government issuing bonds drains reserves by that amount. Government bond sales are reserve-draining operations; in other words, they are operations that assist monetary policy operations. Governments usually run budget deficits, so they are ordinarily in the business of creating reserves. Issuing bonds helps the central bank control the level of reserves. Viewed in this light, government issuance of bonds clearly has nothing to do with borrowing as we usually think of the term, and everything to do with enabling the central bank to do its job.

There is no mechanical or operational limit to the process of the government creating money by running a budget deficit. There are two important economic limits, however—one obvious, the other more subtle.

The obvious one is that the government's ability to run budget deficits and inject new purchasing power into the economy is limited by the amount of real resources in the economy. If the government ramps up its spending too much or puts excessive money in the hands of the public, at some point too much money will be chasing too few goods and high inflation will result. The real constraint on government spending is the availability of real resources, not money. Not that the government should expand its reach until it hits that point. The resources the government commands are unavailable to the private sector (to use for its purposes). Society, through its political process, will want to constrain the government way before it bumps up against the real resource constraints of the economy. Exactly where along the line it does so is the stuff of political battles over "small government" versus "big government." Economists would point out that the real resource constraints of the economy are endogenous to that choice: allow the government to get too big and intrusive in the market economy, and inefficiencies and less innovation will result. Governments trying to control the makeup of the pie and being too proactive in slicing it up will make the pie smaller than it would otherwise be.

The more subtle constraint on the government's money creation relates to the nature of money itself: it needs to be accepted by those to whom it is proffered. When it comes to money being a unit of account and a medium of exchange, it takes two to tango, or more accurately it takes the cooperation of the citizenry. The observation that the government creates money by spending on goods and services (including those supplied by the people it employs) presupposes that the suppliers of those goods and services are willing to provide them in exchange for the checks the government writes.

Most people don't have too hard a time believing that the government can get people to accept the money it creates by fiat. After all, the government has the full coercive power of the state behind it. But that proposition needs to be established rather than just assumed or asserted.

One argument is that the government creates a demand for the currency it issues by requiring that its taxes be paid in it. In this view, a key purpose of taxation is to create a demand for the money supplied by the government.[3] Once that demand is established, the government can leverage it to exercise a near-universal command over society's resources.

This makes for an interesting argument, but it may not pass the test of Occam's razor. If the state can compel its citizens to obey laws and do all the things that are normally associated with being considered a good citizen in a civilized society, it shouldn't be too much of a stretch to believe that it can coerce them into accepting and using the money it creates (or is created by banks with the government's imprimatur). Viewed from another angle, if a government is struggling to get its citizens to accept its sovereign currency, it is likely to have much bigger problems on its hands, such as maintaining basic law and order.

OUR NOT-SO-POOR GRANDCHILDREN

It is widely claimed that government debt represents some kind of burden on future generations. Fiscally conservative politicians and commentators rail against governments racking up big deficits on the grounds that they are loading up future generations with debt and "mortgaging their future." There is a widespread view that budget deficits, particularly large and continuing ones, are bad, or at least a temporary, necessary evil, and that governments over time should strive to run a balanced budget.

This view of government debt and budget deficits rests on fallacious thinking, what logicians call a "category error." The category error here is treating the government as if it were a single household, when in fact it is more akin to an amalgam of *all* households (in that country). There is no reason that governments should always balance their budget, and generally they shouldn't.

When thinking about government debt as a possible burden on future generations, it is important to distinguish between *intra*generational issues (those having to do with the implications for people living at the same time, either now or in the future) and *inter*generational ones (those having implications for people born and living in one period versus those who will be born and live in the future). Arguments that focus on government debt being "a burden on our grandchildren" are explicitly or implicitly intergenerational ones. In examining them, we need to avoid the trap of conflating them with intragenerational issues, such as who wins and who loses among people born and living at the same time.[4] For instance, if the government were to build a big dam over ten years, an intragenerational effect today would be that some people will have to supply the time, labor, and resources to build it, and a more diffuse set of people, without really being aware, will be denied the use of those resources. An intragenerational effect in the future would be that some people will benefit a lot from the use of the water from the dam (for consumption and electricity generation) and others much less so, depending, for example, on where they live. In intergenerational terms, however, one generation sacrificed (invested resources) and a subsequent generation benefited.

One of the overlooked aspects of government debt is that it is a financial asset as well as a financial liability. What future generations inherit in net financial terms, surprisingly enough, is always zero, since the same item on both the asset and the liability sides of a balance sheet must, in aggregate, cancel out. A zero net liability can hardly be a burden on the generation that inherits it.

It is worth laying out at a very intuitive level why the stock of government debt does not represent a burden on future generations. Because we are talking about the current generation taking actions that impose a burden on future generations, we can ignore intragenerational issues (as important and complex as they might be for other issues) and imagine a simple model with two nonoverlapping generations. The period-one generation (call it "generation one") works, consumes, saves, and invests, and the period-two generation ("generation two") inherits the capital stock and financial assets and debts left by generation one. Assume for simplicity that generation two just works and consumes but does not save or invest. After two periods, this simple schematic world comes to an end.

Now, in what sense can generation one impose a burden on generation two by running a budget deficit and leaving the associated stock of government debt to generation two? People who worry about government debt imposing a burden on future generations believe that the government debt, being debt, will have to be repaid at some future point via the government raising taxes. Earlier generations, they maintain, get to enjoy the benefits of overly generous government spending and monetary transfers, and later generations have to pick up the tab. What could be less fair?

However, in our simple example, generation two inherits from generation one the stock of capital associated with generation one's investing and a stock of government debt securities, whose net value to, or burden on, generation two is zero. A government bond is a debt of the government—that is, of society—and an asset for those who hold it. Since we are focusing on intergenerational issues here and ignoring for simplicity what is going on within generations, it is clear that generation two owns government bonds as an asset and a debt, and that the two cancel out.

To use a different viewpoint, imagine a Martian hovering over Earth and observing this simple economy. The Martian would see generation one working, building some infrastructure (investing), and consuming some goods and services they produced. In the next period the Martian would observe generation two using the infrastructure left to it by generation one. The Martian would not see any burden from the government debt.

The way in which generations are linked and can influence one another is governed by the arrow of time, which moves in one direction. Prior generations can bequeath things to later generations but cannot take the fruits of their labor from them or tax them. The current generation produces output using the capital stock and the stock of knowledge it has inherited from previous generations and the blood, sweat, and tears of its own labor. It cannot use any of the labor or the capital that will be accumulated by future generations, since those generations don't exist yet. The current generation cannot take or borrow anything from a future generation; it can only leave something to them. What it can leave is (1) the capital stock that it inherited from previous generations, depleted somewhat by use but augmented by its own investments; and (2) financial assets that, by their nature, have distributional implications for people inside that generation but that cancel out for the generation as a whole.

The current generation can only borrow from itself; never from future generations. Future generations do not exist yet; they have not produced anything yet and so they have nothing to lend to the current generation. Every generation leaves to the next generation a stock of capital, which is almost always bigger and better than what it received from the prior generation. The stock of capital is not just physical productive capital like bridges, roads, airports, factories, and telecommunications networks; it can be thought of more broadly as including the stock of scientific, technological, intellectual, institutional, and cultural knowledge as well as social capital. This is the stuff of economic, technological, and civilizational progress. Each generation is a steward of this planet and, in a civilized society, has a moral responsibility to leave the planet and society in better condition than it received it. Yet, this has nothing to do with the question of whether increasing government debt is a burden on future generations. There are lots of things to worry about in this world, but leaving too much government debt to future generations is not one of them. If there ends up being too much government debt outstanding at some point, macroeconomic policy—monetary and fiscal policy tightening—can take care of it.

PUTTING THE NATIONAL ACCOUNTING IDENTITY TO WORK

The stock of government debt represents the cumulative effect of prior government budget deficits (and any offsetting surpluses). The government runs a budget deficit when it spends more than it takes in by taxing. Let's delve into that a little more.

The national accounting identity, equating two breakdowns of **GDP** or **Gross Domestic Product**, comes in handy here. This identity, which is always true by definition, uses the fact that every dollar of expenditure on the goods and services produced in an economy (in effect, GDP) accrues to someone as income. When economists look at GDP, they usually do so in real terms (i.e., adjusted for inflation) rather than in nominal terms (i.e., using current-period prices, the prices prevailing in that period). **Real GDP** provides a measure of the quantity of output, but in inflation-adjusted (domestic currency) terms. Changes in real GDP attempt to capture changes in the quantity of goods and services produced and consumed. **Nominal GDP** incorporates changes in real GDP but also includes the effect of changes in the price level. Unless stated otherwise, references to GDP and its components will be to real, not nominal, values.

National output can be separated into key categories of expenditure: households invest in houses and buy goods and services to consume; businesses invest in capital equipment; the government consumes goods and services (provides public services) and invests in civilian and military infrastructure; and foreigners buy part of a country's output (exports). On the other hand, part of spending on consumption and investment falls on imported goods and services, and that needs to be taken into account.

Writing this breakdown of output as an identity gives:

$$\text{Output} = \text{Consumption} + \text{Investment} + \text{Government Spending} + \text{Exports} - \text{Imports}$$

This is like a budget constraint for the economy: how much an economy can consume, invest, and export is constrained by how much it can produce and import.

National output can also be decomposed into what those who receive the associated income do with it. This is a bit simpler. National income can be consumed, saved, or taxed by the government. Tax revenue here is net of any transfers the government makes, such as social security payments, welfare payments, or subsidies. If the government takes in $100 in tax revenue, but pays out $25 in transfers, net taxes are $75. The transfers just shift money (or purchasing power) between people; they don't directly enter into GDP. Of course, they influence GDP indirectly because different people have different spending proclivities, or what economists term "marginal propensities to consume": a dollar taken from a rich person and given to a poor person won't dent the consumption of the former but will likely boost the consumption of the latter.

Writing this breakdown of national income as an identity gives:

$$\text{Income} = \text{Consumption} + \textbf{Saving} + \text{Taxes}$$

Combining the two decompositions of GDP gives rise to this identity:

$$\text{Consumption} + \text{Investment} + \text{Government Spending} +$$
$$\text{Exports} - \text{Imports} = \text{Consumption} + \text{Saving} + \text{Taxes}$$

Cancelling and rearranging terms yields a very useful form of this identity; that is, a mathematical relationship that always holds:

$$\text{Savings} - \text{Investment} + \text{Taxes} - \text{Government Spending} =$$
$$\text{Exports} - \text{Imports}$$

That is:

$$\text{Private sector net savings (savings net of investment)} + \text{the}$$
$$\text{budget surplus (if positive) or the budget deficit (if negative),}$$
$$\text{as the case may be} = \textbf{the current account balance}$$

This mathematical identity can be used to infer knowledge of some components based on knowledge of others. For instance, if the current account is in surplus but the country has a budget deficit, private sector savings must exceed investment by the amount the current account surplus exceeds the budget deficit. However, the identity cannot be used to argue causality, such as the current account being in deficit *because* the budget is in deficit and private investment exceeds saving. In economists' language, the identity may describe an equilibrium of the economy but it doesn't say anything about how and why the economy got there.

One Big World

To understand the role that the government running a budget deficit plays in an economy, let's focus on the world as a whole. This allows us to momentarily ignore trade in goods and services between individual economies; on a worldwide scale, one country's exports are another country's imports, so they cancel out.

If there were no government sector, the identity would reduce to a very simple one: Savings = Investment. This is remarkable, but obvious when you think about it.

It is remarkable because the myriad economic agents who decide how much of their income to save are generally different from the myriad economic agents who decide how much investment to undertake. Both sets of agents make those decisions in a highly decentralized manner without coordinating with one another. Yet they still add up to the same amount.

Aggregate private sector saving does not end up being equal to aggregate private sector investment because anyone plans it that way. That would be impossible in a decentralized market economy. In fact, in terms of plans, there is no reason to expect the sum of all the planned *saving* by economic agents to equal the sum of all planned *investment* by economic agents—generally, they will not be. Rather, due to the workings of the world economy—the fact that it is a closed system and that one economic agent's spending is another's income—the two end up being equal.

It is obvious that Saving = Investment in this simplified global economy when we consider what saving is and how it occurs. As with many economic terms in common speech, "saving" and "investing" have a more precise and specific meaning in economists' use. Here we are using the terms in their national accounting sense:

- *Saving* is income that is not spent on consumption or taxed by the government but is being held over for future consumption.
- *Investment* is that part of output that is not consumed today but is used to increase the capacity of the economy to produce more output in the future.

When I take a hundred dollars out of my bank account and use it to buy shares in a listed company, I am neither saving nor investing in the national accounting sense. I am just changing the financial form in which I am holding my earlier savings.

The only way the world as a whole can save—that is, transfer claims on consumption today into claims on consumption tomorrow—is to invest: to add to the capacity of the economy to produce output in the future. Recalling our observing Martians, there's no outside economy on Mars or elsewhere against which to run a current account surplus or accumulate financial claims, in order to transfer purchasing power through time. (Perhaps this will change one day!)

Bringing the Government into the Picture

If we reintroduce the government into the mix, the national accounting identity becomes:

Savings – Investment = Government Spending – Taxes

For the world as a whole, net private sector savings must equal the budget deficit (because we are talking about the world as a whole: technically speaking, the budget deficit arising from summing all national budget balances, since some countries may be running a budget surplus). The only way the private sector in aggregate—that is, all the households and firms in the world—can save more than it invests is if governments in aggregate run a budget deficit.

The government cannot choose how big or small a budget deficit it will run. It can choose how much it *plans* to spend by purchasing goods and services, investing in infrastructure, and employing government workers, and it can choose the *parameters* of its taxation system and social welfare and entitlements programs, but it cannot choose the net outcome of those policy choices, independently of how the decentralized market economy behaves and reacts. As an example, for the government to balance its budget, private savings will have to equal investment, but while the government can influence those two (highly aggregated) variables, it has no way to control them.

Another way of writing the identity for the world as a whole is:

Savings = Investment + the Budget Deficit

There are two ways for the private sector to save for the future: (1) via the investments that companies (plant, structures, and equipment), governments (public infrastructure), and households (houses) undertake; and (2) by governments running budget deficits. This casts budget deficits in a very different light from that suggested by the usual fiscal hawk or "doomsday" economic rhetoric. Rather than being the feedstock of increasing burdens on future generations, the budget deficit here looks more like an additional vehicle for the current generation to save for the future. That sounds like a much more laudatory objective!

Being mathematical identities, the relationships derived from the decomposition of output and income always hold. The only question is, at what level of output will they do so: a full employment level or a lower (possibly much lower) level? Abba Lerner's insightful but much-neglected "functional finance" perspective, building on Keynes's contributions, is that the budget deficit should not be treated as a policy target.[5] Rather, it should be viewed as a policy tool for helping achieve a socially desirable outcome (full employment and low stable inflation).

There are limits to using the budget deficit as a policy tool, however. Fiscal policy, or the size of the budget deficit, cannot be used as a mechanical policy lever. Suppose the budget deficit were $100, meaning that net private savings were also $100, comprising $200 of savings and $100 of investment. If the budget deficit instead were $50, that would mean that the gap between savings and investment must have narrowed by $50 (to $50); we know that as a matter of economic logic. But that does not mean that the government could necessarily cause the gap between savings and investment to be $50 by cutting its spending by $25 and raising taxes by $25. That tightening of fiscal policy will have repercussions throughout the economy, affecting consumption, investment, and savings decisions, which in turn will affect tax revenues and even the government's ability to implement its spending programs. The government can readily set tax rates, but it cannot control tax revenues, which largely depend on decisions taken by the private sector.

Suppose that desired saving by the private sector greatly exceeds desired investment by the private sector at full employment (a situation that Alvin Hansen in the 1930s and Lawrence Summers more recently have termed "**secular stagnation**").[6] Then it makes sense for the government to run a correspondingly large budget deficit. Doing so is the way that the government can satisfy the desire of the private sector to save more than it is willing to invest. The alternative is likely to result in a large budget deficit persisting or the surplus of private sector savings over investment being much smaller, but at a much lower level of output.

The logic works in the other direction, too. Suppose that (desired and realized) private sector investment far exceeds (desired and realized) private sector saving. Then, of necessity, the government would be running a corresponding budget surplus; now the government sector would be saving in net terms, and that saving would serve to offset the deficit of private sector saving. The government would be running down its debt and the private sector would be running down its financial assets, in a sense financing the (relatively) higher level of private sector investment.

This perspective casts government debt in a very different light. When a large surplus of net private sector savings requires the government to run a large and possibly persistent budget deficit in order to maintain full employment, the associated bonds that the government issues represent the supply of the financial assets that the private sector desires to hold. Government dissaving accommodates private sector saving. When the reverse is true, government saving offsets private sector dissaving.

Bringing International Trade into the Picture

Let's return to the level of the individual national economy and bring international trade back into the picture. The national accounting identity can be written as:

$$\text{Saving} = \text{Investment} + \text{the Budget Deficit} + \text{the Current Account Surplus}$$

Now the private sector has three ways to transfer its spending power through time: investing in the real economy, the government running a budget deficit, and the country running a current account surplus.

This makes intuitive sense. If a country exports more than it imports, it must be receiving more money than it is paying out; it is acquiring financial claims on its trading partners (the rest of the world), which constitutes its net national savings—that is, savings over and above what it can achieve by investing in its own economy.

The budget deficit, and the question of how much government debt accumulates over time, is intricately related to that of the private sector's desire to save and invest, and to the public policy imperative of maintaining full employment. The budget deficit and level of government debt are a part of a means to an end, not the end in itself.

GOVERNMENT DEBT NEVER HAS TO BE REPAID

The attraction or plausibility of the idea that "high" government debt levels are problematic because, among other things, they impose a burden on future generations has much to do with a fundamental misunderstanding: that government debt has to be repaid. It doesn't.

To understand this critical point, we need to probe a little bit into the question of what debt is by distinguishing financial and government debt. Financial debt involves a contract in which one party borrows money from another party and agrees to pay the money back in full with interest at some future date. The lender may be a bank making a consumer or commercial loan or an investor buying a corporate bond. A key feature of financial debt is that it is supposed to be repaid in full.

Government debt looks similar to corporate or household debt, but it is fundamentally different. I am talking here about national governments that are able to issue their own currency. Governments do not have to borrow from anybody in order to spend money; rather, they create money by spending. It may look as if governments have to borrow in order to spend, implying that they have to repay what they borrow, because of (1) the widespread separation of monetary and fiscal functions in modern economies and (2) the financial shackles that governments put on themselves by giving their central banks operational independence. And operationally that is how fiscal operations are usually carried out. But that is an artificially constructed system, not the underlying reality.

To make the point clear, it is helpful to imagine life in the mythical Monetary Garden of Eden introduced in chapter one. Imagine there is no separation of the central bank from the treasury: they are one and the same governmental department. Call it the Government Fiscal Bank. The government spends by drawing checks on its fiscal bank, which creates deposits in the banking system and positive balances in the accounts of banks at the fiscal bank (reserves). When the government taxes the public, bank deposits and reserves fall by that amount. If the government writes checks for more than it receives in taxes (i.e., if it runs a budget deficit), there will be net positive balances in bank deposit accounts and bank reserve accounts. The Government Fiscal Bank will have created what we usually call "money": monetary base (reserves) and M1 (bank demand deposits).

As we saw in chapter one, money is created in three ways: bank lending, the government running a budget deficit, and the central bank buying assets or lending to banks. The money created by the government running a budget deficit is called "outside money" in the literature, as opposed to the "inside money" banks create when they lend. The noteworthy feature of outside money is that it is an asset without a counterpart on the other side of the balance sheet; it just *is*, so to speak.

Because the government is running a budget deficit, households find themselves with increased bank deposits, which have bank reserves (deposit balances of the banks at the central bank) as their asset-side counterpart on the balance sheet of the banking system. There is a question of what the balancing item on the balance sheet of households should be. I take the (non-Ricardian) view here that recipients of the government payments to the private sector take them as net worth.[7]

The key point to take from this simple example is that the reserves (base money) created by the government running the budget deficit never have to be repaid. They are just like banknotes. Suppose households decided to hold half of the money they received as a result of the government running a budget deficit as cash (banknotes). Half of the $100 liability on the Government Fiscal Bank's balance sheet created by the deficit would now be reserves and half would be banknotes. The government no more has to repay the $50 reserves at some point in the future than it has to repay the $50 in banknotes. (Recall the earlier example of bringing a $20 bill to the Fed and getting two $10s back.) Or imagine that the public decided to hold the whole amount as cash. It is even clearer now that the government does not have to repay anything.

Of course, in the modern world, things don't work this way. Rather, the "bank part" of the Government Fiscal Bank is separated from the "treasury part." The central bank is made independent of the treasury and fiscal authorities. The central bank is given responsibility for "monetary policy" and the treasury and the political arm of the government are assigned responsibility for "fiscal policy." In this modern setup, laws are typically enacted or rules established barring the central bank from directly "financing" budget deficits, either by directly buying government-issued debt or allowing the government's account at the central bank to go into unlimited overdraft.

The institution of independent, technocratic central banking evolved over the course of the twentieth century, particularly in the second half, to constrain the ability of governments to run inflationary budget deficits. It is this institutional innovation that has created the belief that government debt is something that needs to be repaid and therefore that mounting government debt is becoming an increasingly big burden for future generations.

How do things change when the government can no longer just use its central bank to "print" money? To run a budget deficit, the government now has to issue bonds up front. This drains deposits and reserves at first, but the government running the budget deficit restores them. Imagine now that the central bank, for monetary policy purposes, decides to do $100 of quantitative easing (QE). Looking at things in terms of the consolidated government balance sheet, the impact on balance sheets is exactly the same as in the example of the Government Fiscal Bank.

This underscores a point to be made in chapter four that reserves and government bonds are just two forms of liabilities created by the consolidated government when it runs a budget deficit. One never has to be repaid, the other has a form that makes it appear that it must be. This is not intrinsic but rather is an artifact of the institutional setup. The widespread, large-scale QE by central banks in recent years shows that it is within the power of the central bank, itself part of government, to convert government debt at will into something (reserves or monetary base) that never has to be repaid.

The institution of independent central banking has served a very useful purpose: it has allowed governments to credibly commit to not abusing their ability to create money and purchasing power at will—or, as often put, their access to the printing press. However, it is possible to do away with the fiction that budget deficits lead to the accumulation of a debt that will impose a burden of potential or actual repayment on future generations, while allowing the central bank to keep exerting discipline on government spending, in the following way: the central bank can pay interest on reserves, as most major ones now do. By paying such interest, the central bank can remove the perceived default risk associated with government debt and still maintain control of monetary conditions.

The assertion that governments don't really borrow money might appear to be contradicted by the facts of the bond market. Governments usually issue debt securities with specific maturities— the date on which repayment of the bond is due. Suppose that the US Treasury has a $100 ten-year bond coming due, and imagine for argument's sake that the investors holding that bond want their money back. They may want to invest that $100 in another financial asset. Granted, the Treasury has to repay the $100; in that sense the bond looks and feels like a debt.

Something like the following will happen. The Treasury will issue another $100 ten-year bond to, let's say, the nonbank public. Bank deposits will decline by $100, as will bank reserves, and Treasury deposits at the Fed will increase by $100. The Treasury will use that $100 to pay off the holders of the first bond, resulting in bank deposits and reserves both going up by $100 again. The net effect of all of this will be to leave everything the same in aggregate terms. The bond has come due but the Treasury has simply refinanced it into a new bond; who owns the bond may change, but aggregate balance sheets in the economy don't.

This kind of thing happens continuously in government bond markets and is the way that they operate: as they come due, government debt securities just get rolled over or refinanced. They never have to be repaid and, in net terms, they never actually get repaid. Well, never say never. There is one kind of exception. Suppose, unusually, the government is running a budget surplus, taking in more from the private sector than it is paying out. Then, deposits in the banking system and reserves will fall by the amount of the budget surplus, and government deposits at the central bank will increase by that amount. That's the practical translation of the government taking more money from the private sector in taxes than it is handing over in payment of goods and services and in social welfare transfers. The government will use the budget surplus to pay down its debt by not refinancing debt securities that come due. The net effect on balance sheets will be that government debt securities equivalent to the amount of the budget surplus disappear from the system, with everything else (reserves, government deposits, and bank deposits) unchanged.

What would happen if the government did not use its budget surplus to pay down its debt? Bank deposits and reserves would decline by the amount of the budget surplus and government deposits at the central bank would increase by that amount; the amount of government debt securities outstanding would remain the same. This would be an odd thing for the government to do because, in effect, it would be a "negative carry trade" (i.e., a loss-making proposition). The government would forgo the opportunity to reduce its interest-bearing liabilities by running down an asset (deposits at the central bank) on which it earns no interest.

What the central bank would do in this situation depends on whether it is operating in a binding minimum-reserves regime. If the central bank is targeting a positive overnight interest rate (for interbank loans; see chapter one) and keeping reserves in the banking system in line with minimum reserve requirements, as the Fed and most other central banks were doing before the Global Financial Crisis, it would have to restore to the banking system the reserves that the government drained by running the budget surplus. It would likely do this by buying government debt securities from the public. The net effect of this situation would be for the public to end up with the same amount of deposits, but an amount of government debt securities lower by the value of the budget surplus; the central bank's balance sheet would be larger by the same amount, with government debt securities on the asset side and government deposits on the liability side. From the private sector's point of view, the situation is the same as if the government had used its budget surplus to reduce its debt. From the overall government's point of view, government debt securities and government deposits, equivalent to the amount of the budget surplus, will be sitting on both the central bank's and the treasury's balance sheets, but on different sides; this would beg for them all just to be cancelled out within the overall government, as they already are in effective economic terms.

What would happen if the private sector went on strike and refused to refinance or roll over the maturing government debt securities coming due? Assuming that the government had sufficient deposits at the central bank, or that the legal regime was such that the central bank allowed the government to go into overdraft on its account, government deposits at the central bank and government debt securities would decline, and bank deposits and reserves would rise, all by the amount of debt securities maturing. The public, having refused to roll over or refinance the maturing bonds, will now be holding bank deposits instead. That seems pretty unlikely: government bonds are usually considered the safest asset in the economy, which is why in finance the yield on government bonds is often termed the "risk-free rate." Does it really make sense to imagine that the government could not find anyone who would be willing to trade bank deposits for government debt securities, which is what the government being able to issue new bonds to repay old ones amounts to? Would all investors regard deposits in the banking system as less risky than government debt? That's a stretch.

In this investor bond-strike scenario, from the viewpoint of the overall government's balance sheet, it would be a case of government debt securities being swapped out for central bank reserves. Even if the private sector refused to hold government debt securities, it cannot refuse to hold central bank reserves, either directly (if banks held the maturing bonds) or indirectly (if the nonbank public did), as this is what the overall government gives them, again directly or indirectly, when it makes good on its debt securities. Government-produced money, once created, is trapped in the system, unless it is destroyed by the government running a budget surplus.

What if, on top of an investors' bond strike, the government could not go into overdraft on its account at the central bank and the central bank was barred from buying government bonds directly from the government? The government would be imposing these constraints on itself, or society, via the legislature, would be forcing it to do so. Then the government would be stuck and unable to repay its debt. Operationally, the government repays its maturing debt by having its bank account at the central bank debited (for the remittances it makes into the bank accounts of the holders of the maturing bonds). If its account balance hits zero and, by assumption here, the government is unable either (1) to have its account go into overdraft or (2) replenish it by issuing new debt securities either to the public or the central bank, it will not be able to repay its debt.

The only scenario in which the government is unable to roll over or refinance its existing debt is one in which it is assumed that the public prefers bank deposits to less risky government debt securities and the government itself (or society) has arranged the institutional deckchairs to make this artificially the case.

THE PURPOSE OF TAXATION

If this is the case, why do governments raise money by taxing the public? Government taxation actually has nothing to do with a mooted need of the government to finance itself. Government taxation serves three distinct purposes: mitigating negative externalities, redistributing income or purchasing power, and controlling **aggregate demand**.

A classic reason for governments to levy taxes is to mitigate negative externalities (or, in the reverse case, to give subsidies to promote certain activities). Negative externalities occur when market prices do not fully reflect the harm that an activity has on people other than the person engaging in it. In a sense, all economic activities have a negative impact or (opportunity) cost in the sense that the resources consumed are not available for other purposes. A central tenet of economics is that the price system of the market mechanism usually does a good job of internalizing those costs. But sometimes it doesn't. The government may want to tax activities that pollute or degrade the environment, raise the risk of damaging or cataclysmic climate change, pose risks to others' physical safety, or impose high costs on the healthcare system. The purpose is not to raise tax revenue per se, but to change relative prices in a way that promotes or deters certain economic activities and thereby putatively enhances welfare for society.

A second reason for government taxation is to redistribute purchasing power or income among its citizens, ostensibly from those who have more than they need to those who have too little. The market economy is very efficient at producing goods and services and at incentivizing technological innovation, but it is largely oblivious to issues of equity and fairness. I say "largely" because the market mechanism does seem to have some stabilizing mechanism to prevent income and wealth inequality from reaching too egregious an extreme: harking back to an insight attributed to Henry Ford, households need to be paid enough for supplying their labor services to afford to purchase the output that firms produce.

The third, and least commonly recognized, reason for taxation is to modulate the amount of aggregate demand. Raising taxes drains household purchasing power and vice versa. If the economy is overheating or risks doing so, the government can cool it down by raising taxes. If economic activity is stalling or looks about to, the government can cut taxes to give households more purchasing power and buoy the economy. In this regard, taxes are to fiscal policy what interest rates are to monetary policy: a knob that the authorities can turn to try to keep aggregate demand in line with aggregate supply, and therefore the economy at full employment with low and stable inflation.

Popular discussion of government spending and taxing is commonly framed in terms of the government needing to raise money to pay for its new spending. That cannot be right because the government, in principle, can always create the money it needs to spend. In such circumstances, the government doesn't need to raise taxes in order to pay for the new spending, but it will likely need to free up resources in the economy in order to absorb the new spending without generating inflationary pressure. The way that society pays for new government spending is by forgoing other spending that otherwise would have occurred. The purpose of taxing in those circumstances is not to raise money per se, as if the government needed that money and was going to use it again; rather, it is to withdraw purchasing power so as to free up the necessary resources.

WHAT IF FOREIGNERS OWN THE MORTGAGE?

The implicit assumption up until now has been that the government debt is held by the citizens of that country. Any distributional issues associated with the people (typically more affluent ones) owning the government debt as an asset being different from those liable for it as a liability (taxpayers in general) will be intragenerational, not intergenerational. But if a country has been running a sustained budget deficit and a current account deficit, foreigners will have been accumulating significant financial claims on the country, likely including holding its government bonds. Does this mean that government debt can be a burden on future generations of that country if much of it ends up being owned by foreigners?

"Burden" does not seem to be the right word to describe this situation. The US has been running large budget and current account deficits for years, and countries like Japan and China now hold a significant amount of US Treasury securities. The Treasuries that the Chinese hold give them a future claim on US goods and services, a claim they have earned by selling more to the US than they bought from it in the past. Imagine that Chinese holders of US Treasuries choose to sell them in the future in order to consume more US goods and services. The Chinese consumers still have to pay for the output they consume. For the producers of those goods and services, and for their workers, the demand from Chinese consumers is indistinguishable from demand that might come from US consumers.

If the output of US businesses is going to satisfy foreign rather than domestic demand, there may be subtle effects on the current account balance and exchange rate and on the pattern of domestic production, investment, and consumption. However, these are all probably better thought of as part and parcel of the complex workings of a decentralized and globalized market economy than as representing a burden that one generation bequeaths another because of its own consumption, savings, and investment decisions.

PROBLEMATIC DEBT-TO-GDP RATIOS

The most common metric used in discussions of the sustainability of government debt levels is the debt-to-GDP ratio. This is a very misleading statistic. The higher the debt-to-GDP ratio of a country, the more concern is expressed about the sustainability of its fiscal finances. Keeping the debt-to-GDP ratio below a certain level is often an explicit or implicit target of macroeconomic policy. The Stability and Growth Pact underlying the fiscal rules of the **euro area** requires countries to keep their debt-to-GDP ratio below 60 percent. A ratio approaching 100 percent is generally regarded as flashing amber, and a country such as Japan, with a gross debt-to-GDP ratio of some 240 percent, elicits despair (among Japan's fiscal hawks) or bewilderment (at why a fiscal crisis has not already occurred). Japan's net debt-to-GDP ratio, at about 130 percent, is much less scary, although still worrying to many.

A big problem with the debt-to-GDP ratio is that it mixes up units. Debt-to-GDP ratios are universally quoted, as I just did, in percentage terms. The correct unit, however, is "number of years of GDP." A debt-to-GDP ratio divides a stock by a flow; that is, something measured in dollars, say, divided by something measured in dollars per year. The correct units for a ratio whose numerator is measured in dollars and whose denominator is measured in dollars per year is number of years of what is being measured in the denominator. Measuring debt-to-GDP ratios in percent terms when the correct unit is "number of years" (of GDP) makes for confusion and unnecessary alarm.

Take a debt-to-GDP ratio of 100 percent, which in this context is what economists call a "focal number," a number that attracts attention beyond any intrinsic meaning it might have. When a percentage is the correct unit to use, 100 percent is often the maximum amount possible: for instance, when measuring performance on a test, compliance with a rule, or attendance at an event (relative to the number invited or the capacity of the venue). A value of 100 percent, let alone one above it, invokes a sense of reaching or exceeding some kind of natural limit, subtly underscoring the sense of unsustainability.

As mentioned, the correct unit in our debt-to-GDP example is "one year." A debt-to-GDP ratio of 1 can be thought of as indicating that, were it necessary to completely "pay off" the stock of government debt, one year's worth of GDP would need to be allocated to the purpose. "One year" seems to be a much more benign prospect than "100 percent," particularly for an entity—the government of a nation state—that, in principle, continues to exist indefinitely. Even so, the image invoked is one of the country's citizens toiling away for a whole year and the entire fruits of their labor being expropriated to pay down the national debt.

This is misleading. The government debt does not have to be paid off. Rather, it represents an asset that can be converted into purchasing power. A large stock of government debt implies a large amount of latent purchasing power. The real issue is whether the economy is capable of producing the goods and services that the holders of that asset might want to consume. If at any point in time it is not, there will be upward pressure on prices across the economy and the overall price level or cost of living will start to rise at an acceptable rate. That is called inflation; it, and the role of monetary policy in controlling it, is a topic we turn to next.

3

THE POWER OF CENTRAL BANKS

It follows from these propositions that *inflation is always and everywhere a monetary phenomenon* in the sense that it can be produced only by a more rapid increase in the quantity of money than in output.

Milton Friedman, 1994[1]

What causes inflation, and what tools do policymakers have to control it? That's a core question about money, because "too much money chasing after too few goods," as Milton Friedman famously put it, causes inflation,[2] and high inflation erodes the value of money. The policy key to controlling inflation must lie in ensuring that just the right amount of money is created: too much and you get (too high) inflation, too little and you get **deflation**. In this chapter, we explore what inflation is, what monetary policy is, and how central banks use those policies to try to control inflation.

We also examine why society assigns the primary responsibility for controlling inflation to the central bank and to monetary policy (rather than to the budgetary authorities and to fiscal policy).

Central banks have evolved over the centuries, the earliest ones starting as privately owned government-chartered banks, and there are many fascinating histories of how they have changed (see chapter one). In the modern era, central banks are part of the government, but they occupy a special place in it. They act largely independently within the government, accountable to but not controlled by it: "'Independent within the government' rather than 'independent of government,'" as the Federal Reserve itself has put it. The notion of central bank "independence" is paramount in the modern economic system, so much so that central banks appear to be closer to financial markets than to the rest of the government. Herein lies the linguistic trickiness: central banks are such important and visible actors in the financial markets and the economy, and their independence is so cherished, that they are spoken of as if they were *not* part of the government, when in fact they are.

DEFINING INFLATION

"Inflation" is a treacherous word because it means different things to different people, and sometimes even different things to the same person. That's a problem for a word on which so much hangs. Inflation is often used as a synonym for "high inflation." To the everyday person, inflation means that the cost of the things they buy day to day is going up. That's bad.

But to central bankers and economists, inflation in that sense is not necessarily a bad thing. They consider a little bit of *measured* inflation a good thing, the operational equivalent of there being no inflation, and a force that helps grease the wheels of the economy. Central banks are tasked to maintain "stable prices" or "price stability." This does not mean stability of individual prices—quite the opposite. Central bankers are generally card-carrying members of the "Washington Consensus": they support free markets, those in which supply and demand are free to change and market prices fluctuate accordingly. It is the average level of prices—a carefully constructed index of the *overall* price level—that central bankers seek to stabilize, and they do so at a slightly positive rate of change, usually 2 percent. For most central bankers, "zero inflation" in effect means 2 percent measured inflation; zero percent inflation, as it is measured, would mean the price level was slipping.

Pressed on whether they would prefer the prices of things they buy to be going down, most people would say, "Yes, please." A lower price level means a higher standard of living. Not so for central bankers and economists. A falling price level (or negative inflation rate) is just as bad as, if not worse than, one that is rising too fast. There are a few reasons for that. One is definitional: central bankers want price stability, which means a price level that is neither rising (at a rate faster than the target) nor falling.

A deeper reason is that economists think in "general equilibrium" terms. They don't look only at the impact of one thing changing on another (that is, in "partial equilibrium" terms); they try to trace through all the interactions and implications of one thing changing on everything else and how these changes impact the original thing that changed or was changed. (More technically, they compare the new equilibrium of the economy with the old one and look at what has changed once everything has adjusted.) Economists recognize that one person's spending is another person's income, so what is good for one person (lower prices) may be bad for another (lower income), and that may come back to bite a consumer who thought they were benefiting from falling prices . . . until they found out that this was because of a weakening economy and they no longer had a job. There was deflation in the Great Depression, but few people were celebrating.

A third reason is that central bankers and economists generally recognize that it is easier for central banks to bring down inflation when it is too high than raise it when it is too low. Having to deal with a falling price level is not something central bankers relish. Fiscal policy, which is out of the hands of central banks, is better at that.

When it comes to measuring inflation rates, four zones can be distinguished:

1. inflation at target (plus or minus a few **basis points**, perhaps, one basis point being one-hundredth of a percent)
2. inflation above target
3. inflation below target but zero or above
4. inflation in negative territory (outright deflation)

Inflation in the third zone is sometimes called "**disinflation**" to distinguish it from deflation, although the term "disinflationary" is often used in a directional sense, such as when high inflation is coming down due to "disinflationary forces." Central bank watchers have to be accomplished linguists.

WHY 2 PERCENT INFLATION?

Why do central bankers choose 2 percent (or some other positive number or range) as their target rather than zero? A lot of this complexity and ambiguity of language could be avoided if central banks adopted an inflation rate of zero percent as their target, perhaps with a bit of leeway above or below. The price stability target would be zero percent; anything above that would be inflation and anything below would be deflation. Central bankers would be in the business of avoiding both inflation and deflation. Life would be simple.

Here the monetary plot thickens. Economists usually recommend that central banks target a somewhat positive *measured* inflation rate, for three reasons.

The first is that the measured inflation rate is believed to overstate the *true* inflation rate. The arguments behind this that can get quite technical, quite fast. Inflation is measured by the rate of change of an index (collection) of prices: a **consumer price index** (CPI). A CPI usually has a base year at which the weights of the various goods and services included in the index are fixed. Consumers react opportunistically to price changes, buying more of the goods whose prices fall and less of the ones whose prices rise. This leads the CPI to overstate somewhat the rise in the cost of living because it implicitly assumes that consumers do not react to price changes. Statisticians attempt to incorporate quality improvements in CPIs so that a product whose price has not changed but whose quality has will be judged to have experienced a fall in price. To the extent that such quality improvements are underestimated, as they likely are, CPIs will have an upward bias.

A second reason for the target inflation rate being a positive number involves human psychology and what economists call "wage rigidity." Generally, people like their wages to go up but not down. What should matter to workers is not what happens to their *nominal* wages but what happens to their *real* wages, their nominal wages adjusted for inflation. If inflation is running at 2 percent a year, and my wages are going up by 2 percent a year, my real wages are unchanged. But let's say economic circumstances are such that my wages need to go down by 1 percent in real terms for my employer to remain competitive enough to stay in business and for me to keep my job. If the central bank is successfully targeting 2 percent inflation, then my employer can offer me a 1 percent pay raise and I probably won't be too unhappy. But if the central bank is targeting a zero percent inflation rate, my employer will have to cut my wages by 1 percent to achieve the same effect. It might be irrational for *Homo economicus* to do so, but I might object to that.

Why 2 percent and not 3 or 4 percent? There is little science behind the answer, but legendary central banker Alan Greenspan famously put it this way: "Price stability is that state in which expected changes in the general price level do not effectively alter business and household decisions."[3] Two percent was the nice round number that was above zero but deemed to be not high enough for people to notice and take umbrage with.

A third reason is a bit more technical but has to do with what economists call the **"zero lower bound"** on interest rates. The principal tool that central banks use when they need to stimulate the economy and try to prevent the inflation rate from settling below its target is the overnight interest rate. To rein in economic activity and quell inflationary pressures, central banks can hike the overnight interest rate; there is no upper limit on their ability to do so. Not so in the other direction, however: central banks can cut the overnight interest rate to zero or close to it, but that's about it—this is the zero lower bound. "Zero" needs an asterisk, however: recent experience has shown that central banks can push the overnight interest rate into negative territory to a limited extent, and even some market interest rates may follow suit, but there are still technical and operational limits, not to mention ones of political and public acceptance. So, the zero lower bound has become the **"effective lower bound"** with an implicit bit of downside flex into negative territory.

An inflation target of around 2 percent helps loosen the constraint of the effective lower bound on interest rates. Suppose that the inflation rate is 2 percent and the overnight interest rate, as set by the central bank, is 3 percent, implying a real interest rate of 1 percent (3 percent minus 2 percent). Imagine now that the economy goes into a slump and the inflation rate falls by half a percentage point, to 1.5 percent. The central bank wants to stimulate the economy and bring the inflation rate back up, so it cuts the overnight rate to 1 percent. The real interest rate is now negative (minus half a percent), even though the nominal interest rate is in positive territory. That might do the trick.

Suppose instead that the central bank is targeting an inflation rate of zero percent but other conditions are analogous: the overnight rate is 1 percent, the real interest rate is 1 percent, and inflation falls by half a percentage point. For simplicity, assume also that the effective lower bound is zero percent. Now there is a hitch: the central bank cannot cut the interest rate by 2 percentage points as in the prior case because it hits the zero bound. The lowest real interest rate the central bank can engineer to try to stimulate the economy is 0.5 percent. The zero lower bound means that a 2 percent inflation target gives the central bank more leeway to cut real interest rates and stimulate the economy.

That logic applies even more so for an inflation target of 3 or 4 percent, and some economists have argued for higher inflation targets because of the greater leeway they would afford. But nothing comes for free: the higher the inflation target, the more dubious the claim becomes that the central bank is acting to preserve the purchasing power of money, and the less likely that central banks will be able to maintain political and public support.

HOW CENTRAL BANKS CONTROL INFLATION

Monetary policy works as a three-step process:

- The central bank sets its monetary policy.
- Financial markets react, thereby "transmitting" the monetary policy to the real economy.
- The real economy reacts.

Monetary policy works in a very indirect or roundabout way. A change in monetary policy settings may translate into a change in financial conditions fairly quickly, but it can take quite a while for a change in financial conditions to affect economic activity. Hence the idea that monetary policy works with long and variable lags.

Central banks set monetary policy with a view to influencing financial conditions, depending on whether they think that economic activity and inflationary pressures need to be restrained or buoyed. Conceptually, monetary policy is very simple: the central bank has knobs, which it turns in one direction (down) when it needs to stimulate the economy and in the other direction (up) when it needs to restrain it.

By saying monetary policy works in roundabout fashion, we mean that the central bank doesn't have any tools that directly impact economic activity. The central bank is in the business of coaxing, nudging, persuading, and sometimes even threatening, but it cannot dictate or control economic outcomes. The biggest strength of monetary policy—the fact that it relies maximally on a decentralized market economy—is also its biggest limitation.

Monetary policymaking is also plagued by uncertainty. The central bank has to correctly assess the state of the economy, a highly complex and dynamic entity. It requires a good understanding at every point in time of the economy's trajectory and how it is likely to respond to changes in its monetary policy settings. It also has to correctly diagnose the patient and prescribe and administer the right medicine. This task is complicated by the fact that monetary policy works on the economy with a lag, whereas much of the data the central bank has come to it with a lag, those two lags compounding one another: monetary policymaking has to be forward looking but most of the available data is backward looking.

Before the 2008 Global Financial Crisis, for most developed-world central banks, monetary policymaking was operationally very simple. The Bank of Japan was the main exception because it was forced to the zero lower bound a decade before the Fed and other major central banks, after Japan's massive 1980s asset price bubble burst. In normal times, the central bank has one knob—the short-term interest rate—and it turned it one way or the other, depending on what kind of fine-tuning it judges the economy to need. Since the financial crisis and even more so with the COVID-19 pandemic, monetary policymaking has become much more complicated, but we will discuss that in the next chapter.

INFLATION TARGETING

The period immediately before the financial crisis was the heyday of "inflation targeting," an approach to monetary policymaking that had evolved in the prior two decades and has continued to evolve since.[4] In an inflation-targeting framework, the central bank seeks to control inflation by announcing an explicit inflation target and establishing credibility in the eyes of the public. I am using the term "public" here to include financial market participants, notably traders, money managers, and investors. Having credibility as an inflation targeter means that the public believes the central bank is both able and willing to achieve its inflation target: that the central bank has the necessary tools and requisite operational independence to use them, and the determination to do so.

The working assumption of the inflation-targeting framework is that the central bank, using its monetary policy tools, should be able to control inflation, and therefore it makes sense to give it that job. That the central bank should be able to control inflation with monetary policy used to be almost an article of faith among economists and central bankers; fiscal policy, as a tool to stabilize the macroeconomy, was widely seen as being unnecessary or ineffective, or even as counterproductive by some. Since the financial crisis and again with the COVID-19 pandemic, the realization has grown that fiscal policy has an important role to play, too, and sometimes may need to take the lead. The problem is that the macroeconomic policy framework, resting as it does on central bank independence and the presumed primacy of monetary policy, is not conducive to the optimal coordination, let alone joint mobilization, of monetary and fiscal policy.

The goal of macroeconomic policy is to keep the economy at "full employment" and the price level stable. Full employment, to economists and policymakers, is a notional state of the economy in which everyone who wants to work can find a job (there is enough demand); it doesn't mean a zero or near-zero unemployment rate, because there will always be some people in the labor force and in the process of changing jobs or looking for work.

Macroeconomic policy orthodoxy holds that seeking to control inflation, to keep it in line with the (usually) 2 percent target, is the best way to achieve the other goal of full employment. Scratch a macroeconomist and they will start talking about "the Phillips Curve." In the jargon, the long-run Phillips Curve is held to be vertical: that is, in the long run (when everything is settled) there is no trade-off between inflation (on the y-axis) and unemployment (on the x-axis). Attempts to push employment higher than its natural limit, or the unemployment rate lower than its "natural rate," ultimately will only result in higher inflation at the same level of unemployment.

Politicians, however, operate in the short run, with one eye on the next election, and may be tempted to "juice up" the economy even if the long-term effect of that may just be the same unemployment rate but with higher inflation. It is a key tenet of modern macroeconomic policymaking that, in managing monetary policy, central banks need to be insulated from political influence. Governments giving central banks operational "independence" is the way that they credibly commit not to interfere in monetary policymaking, with counterproductive effects. The government assigns the central bank the job—control inflation and keep the economy at full employment—and gives it the tools but promises not to interfere with the central bank's deployment of those tools to do its job.

In doing that job, central banks strive to "manage" the inflation expectations of the public or "anchor" them at their inflation target. Managing the public's inflation expectations plays a critical part in helping the central bank achieve its goal because inflation expectations largely drive inflation outcomes. Over the medium term at least, there is a significant self-fulfilling-prophecy aspect to inflation targeting. If the central bank can convince the public that it is both able and determined to achieve its inflation target, then it is rational for the public to adopt the central bank's inflation target as its own expectation of future inflation, which in turn helps guarantee success. It sounds almost too good to be true, which probably means it isn't, or at least not in all circumstances.

Communication and transparency lie at the heart of the central bank's management of inflation expectation. The central bank communicates with the public transparently, not just by announcing an explicit inflation target but also by communicating its view of current and likely future economic developments, its monetary policy decision-making process, and its "reaction function"—that is, how it is likely to respond to future developments. The central bank communicates almost constantly in all manner of ways: formally announcing monetary policy decisions; publishing regular reports detailing its economic forecasts, often including expectations of its future monetary policy decisions; releasing the minutes of monetary policy meetings (and often, after a few years, the full transcripts); having key officials give speeches and interviews; and publishing the results of analysis by its research staff. Inflation targeting is said, without too much exaggeration, to be all about communication, communication, and communication.

CONTROLLING THE SHORT-TERM INTEREST RATE

But how exactly can the central bank implement monetary policy in this framework? It simply raises or lowers the overnight interest rate, depending on whether it wants to restrain or stimulate economic activity, respectively. The mechanics of this are simple. Here is a simplified version of the Federal Reserve's balance sheet as it was on September 12, 2007, just before the Fed started to cut interest rates as the first tremors of the Global Financial Crisis started to be felt:

Assets ($ Billions)		Liabilities and Capital ($ Billions)	
US Treasury securities	779.6	Banknotes	775.4
Repurchase agreements	45.0	Reserves	31.7
Gold certificates	11.0	US Treasury deposits	5.2
Loans	7.4	Other items	43.3
Other items	47.2	Capital	34.6
Total	890.2		890.2

Federal Reserve Statistical Release, H.4.1; federalreserve.gov/releases /h41/20070913/.

In normal times, central banks like the Fed use the shortest-term interest rate in the economy as their main tool of monetary policy. That rate is called different things in different countries, but is the interest rate that commercial banks charge other banks for lending them their deposits at the central bank overnight (from one day to the next). It is worth taking a mini deep dive to understand how it all works.

As noted, the central bank is the banker to banks, which means that banks have deposit accounts at the central bank and these accounts are used to settle transactions between banks. There are hundreds of millions of noncash financial transactions every day, many of which are settled between banks. Suppose I pay for a fifty-dollar meal at my local restaurant by credit or debit card, and the restaurant and I maintain bank accounts at different banks. Fifty dollars moves from my bank account to the restaurant's; my bank does that by debiting my account by fifty dollars (liability side of its balance sheet) and transferring fifty dollars of its reserves at the Fed to the reserve (deposit) account of the restaurant's bank. Neither the total amount of deposits in the banking system nor the total reserves at the Fed changes; they just move between banks. Because so many transactions are settled between a relatively small number of banks, the bulk of transactions between banks net out, so it is only the net balance between banks per period that needs to move between reserve accounts.[5]

The reserve accounts of banks at the central bank underpin the whole payments system, without which a modern economy could not function. They also play a key role in monetary policymaking. How they do so today has evolved since the financial crisis, but to understand how, it is necessary to start with the system as it operated before the financial crisis. I will call it the "pre-crisis" system for short.

Financial Conditions

The key idea underlying monetary policymaking is that, by controlling one financial variable (the overnight interest rate), the central bank can indirectly influence the whole array of interest rates and asset prices—that is, financial conditions in the whole economy. "Financial conditions" is a broad term of art among monetary policymakers and economists that refers to the degree to which conditions in financial markets are or are not conducive to economic activity. Financial conditions are said to be "easy" or "loose" when interest rates are low and/or falling, when banks are eager to lend, when stock prices and the prices of other risk assets are high and/or rising, when "credit spreads" (the difference between yields on corporate debt of varying degrees of riskiness compared to one another and to the yield on government bonds) are narrowing, and when the foreign exchange rate of the currency is weak and/or weakening. Financial conditions are said to be "tight" when the reverse is true: interest rates are rising, banks are more reluctant to lend, risk asset prices are falling, credit spreads are widening, and the exchange rate is strengthening.

Arbitrage Connects Everything

What kind of alchemy allows central banks to influence such a wide array of interest rates and asset prices and lending conditions by moving one short-term interest rate? The answer: "arbitrage." All interest rates and asset prices are indirectly linked by a process called "financial arbitrage," which is driven by traders and investors seeking better financial returns. If the price of one asset starts to look low relative to the price of another that looks high, given their respective prospects or "fundamentals," investors will start to sell the more expensive asset, putting downward pressure on its price, and buy the cheaper one, putting upward pressure on its price. This arbitrage process will continue until the first asset no longer looks cheap relative to the second one. Arbitrage drives trading activity in financial markets every second of the day. And central banks likewise can exploit it for their own ends—that is, for the collective benefit of society.

For monetary policy transmission, the arbitrage process operates first and foremost along the "**yield curve**," the array of interest rates (yields) corresponding to government bonds of increasing maturity, out to thirty years or more. The yield on the bond of a given maturity can be thought of as the market interest rate, which can constantly change as traders buy and sell the bond. (This rate is different from the interest rate given by the coupon, the promised annual payment relative to the principal amount, or the amount initially raised by the issuance of the bond). Bond prices and yields move in opposite directions: yields fall as bond prices rise and vice versa. The overnight interest rate, being the interest rate of shortest maturity, is the first point on the yield curve, the "anchor point"; all other interest rates along the curve are indirectly influenced by the overnight rate because they incorporate the market's expectations of its future path.

Arbitrage again does the work, but in a subtle way. The central bank can control the overnight interest rate. Here's how.

The central bank announces a target for the overnight rate, often called the "policy rate," and then adjusts the amount of reserves in the banking system so that the prevailing rate in the interbank market for reserves aligns with that. In the US, these are the federal funds target rate and the federal funds rate, respectively. Pre-crisis, most central banks, including the Fed, did not pay interest on reserves, in the same way that they do not pay interest on banknotes. This meant that all the central bank needed to do was to adjust the amount of reserves in the banking system to be more or less in line with the total of all the individual banks' minimum reserve requirements. If the amount of reserves were much above that amount, banks would be eager to lend their "excess reserves" to other banks, which would put downward pressure on the overnight rate; if it were much below, some banks would be scrambling to borrow reserves in order to meet their minimum reserve requirements, which would put upward pressure on the overnight rate. By adjusting the amount of reserves, the central bank is able to control the shortest-term market interest rate, guiding it up or down as needed to hit its target.

If the central bank can control the overnight interest rate today, then it can do so tomorrow, and the next day, and every day into the future. Market participants know this. These two things—the central bank being able to control the overnight rate and investors knowing and acting on that—together drive arbitrage along the whole yield curve. Arbitrage ensures that every point along the yield curve incorporates market expectations about the future course of policy rates.

Now, suppose that it didn't. To take the simplest example, suppose a bank wanted to borrow reserves for two days, and the prevailing two-day interest rate was higher than that obtainable by borrowing at the prevailing overnight rate and again the next day at the overnight rate expected to be prevailing then, which will be determined by the policy rate of the central bank. In that case, the bank rationally will not borrow at the two-day rate and instead borrow at the overnight rate, planning to do so again the next day to achieve the same effect of securing reserves on a two-day basis. That will put downward pressure on the two-day interest rate and upward pressure on the overnight rate (although the central bank will offset any such upward pressure). Arbitrage, driven by the profit motive, will ensure that the two-day interest rate will reflect both today's policy rate and the market's expectation of the policy rate tomorrow. What is true for two days is true for three and true all along the yield curve.

This is the subtle point about central bank interest rate setting: the overnight rate does not *directly* affect the borrowing rates on loans that matter most for economic activity, such as those for consumer loans, home mortgages, and corporate borrowing for investment, which range from two to thirty years. But *indirectly* it does. Harvard economist and former Fed governor, Jeremy Stein, famously observed that monetary policy "gets in all of the cracks."[6] It could also be said that monetary policy has a long invisible hand.

Yields typically increase slightly with longer maturities because investors are committing their money for longer and need to be compensated for that. This is called the **"term premium,"** and it is normally positive. This and other nuances along the yield curve do not change the basic mechanism; arbitrage just incorporates them into its relentless profit-seeking process. Nor is the arbitrage effect limited to the yield curve; it extends to all financial assets, loosely tethering them all to one another and to the policy rate. Suppose that bond prices rise because the central bank lowers the policy rate and signals to the market that interest rates will likely be low for a long time; suppose also that this prospect had not already been factored into asset prices. All other things equal, which of course they never are, stock prices will now be more attractive.

Economists use the *ceteris paribus* or "all other things equal" assumption as an analytical device to try to isolate the effect of one thing on another, not as a description of reality. Some of the other things held constant can easily swamp the change under consideration, particularly if one is driving the other. Although, all other things equal, lower interest rates should buoy stock prices, it is a weakening of the economy that leads the central bank to cut interest rates. This weakening economy effect, initially at least, is likely to overwhelm the monetary easing effect and lead to lower stock prices. But in markets, timing is everything, and if the stock market has already discounted the weaker economic outlook but not the monetary easing, then the cut in interest rates may well cause stock prices to rally.

Central banks built this inflation-targeting framework on earlier thinking about how they can use monetary policy to manage the macroeconomy. Prior to this framework becoming predominant in the 1990s and beyond, economists had made an important intellectual breakthrough in their understanding of the macroeconomy and the relationship between the level of economic activity and inflation. In 1958, economist William Phillips pointed out that wage inflation and changes in the unemployment rate moved in opposite directions, declines in the unemployment rate being associated with faster wage growth. This was later recast as a similar relationship between price inflation and unemployment, which became known as the Phillips Curve.

The implication for central bankers was that, in operating monetary policy, they might be able to exploit a trade-off between inflation and unemployment, meaning that they could push the unemployment rate a bit lower at the cost of tolerating a slightly higher rate of inflation. There was also an implication for central bank independence: if politicians were able to influence or control monetary policy, they might be tempted to stoke the economy and push down unemployment, particularly ahead of elections. This would come at the cost of higher inflation down the line, but hopefully after those politicians had been reelected!

Economists Milton Friedman and Edmund Phelps pointed out in separate works that pursuing this trade-off was a fool's errand. They argued that, while it was possible to push the unemployment rate below its "natural rate" temporarily by overstimulating the economy, as the economy adjusted over time, this would just push up inflation and entrench it at a higher level as the public revised up its inflation expectations. In the long run—that is, once the economy had fully adjusted—the unemployment rate would still be at its "natural" or full employment rate; the inflation rate just would have been ratcheted higher, how high depending on how persistently policymakers tried to exploit the trade-off between inflation and unemployment that they falsely believed existed. This further increased the case for central bank independence: better to keep the politicians' hands off the levers of monetary policymaking and leave it to technocrats who understand the intricacies of such things.

The inflation-targeting framework incorporated these insights, as well as insights from the "rational-expectations" revolution of the 1970s and 1980s. Economists like to use models, sometimes quite complex ones, to help them understand the economy and forecast its future path. The key insight of the rational-expectations revolution was that, in building and using models for policy purposes, economists had better assume that the public had the same model of the economy as the government, or at least behaved as if it did. If policymakers were using a model of the economy that assumed the public could be fooled or tricked in some sense, the joke was on them.

Inflation targeting revolves around the idea that the central bank is able to control the public's inflation expectations. Transparency and communication are key. The central bank does not try to spring things on the public or keep anything up its sleeve. Rather, it tells the public that it is aiming for a certain rate of inflation and keeps the public informed about its views on the economy. The credibility of the central bank in the eyes of the public is also key. Two things are necessary to cultivate this. First, the public needs to believe that the central bank has the tools to keep inflation in line with its target over time. Second, the public needs to have confidence that the central bank will use its tools to try to achieve its inflation target, importantly including the bank being given the necessary operational independence and insulation from political interference. If these two conditions are satisfied, the public should reasonably expect the inflation rate to be whatever the central bank announces as its target. If the public believes that the central bank can and will control inflation, why would it expect the inflation rate to be anything other than what the bank says it is shooting for?

If the central bank's model of the economy implies that it can control inflation, the public needs to embrace that model, too. The inflation target of the central bank also has to accord with the inflation rate the public expects to prevail, and both need to be vindicated after the event.

This is not to suggest that the central bank can control the inflation rate in the short run—that is, at every point in time. It can't, as the recent global post-COVID spike in inflation has brutally shown. The actual inflation rate at any and every point in time will be subject to noise or random shocks that push it one way or the other. Over the medium term, however, the public's inflation expectations help to anchor inflation outcomes because they become embedded in wage- and price-setting behavior. When workers are bargaining for pay raises with their employer, it is rational for both parties to build in a baseline expectation that inflation will run at around 2 percent (or whatever the central bank's target is) over the horizon of the agreement. Similarly, when the myriad individual businesses in the economy are setting the prices of the goods and services they sell, they will factor in that same inflation rate. Individual prices will be moving relative to one another, in response to changes in supply and demand, but they will not be building in expectations of the overall price level rising at a rate different from what the central bank is aiming for. "Anchoring" the public's inflation expectations in this way helps to keep inflation in line with the central bank's target.

The inflation-targeting framework incorporates some ingenious features and works very well in many circumstances. But it has proved to have some serious limitations and downsides. The framework presupposes that the central bank alone can control inflation. This might be true when the economy is operating near full employment and inflation is in line with the central bank's target. Monetary policy works reasonably well when all that is needed to keep the economy on an even keel is for the central bank to make occasional minor adjustments in its policy settings. Plus, the policy rate is a long way away from the effective lower bound, meaning that the central bank has lots of interest rate ammunition in its arsenal.

However, there are several circumstances in which monetary policy is much less effective and may need considerable help from fiscal policy, if not hand over the reins to it. One is when the economy endures a big negative shock to demand and actual GDP is pushed far below its potential level. Then a quick, big infusion of aggregate demand is needed; fiscal policy, which can put money directly in people's pockets and put people to work on major infrastructure programs, is better suited to that task than monetary policy, which relies on demand being generated indirectly, incrementally, and in a decentralized fashion.

Monetary policy is also stymied when too much debt has built up and the economy enters a secular (that is, structurally-driven, long-term) deleveraging cycle, such as what happened in Japan in the 1990s after its 1980s asset price bubble burst. Monetary policy relies principally on creating incentives for households and businesses to borrow money to finance an expansion of economic activity, such as via purchases of consumer durables, housing investment, and business capex (capital expenditures). However, if households and businesses are focused on paying down existing debt or on not taking on too much new debt, monetary policy loses much of its potency.

Another circumstance in which it may not pay to rely solely or mainly on monetary policy is when the equilibrium real natural rate, also known as the "natural rate of interest," is very low. Then the central bank, much of the time, is likely to be operating quite close to the effective lower bound. The natural rate of interest refers to the real rate of interest associated with the economy being at full employment with low and stable inflation. For various reasons, which are the subject of much speculation and debate, the natural rate of interest seems to have been on a secular decline over the past few decades, although post-COVID that may be reversing. The Federal Reserve currently reckons the natural rate in the US to be around half a percent. This means that the "neutral federal funds rate"—the policy rate prevailing when the Fed neither has to tighten nor ease monetary policy to keep the economy humming along—would be around 2.5 percent. Thus, the Fed, starting from that position, would have just 250 basis points of interest rate ammunition should it need to cut rates during a recession, or to stave one off. In the post–World War II period, the Fed has cut rates by an average of about 500 basis points in a recession.

In these circumstances, the assumption underpinning the inflation-targeting framework—that the central bank has the tools to control inflation—starts to look shaky. That is not necessarily a problem if fiscal policy can come to the rescue, but a key tenet of inflation targeting is that the central bank needs to be independent of the government and not subject to "fiscal dominance." Close communication between the monetary and fiscal authorities and close coordination, if not joint mobilization, of monetary and fiscal policy may be called for, but to advocates of inflation targeting, this kind of thing is like a red rag to a bull. Such coordination and joint mobilization does occur in crises—chief examples being the Global Financial Crisis and the COVID-19 pandemic—but does so in an ad hoc way and with a sense of unease, if not embarrassment, all around.

MONETARY POLICYMAKING AS GAME THEORY

Inflation targeting can be interpreted through game theory, which models strategic interactions between (usually) two parties. A key concept in game theory is that of a "credible threat." A threat is credible when it is in the interests of the party making the threat to carry it out when the other party takes the action that the threatening party is warning against. A noncredible threat is one that is made but would not be carried out if the threatened party called the other party's bluff. If an employer is looking for a good excuse to fire an employee, telling the employee that they will be fired if they don't raise their game might be a credible threat; if the employee thinks so, they may redeem themselves and avoid getting the sack. On the other hand, if an employee, on the verge of being sacked and hoping to avoid that fate, threatens to sue the employer if it sacks them, the employer may go ahead and do so, realizing that the employee's threat is not credible—that the employee, once sacked, may realize they don't have a leg to stand on and would just earn a damaging reputation as a problematic, disgruntled employee, and just move on.

The key point about a credible threat is that, if both parties see it as such, the threat has its desired effect and never has to be carried out. The credible threat of one party has the powerful effect of altering the behavior of the other party, yet it is never observed.

An inflation-targeting central bank can be thought of as "threatening" the public should the public not adopt as its inflation expectations the target inflation rate of the bank. Suppose inflation rises significantly above the central bank's target, say from 2 percent to 4 percent, and the public increases its inflation expectations accordingly, which in turn causes inflation to run at around 4 percent into the future. To prevent this, an inflation-targeting central bank threatens to punish the public for its expectations by tightening monetary policy sufficiently to bring inflation down to target, pushing the economy into recession in the process if necessary. If the public regards this threat as credible, it will not raise its inflation expectations, inflation will come down to 2 percent, and monetary policy will not have to be tightened (as much). The central bank can hike interest rates as high as it needs to because it has the mandate and the tools to do so. Is the threat to deploy them credible? Most likely yes, if the central bank is independent and not subject to political control.

At the time of writing, this theory was being put to the test, as the Federal Reserve, having gotten itself way behind the inflation curve, aggressively moved to hike interest rates. Annual CPI inflation was 1.5 percent in March 2020, when the Fed started pulling out all the stops in response to the pandemic, after having averaged 2 percent in the preceding twelve months. Inflation averaged 1.2 percent over the next twelve months, and started to rise from March 2021, reaching an eye-popping 8.5 percent by March 2022, when the Fed started to reverse course, and peaking at 9.1 percent in June 2022.[7] The Fed maintained a target range for the overnight interest rate (the federal funds rate) of zero to 25 basis points between March 2020 and March 2022, but at seven meetings between then and the end of 2022, it raised the target range by a cumulative 425 basis points, to 4.25 to 4.50 percent.

What if inflation falls significantly below the central bank's target, say from 2 percent to zero percent, and the public revises its inflation expectations accordingly, which in turn causes inflation to run at around zero percent into the future, a situation not unlike post-1995 Japan? The game theory interpretation would be that an inflation-targeting central bank, faced with such a prospect, would threaten to punish the public for not aligning its inflation expectations with the bank's target by cutting interest rates and taking other measures to reflate the economy (i.e., stimulate the economy and push up the inflation rate). The notion of "punishing" here may sound a little odd, but think of the public suffering some inconvenience or financial losses by being wrong-footed by the central bank's management of the economy and inflation. The real question is whether the central bank's threat is still credible. It has the mandate and the independence, but does it have the tools? The fact that it has limited interest rate ammunition casts some doubt on this and suggests that it may need considerable help from fiscal policy. The key to the central bank's threat being credible may be that it has to be a joint threat of the central bank and the government. The inflation-targeting framework, revolving as it does around central

bank independence and the primacy of monetary policy, is not con-
figured to make that a foregone conclusion.

THE MISLEADING TEXTBOOK MODEL

The way monetary policy works differs from the common textbook
portrayal, which has shaped popular understanding. The textbook
story has a strong "monetarist," or "money drives everything," flavor
to it: the central bank controls the "money supply," either expanding or contracting it as deemed necessary, depending on whether it
judges it needs to stimulate or restrain the economy, respectively.
Economists are congenitally vague about what they mean by the
"money supply," given that there are numerous "monetary aggregates" or categories of money supply (as discussed in chapter one).
Sometimes they mean reserves or the monetary base (reserves plus
banknotes) but more often they have something like M2 in mind
(banknotes, demand deposits, savings deposits, and some money
market funds). There are two versions of the story about how the
central bank adjusting the money supply works, corresponding to
the two sides of the banking system's balance sheet: loans on the
asset side or deposits on the liabilities side.

One version focuses on the bank lending or credit channel (the
asset side). The central bank increases (decreases) the money supply
by increasing (decreasing) reserves, and this "multiplies" through to
a proportionate increase (or decrease) in bank lending. This is the
famous "money multiplier" model that fills the pages of economics textbooks and is the stock-in-trade of generations of economics
teachers. In this world view, increases in reserves by the central bank
translate mechanically into increases in bank lending, with the associated stimulus to economic activity. This model rests on two key
assumptions, which unfortunately for the model are at odds with
reality: banks target a fixed deposits-to-reserves ratio, and so keep
increasing their lending until this target ratio is hit; and the public
maintains a fixed ratio of currency (banknotes and coins) to deposits.[8]

The other version is purely monetarist and focuses on the public's demand for money (the liability side of the banking system). It follows Milton Friedman in arguing that the central bank can control, via the money multiplier process, the nominal money *supply*, but it cannot control the money *demand* of the public, which is a *real* demand. Friedman's key idea is that the public wants to hold just enough money to satisfy its demand for a certain amount of goods and services in a given period. The demand for money has to equal the supply of it in real terms, but what equilibrating mechanism makes this so, given that the central bank controls one (nominal money supply) but not the other (the public's real money demand)? The answer, to Friedman, is simple: the price level will adjust until the two are equal to each other in real terms. This is how the central bank controls inflation. Suppose the central bank has supplied too much money; the public in aggregate is holding too much money relative to their real demand and will try to get rid of the excess by spending it on goods and services. But, in aggregate, the public has to hold the stock of (nominal) money supplied by the central bank; the excess money just gets passed around the economy. As it does, the demand for goods and services continues to rise, pushing up the price level. This process continues until the public is happy to hold the amount of money supplied by the central bank, which happens when enough inflation has occurred to make the real money supply equal to the public's (real) money demand.

There is a fatal problem with this story, however: central banks do not operate monetary policy this way. Prior to the 2008 financial crisis, the Fed and most other major central banks did not pay interest on reserves, and economic conditions were such that they targeted a positive interest rate—that is, they operated well away from the zero bound. That being the case, they did not use the amount of reserves as an active instrument of monetary policy. If a central bank had attempted to increase the money supply by increasing the amount of reserves beyond the amount corresponding to total minimum reserve requirements, the overnight interest rate would have fallen to zero, as banks tried to offload their excess reserves to other banks but found there were no takers.

This all changed with the 2008 financial crisis (and, in the Bank of Japan's case, even earlier, in March 2001, as it battled deflation) when the Fed and other major central banks cut their policy rates to, or close to, zero. Then, these central banks could supply excess reserves in large quantities without having to worry about sending their policy rate toward zero. A new era of large-scale quantitative easing was beginning, a topic we turn to now.

4

THE POWER OF QUANTITATIVE EASING

The US government has a technology, called a printing press (or, today, its electronic equivalent), that allows it to produce as many US dollars as it wishes at essentially no cost.

Ben Bernanke, then governor of the Federal Reserve Board, Washington, DC, November 2002[1]

W hy in the past two decades have central banks been ramping up the size of their balance sheets by buying (mainly) government bonds, in a policy that has become known as quantitative easing, or just QE? How does this policy work and what do central banks hope to achieve by doing it? What problems if any lie in wait for central banks when they try to unwind QE? And why does QE attract so much criticism?

QE is now an established part of developed-world central banks' toolkit. The Bank of Japan (BOJ) pioneered QE in the early 2000s, in an attempt to end Japan's chronic deflation. At that time, most observers thought QE was just a Japanese curiosity, but after the Global Financial Crisis erupted in September 2008, QE went global. The Federal Reserve, the European Central Bank (ECB), the Bank of England, and again the BOJ all adopted variants of QE. Then, with the COVID-19 pandemic, these major central banks pulled out the QE stops again and some new banks joined in.

A word on language. The Fed has never described its balance sheet expansion formally as QE, describing it instead as "large-scale asset purchases," or LSAPs—one of the uglier monetary acronyms. The Bank of England, on the other hand, from the beginning unabashedly called its asset purchase program QE. The BOJ, awkwardly, described its October 2010 QE-like move as an Asset Purchase Program within its Comprehensive Monetary Easing; more deftly, it called its dramatic April 2013 policy shift Quantitative and Qualitative Easing (QQE). The ECB does not use the term QE to describe its various asset purchase programs. But QE they all are.

QE has been highly controversial. Critics have opposed it variously as being potentially reckless money printing and therefore an inflation accident waiting to happen; as being too intrusive into, and overly distortive of, financial markets; as blurring the lines between monetary and fiscal policy, with central banks veering too much into the fiscal lane; or as being ineffective and not worth doing. While some of these criticisms have merit, most reflect misunderstanding of what QE is and how it works. Abstruse explanations by central bankers have not generally helped. In this chapter, I attempt to dispel some of the myths surrounding QE by going back to economic basics. QE blurs the line between monetary and fiscal policy, because that line is not so bright to begin with. When central banks are having to do full-fledged QE in order to achieve their objectives, it is a surefire sign that fiscal policy needs to be mobilized in tandem with monetary policy, if not take the lead.

QE: IT'S WHAT CENTRAL BANKS DO WHEN THEY RUN OUT OF INTEREST RATE AMMUNITION

What exactly is quantitative easing? Put simply, a central bank does QE when it purposefully buys assets, usually government bonds, financed by creating central bank money (reserves). That is, it purposefully expands the size of its balance sheet in order to ease monetary policy.

A picture speaks a thousand words. Figure 4.1 shows the size of the Fed's balance sheet since 2002. Up until September 2008, the Fed's balance sheet was growing at a steady rate of about 4 percent per annum, as nominal GDP and the public's demand for money increased. The size of the balance sheet was not a tool of monetary policy; it was a by-product of it. Recall the bucket explanation in chapter one. Before

FIGURE 4.1 SIZE OF THE FEDERAL RESERVE'S
BALANCE SHEET, 2002–2022

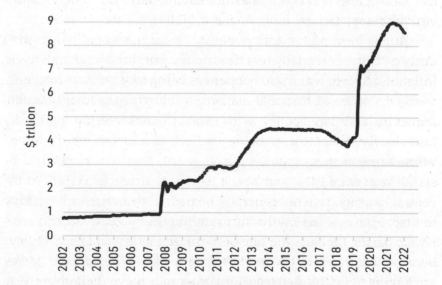

Board of Governors of the Federal Reserve System, retrieved from FRED, Federal Reserve Bank of St. Louis; weekly data.

central banks started paying interest on reserves during or after the financial crisis, and they were targeting a positive short-term interest rate, they had to keep the aggregate amount of reserves in line with the amount corresponding to the minimum reserve requirements they themselves set—the waterline in the bucket. Under QE, central banks fetch themselves a much bigger bucket and keep pumping in more water, oblivious to the old waterline.

Why did central banks start doing QE? Put simply, QE is something that central banks can do to try to stimulate economic activity when they are out of interest rate ammunition or have reached the "effective lower bound" on interest rates. This lower bound used to be taken to be zero or a little above, but, with several major central banks pushing their policy rates into negative interest rate territory, the effective lower bound is now reckoned as being in slightly negative territory (up to about −75 to −100 basis points).

Monetary policy works on the economy by influencing "financial conditions": the ease or difficulty of borrowing and the size of "wealth effects" relating to the value of assets, such as equities or real estate. Central banks need a tool or tools that allow them to either tighten financial conditions or loosen them, depending respectively on whether they need to restrain economic activity in order to achieve their macroeconomic policy targets or to boost it.

The workhorse tool of monetary policy, in the modern "flexible inflation-targeting" era, is the overnight interest rate. But there is an inherent asymmetry in the efficacy of the policy rate to restrain or stimulate economic activity.

When the central bank needs to tighten financial conditions to rein in a potentially overheating economy and quell inflationary pressures, it can raise the policy rate; there is no upper limit on its ability to do so. Paul Volcker's actions as chairman of the Federal Reserve in the early 1980s made this clear. If a 10 percent interest rate is not enough to rein in the economy, try 15 percent; if 15 percent is not enough, what about 20 percent? And so on without limit. Knowing that the central bank has unlimited leeway to raise interest rates, the public's inflation expectations—a key driver of inflation outcomes—are likely to remain well "anchored" in the vicinity of the central bank's announced, typically 2 percent, inflation target.

However, the situation is decidedly different when the central bank needs to cut interest rates to stimulate economic activity and counter disinflationary or deflationary pressures. Whatever the starting point policy, the central bank has a finite amount of room to cut interest rates before it hits the zero (interest rate) bound. For instance, in the easing cycle the Fed began on July 31, 2019, it started with only 225 basis points of interest rate ammunition, and, thanks to the COVID-19 shock, hit the zero bound on March 15, 2020.

As the ECB, BOJ, and some others have shown—but other central banks have been reluctant to emulate—a central bank can set the policy rate below zero. The Swiss National Bank set its policy rate at −75 basis points (that is, −0.75 percent) for fifteen years, until it raised it to −25 basis points in June 2022, and then to 0.50 percent in September 2022. The ECB maintained a negative deposit rate (ranging from −10 to −50 basis points) from June 2014 to July 2022. Likewise, the BOJ has pegged its overnight rate at −10 basis points since January 2016. It might seem odd that a central bank could set a negative interest rate, but this is a corollary of the fact that, at any point in time, the central bank can determine the aggregate amount of reserves in the banking system; if it can control the quantity, it can also set the interest rate.

Pushing the policy rate much below −75 basis points is likely to prove difficult, if not impossible, particularly politically. Negative interest rates imposed by the central bank are essentially a tax on banks, and banks will want to pass on that tax to depositors; otherwise they will be earning "negative carry" on that part of their balance sheet. But whereas a central bank, in theory, could impose as negative an interest rate as it wanted to on banks (because they have to hold the reserves it supplies), this is not so for depositors in banks. They have the option of moving from negative-yielding bank deposits into non-interest-bearing banknotes. This limits the ability of banks to pass on the negative rates to depositors.

Enter QE. At the effective lower bound, central banks have a tool they can use to try to ease monetary policy: they can start to buy up assets (typically government debt securities) financed by the creation of central bank money. And there is no theoretical (as opposed to legal) limit on a central bank's ability to do this, other than the supply of available assets in the world.[2] Thus QE restores the symmetry to the monetary policy tools of the central bank, in principle giving it an unlimited ability to ease monetary policy analogous to the unlimited ability it has to tighten monetary policy by hiking interest rates. The question is: Is there any reason to believe that QE works in terms of easing monetary policy, and, if so, in what way? We answer that question now.

HOW QE WORKS

There are several prominent narratives about how QE works as a monetary easing mechanism.

We can dispense with one right up front: the idea that QE provides money (reserves) to banks that they can then lend to households and firms. Banks cannot "lend on" or "lend out" the reserves supplied by the central bank; although individual banks can lend their reserves to other banks, banks in aggregate have no choice but to hold these reserves. Despite the popularity of the concept in textbooks, in the real world there is no "money multiplier" process: the idea that, when the central bank increases the amount of reserves (narrow money), this multiplies at a fixed rate into a larger amount of bank credit (broader money) creation.[3]

If this theory held, QE, by massively increasing the base of money creation, would lead to an explosion of bank credit. This has not happened because QE and credit creation do not work this way. Many commentators, and even some monetary policymakers who are schooled in the theory, responded to this by observing that "the money multiplier has collapsed," with the implication that the collapse may have just been temporary or anomalous (see figure 4.2). Banks were just "parking" their excess reserves at the central bank, these commentators believed, but when demand for funds picks up, they might start "lending them out," and, because the amount of excess reserves is so massive, there may be a burst of inflation.

FIGURE 4.2 US M2 "MONEY MULTIPLIER," 1990–2022

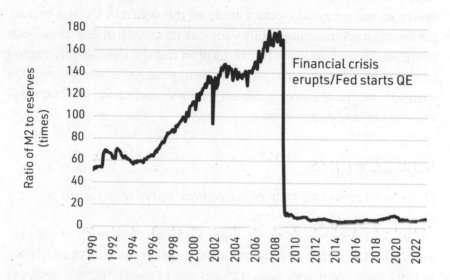

Board of Governors of the Federal Reserve System, retrieved from FRED, Federal Reserve Bank of St. Louis; monthly data.

But the money multiplier did not collapse because it was never there in a meaningful sense to begin with. Rather, a ratio of two loosely connected numbers collapsed because the Fed jacked up the denominator (by doing QE).

An easy way to see that banks cannot lend their reserves to potential borrowers is to revisit the central bank balance sheet identity from chapter one: the change in central bank assets equals the change in reserves plus the change in banknotes plus the change in government deposits. Nowhere does bank lending appear: the idea that banks can convert their reserves into loans (to nonbank borrowers) is a balance sheet non sequitur. Rather, banks lend by creating deposits. Only to the extent that depositors withdraw their deposits and do not redeposit them in other banks—that is, they turn them into banknotes—does new lending cause reserves to decline.

Banks need three things to be able to lend, reflecting economic and regulatory factors: willing borrowers on the terms that banks find profitable to lend; sufficient equity to maintain regulatory capital ratios when the bank's balance sheet expands; and sufficient reserves to satisfy minimum reserve requirements when deposits increase, as the balance sheet counterpart to the new loan. But, whether the central bank is doing QE or not, in the modern monetary and banking system banks are never "reserve constrained." In a non-QE world, the central bank will also supply whatever reserves are demanded; otherwise it will not be able to meet its interest rate target, as explained in chapter one. In a QE world, central banks are "oversupplying" reserves, by definition, so banks are even less reserve constrained.

Two QE Narratives

The two main narratives about how QE operates are what I call "the trading floor narrative" and "the central bank narrative." Both are valid enough, as far as they go, although I prefer some other explanations of my own.

In principle, abstracting from legal constraints, a central bank could buy any kind of asset when it does QE. Sometimes central banks buy such private sector risk assets as corporate bonds, asset-backed securities, equities, and real estate investment trusts. Most notable in this regard is the BOJ. It has been buying equity exchange-traded funds (ETFs), among other private risk assets, for monetary policy purposes since October 2010 and, as of the time of writing, held ¥36.91 trillion (about $265 billion), comprising about 5.1 percent of total Tokyo Stock Exchange market capitalization.

In the overwhelming majority of cases, however, partly for legal reasons and partly because of central bank preferences, QE involves the central bank buying government debt securities. I term this "plain vanilla QE."

In such cases, the trading floor narrative is that the flow of central bank purchases of government bonds represents a new and continuous bid in the bond market that puts upward pressure on government bond prices (and downward pressure on yields). When plain vanilla QE is in train, bond traders themselves feel more comfortable buying and holding bonds because they "know" that the central bank will be there "in the market" as a steady, reliable buyer.

The dominant central bank narrative is a bit more sophisticated and academically grounded, and focuses more on the "stock" effect of QE than the "flow," although the stock of bonds held by the central bank is a direct result of the flow of its purchases. It goes by the (ugly) name of the "portfolio rebalance effect."

The idea is that by doing QE, the central bank alters the composition of the aggregate portfolio held by the private sector, removing a large chunk of government debt securities and supplying reserves (central bank money) in their stead. Banks now find themselves with a lot of excess reserves and nonbanks that have sold bonds to the central bank find themselves with more bank deposits than they had or may want to hold. This fosters a process of portfolio rebalancing, as banks and investors (e.g., hedge funds, asset management companies, insurance companies, and mutual funds) use their extra reserves and bank deposits, as the case may be, to buy other yielding assets.

Banks that end up with more reserves as a result of QE may turn around and buy more bonds with those reserves. At any point in time the inventory of bonds is fixed, so the only way a bank can get its hands on more bonds, and offload its reserves to other banks, is to bid up the price of those bonds, making it sufficiently attractive to the other party to sell them and receive reserves (or bank deposits if the seller is not a bank) in exchange.

This portfolio rebalance effect of QE is often characterized in terms of QE causing investors to "search for yield" or, in more technical terms, as QE either "suppressing the term premium" along the yield curve or "extracting duration" from the bond market.[4]

The logic of the portfolio rebalance effect is not confined to the assets bought by the central bank—in the case we're considering, government bonds. It extends to all kinds of securities and assets, via arbitrage effects. Finding their portfolios more flush with reserves or bank deposits, banks and investors may decide to reallocate part of the cash to other asset classes such as corporate bonds, equities, or foreign exchange. So, in this reckoning, QE has a more pervasive impact on the easing of financial conditions.

Asset Price Equilibrium

I prefer to think about the portfolio rebalance effect in the more finance-theoretic terms of "asset price equilibrium." Think of asset price equilibrium, at any point in time, as being a hypothetical state in which the prices of all assets (government bonds, corporate bonds, equities, foreign exchange, etc.) have adjusted as a result of investors rebalancing their portfolios—that is, buying and selling securities— such that at the new set of asset prices, the marginal investor (trader) is indifferent regarding which of the set of assets available to hold (although there may be "corner solutions," in which an investor chooses to hold none of a particular asset class). In intuitive terms, all the new information in the market has been reflected in asset prices and investors are happy with the portfolios they hold.

Now enter the central bank doing QE. QE can be thought of as a process whereby the central bank alters the composition of the aggregate portfolio of assets held by the private sector, akin to an asset swap the central bank forces upon the private sector. Because, and inasmuch as, the assets taken out of the private sector's portfolio by the central bank (say government bonds) are different from the assets it supplies in exchange (central bank money), this enforced asset swap will disturb the prevailing asset price equilibrium. Asset price equilibrium will be restored as investors rebalance their portfolios by trading with one another. The resulting change in asset price equilibrium is none other than the monetary easing effect of QE.

An illustrative example might be helpful. Suppose the central bank implements (or announces its intent to implement) a certain amount of QE. Whatever asset price equilibrium initially prevailed will be disturbed, and bond and other asset prices will need to shift in such a way as to restore asset price equilibrium—that is, bring about a new equilibrium.

A feature of asset price equilibrium is that investors necessarily must be indifferent to holding the stock of central bank money supplied versus holding other assets. In a world of QE, central bank money (reserves) is an unattractive asset for the private sector to hold because there is much more of it than the private sector demands, and, depending on the specific decisions of the central bank concerned, this money will carry an interest rate that is close to zero, zero, or slightly negative.

Even though, in aggregate, the private sector has to hold the total amount of reserves supplied to it by the central bank, asset price equilibrium requires that asset prices have adjusted such that the private sector is indifferent about holding that stock of money versus holding any other assets. Somewhat counterintuitively this means that bond and other asset prices must rise to make them sufficiently unattractive for investors to want to switch out of the central bank reserves into those assets. This means, in theory, that an increase in QE should lead to (perhaps a very small) increase in the prices of bonds, equities, real estate, and foreign assets—that is, in a depreciation of the domestic currency. As asset price equilibrium is restored, financial conditions are eased.

QE AS A DEBT REFINANCING OPERATION OF THE CONSOLIDATED GOVERNMENT

This is all very well and good, but readers' eyes may be starting to glaze over. There is a much more intuitive and revealing way to understand plain vanilla QE.

The central bank is part of the "consolidated government": the government plus the central bank. When the central bank buys government bonds as part of QE, those bonds are now held within the consolidated government, and the private sector now holds an equivalent amount of central bank money instead. From the consolidated government's point of view, the QE has resulted in the government bonds sitting on both sides of its balance sheet—that is, being held *within* the consolidated government. Central bank money therefore replaces government bonds as the liability issued to and held by the private sector. *Plain vanilla QE is nothing other than a debt refinancing operation of the consolidated government whereby the consolidated government, via the central bank (rather than the treasury), retires government debt securities and refinances them into central bank reserves.*

Viewing QE as a consolidated government debt refinancing operation yields several valuable insights. First, it highlights the fact that QE should not be expected to be a very potent form of monetary easing, under circumstances in which it makes sense for the central bank to implement it. QE is often described as the central bank "printing" vast amounts of money or "pumping" huge amounts of **liquidity** into the banking system—shown in figure 4.1 as a dramatic increase in the size of the central bank's balance sheet. This is liable to conjure up an image of being a dramatic or highly reflationary monetary easing measure.

However, when QE is viewed more accurately as the consolidated government merely shifting between two forms of liability—that is, two forms of broadly conceived government money—it starts to sound much more innocuous or even impotent as a form of monetary easing. Descriptions of QE as pumping liquidity into the banking system are commonplace, but rarely if ever is it noted that for every dollar (euro, yen, etc.) of reserves the central bank "pumps into" the system, the same amount of government bonds is "sucked out." QE does not inject one iota of new purchasing power into the economy; it just changes the form in which it is manifest.

Second, viewing QE in this way highlights that the line between monetary policy and fiscal policy is nowhere near as bright as commonly held. The conventional macroeconomic policy framework rests on a sharp distinction between "monetary policy" and "fiscal policy," the former being the preserve of the central bank, the latter that of the government (i.e., the polity and the treasury within the government). Moreover, under the system that has developed and gained ascendancy in the past thirty to forty years, the primary responsibility for macroeconomic stabilization (price stability and full employment) is assigned to a technocratic central bank that, to insulate it from political pressures, is made independent of the government.

One of the common criticisms of QE, and a prevalent source of discomfort with QE among central bankers themselves, is the observation that QE blurs the line between monetary and fiscal policy. This might be better viewed as a design feature of QE than a design flaw. QE blurs the line between monetary and fiscal policy because that line is blurred to begin with. QE pulls back the curtain on the fact that the strict separation of monetary and fiscal policy is more of an institutional artifact than a God-given feature. It is a means to an end, and should not be seen as an end in itself.

QE can now be seen for what it (partially) is: a step back into the Monetary Garden of Eden of chapter one. Consider a three-stage evolutionary process. In the Monetary Garden of Eden (first stage), a government running a budget deficit creates reserves (the most fundamental component of monetary base). In the standard version of the modern world (second stage), the government issuing debt securities expunges those reserves. When economic circumstances then push monetary policy past its conventional limits into QE territory (third stage), those government debt securities are converted back into reserves. No wonder it looks like QE blurs the line between monetary and fiscal policy!

No More Debt Due-by Dates

The third benefit of viewing QE as a debt refinancing or reprofiling operation of the consolidated government is that it starkly reveals that the government, via the central bank, has the power to do away with the apparent need to repay its "debt." Central bankers almost never describe QE in these terms; nor do governments. Incumbent policymakers, with all due respect, are too steeped and socialized in the existing conventional macroeconomic policy framework to enthusiastically embrace the solution to both chronic deflation (or "secular stagnation") and excess burden being placed on monetary policy that is staring them in the face: much closer communication, coordination, and joint mobilization—or even effective fusion—of monetary and fiscal policy, when circumstances call for it.

Although viewing QE as a debt refinancing operation highlights how much less dramatic it is than narrow characterizations from the monetary trenches would suggest, there is one crucial difference between government debt securities and central bank money whose import is potentially game changing. Government bonds have a maturity date attached to them, whereas central bank money is a liability of the government that never has to be repaid. By converting government bonds into central bank money, QE relaxes the fiscal constraints on governments and paves the way for the government to be able to run a much more expansionary fiscal policy, if circumstances warrant.

If the consolidated government can turn its liabilities into ones that by their nature cannot default, where is the risk of "fiscal crisis," and in what sense do fiscal finances become "unsustainable?" The real unsustainability is that too much government spending can lead to runaway inflation, but the circumstances in which central banks reach for QE are ones in which such spending looks more like a solution than a problem.

The orthodoxy of fiscal probity is so entrenched, and in the case of the euro area so institutionalized, that governments generally have not used the arrival of QE on the macroeconomic policy scene, let alone the prodding from MMT, to fundamentally rethink the relationship between monetary and fiscal policy, and to refashion the macroeconomic policy framework accordingly. The time has surely come to do so.

Quantitative Tightening

There is even a fourth stage in the evolutionary toggling between reserves and bonds: the reversal of QE, which goes under the name of **quantitative tightening (QT)**. When the central bank exits from (or "unwinds") QE by refinancing excess reserves back into government bonds, it is returning the state of affairs to that obtaining in the second stage. The third stage is really the first stage reincarnated, and the fourth stage replicates the second stage. QE and QT as debt refinancing operations of the consolidated government are really just processes of toggling between two stages: an MMT-type world (the Monetary Garden of Eden) and a monetary–fiscal separation world (the conventional framework).

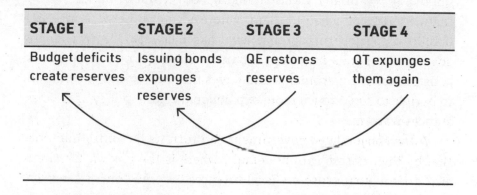

STAGE 1	STAGE 2	STAGE 3	STAGE 4
Budget deficits create reserves	Issuing bonds expunges reserves	QE restores reserves	QT expunges them again

In principle, there are two ways in which a central bank can do QT: it can (passively) let maturing bonds roll off its balance sheet or it can (actively) sell them back into the market; in both cases, reserves fall by the amount of the bonds leaving the asset side of the balance sheet. The latter is really just a more active or aggressive form of the former. Unless, unusually, they are running a budget surplus, governments have to refinance their maturing bonds into new ones.[5] Issuing new bonds to replace the old ones drains reserves; the government then uses the proceeds, now sitting in its deposit account at the central bank, to "repay" the central bank, extinguishing the maturing bonds on the asset side of the central bank's balance sheet and its deposits on the liability side.[6] The net effect is for bonds and reserves to disappear from the central bank's balance sheet and for the private sector to now hold bonds instead of reserves (if banks buy the newly issued bonds) or bank deposits (if nonbanks do).

QT seems to excite as much passion and invite as much confusion as QE does. Most QT worrywarts were never keen on QE to
begin with. Concerns come in several versions, but the common
thread is that, having pumped up their balance sheets with QE (see
figure 4.3), central banks are trapped, and will find it impossible to
do QT without crashing the markets and tanking the economy. QE
is like Hotel California: you can check in (start doing it), but you can
never check out (bring it to an end). That's a nice line,[7] but not true:
there is nothing inherently fraught about QT, either conceptually
or operationally.

FIGURE 4.3 EXPANSION OF CENTRAL BANK BALANCE SHEETS, 2003–2022: FED, ECB, BOJ

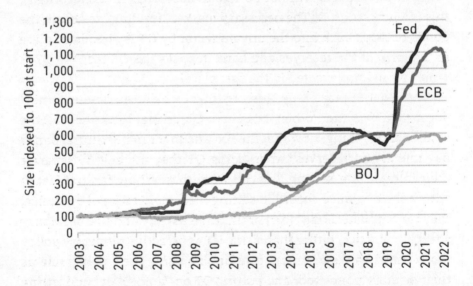

Bank of Japan (BOJ), Board of Governors of the Federal Reserve System (Fed),
European Central Bank (ECB) retrieved from FRED, Federal Reserve Bank of St.
Louis; monthly data.

That is not to say that QT is easy for central banks to do. Monetary policymaking is inherently tricky to do, and monetary tightening is particularly so. Central banks don't have a crystal ball and

the levers they pull are only loosely and unreliably connected to the object they aim to move.

QT is just the reverse of QE—the central bank shrinking its balance sheet rather than expanding it—so everything that pertains to QE should pertain to QT in reverse. QE takes bonds out of private sector portfolios, QT puts them back in; QE creates reserves, QT expunges them; QE refinances bonds into reserves, QT refinances reserves back into bonds; QE eases financial conditions (a bit), QT tightens them (a bit); QE reduces the term premium, QT increases it. There's nothing mysterious about QT—it's just QE with the opposite (mathematical) sign.

One common misconception about QT is that central banks will have a hard time offloading the bonds because, the amounts involved being huge, markets will not be able to absorb them. Conceptually, this is a non sequitur. The necessary market "funding" to absorb the bonds released back into the private sector by QT is already in place in the form of the reserves and bank deposits the QE that the QT is aimed at undoing created in the first place!

But even if practically this argument holds to some extent, it doesn't really matter. When it comes to QT, central banks hold all the cards. For one thing, now that the Fed and other major central banks pay interest on reserves, when doing QT they are able to separate their interest rate-setting decision from that of how far and fast to shrink their balance sheet.[8] In setting their monetary policy stance, they can calibrate along two margins (interest rate and size of balance sheet). In practice, rather than using QT as an active monetary policy tool, central banks are more comfortable using their policy rate as their primary policy tool and putting QT on "auto-pilot" and letting it run quietly in the background, relying on some combination of passive runoff (of maturing bonds) or a pre-announced program of monthly sales of bonds in preset amounts. The Fed established this template when it embarked on its first round of QT, or QE-unwind, in October 2017 to September 2019 period and has been using it again since June 2022 in its post-COVID-19 QT.

The hidden secret of QT is that central banks don't really need to do it (but if they want to, that's no problem either). Indeed, with relatively little fanfare, the Fed drew down the curtain on its first round of QT (associated with its post-financial crisis QE) in January 2019 by announcing that, rather than completely drain the excess reserves created by its QE, it would henceforth operate an "ample reserves" regime whereby it would not actively manage the supply of reserves.[9] At the time, the Fed's balance sheet was $4.04 trillion (compared to its pre-financial crisis level of around $900 billion) and banks held some $1.48 trillion of excess reserves.

From the consolidated government's point of view and from the economy's point of view, if the central bank is targeting a positive interest rate, it doesn't really matter whether the "money" created by past and ongoing government budget exists in the form of central bank reserves or government bonds and whether the interest paid on them comes from the central bank or from the government treasury.

QE AND INEQUALITY

A common criticism of QE, and sometimes of monetary policy more broadly, is that it leads to asset price bubbles and exacerbates wealth inequality. We will consider asset price bubbles in chapter six. Those who assert that QE exacerbates inequality point to the fact that QE involves a massive amount of "money printing" and that this money "has to go somewhere," that somewhere usually being asset prices. They note that it is mainly the rich who own financial assets and, therefore, who benefit from QE.

This line of argument has more than a grain of truth in it but is simplistic and misleading. This chapter has noted how QE does not really create new money; it merely changes the form it takes. QE, like all monetary easing, does buoy asset prices, but in and of itself this is a desirable thing, because higher asset prices help stimulate economic activity, which is what monetary easing seeks to achieve. If QE creates disparities in wealth inequality that the government, acting for society, deems undesirable or unacceptable, it can address them with fiscal policy. This would seem to be an argument for society to establish a better framework for coordinating monetary and fiscal policy. Then, fiscal policy could be mobilized earlier and on a bigger scale—so as to obviate the need for monetary policy to have to venture into QE territory in the first place—and redistributive fiscal measures could be implemented to help offset some of the putative wealth-inequality-exacerbating impact of QE.

Another thing to bear in mind: equity and other asset prices reflect investors' assessments of future prospects. To the extent that QE is successful in improving future economic prospects, asset prices should respond favorably. Blaming rising asset prices on QE is a bit like shooting the messenger, when a word of thanks might be more warranted.

Last, policies need to be assessed not in terms of their effects per se, but in terms of whether the totality of the situation they create results in a better outcome for society than the status quo or pursuing other feasible policies. Just saying that QE might exacerbate inequality doesn't say very much, if inequality is an intrinsic part of economic life, let alone if increased inequality can reflect positive societal processes as well as more concerning ones. Inequality being created is a complex and controversial topic and aspect of monetary affairs, to which we now turn.

5

THE POWER OF MONEY TO CREATE
INEQUALITY–AND WEALTH

*For society as a whole money is just an artificial device
to facilitate real things that constitute real wealth.*

Thomas Sowell, 2015[1]

At the time of writing, Elon Musk, serial entrepreneur and larger-than-life character, is the richest man in the world, with a net worth estimated at $187.0 billion.[2] Being a mere millionaire used to be a big deal, and for many people it still is; by contrast, Musk is the equivalent of 187,000 millionaires. Such amounts of wealth for an individual to possess are almost impossible to comprehend. Jeff Bezos, founder and executive chairman of Amazon, comes in fourth, with a reported net worth of 112.6 billion, equal to 112,600 millionaires. Ken Griffin, owner and founder of the hedge fund Citadel, reportedly has a net worth of $31.9 billion; that's still the equivalent of 31,900 millionaires.[3]

Jamie Dimon, chairman and CEO of JPMorgan Chase, reportedly received total compensation of $34.5 million in 2021.[4] His net worth is reported to be $1.6 billion, not bad for a fellow who has drawn a salary all his working life.[5] Star basketball player LeBron James is reported to have an annual base salary of $44.475 million and a net worth of $1 billion.[6] Meanwhile, it is estimated that in 2021, more than half a million people in the US were homeless.[7] A few years ago, academics Kathryn Edin and Luke Shaefer wrote a book depressingly titled *$2.00 a Day: Living on Almost Nothing in America*.[8] That is the plight of too many people.

Most people, me included, when confronted with such extreme disparities in wealth and income and reminded of the abject poverty that many people endure, feel sick to their stomachs. Something seems grossly unfair and intolerable about extreme wealth and income inequality. Feelings of indignation, anger, and helplessness may start to well up. There may even be a sense of fear and foreboding about how this may all end if we don't do something to redress the situation. French economist Thomas Piketty, convinced that the modern capitalist system creates "a large upward redistribution from the middle and upper-middle classes to the very rich," warned in his influential 2019 book *Capital in the Twenty-First Century* that "such an impoverishment of the middle class would very likely trigger a violent political reaction."[9] My reading of Piketty, someone well versed in the history of his own country, is that he was using the term "violent" in a literal sense, not just metaphorically.

It is easy to express moral outrage at inequality and argue for all kinds of redistributive policies to reduce it. Doing so can engender a sense of moral satisfaction, and is safe ground to stand on. But, is there another side to the coin? Is inequality largely a natural outcome of the workings of a modern market economy, and to the extent that it is evil, is it a necessary one in some sense? Does trying to lessen inequality involve an element of tilting at windmills? What is the best way to address this problem without throwing the (prosperity-generating) baby out with the (inequality-reducing) bathwater?

These are treacherous waters to wade into. There is not a lot of social or reputational upside in opening yourself up to the charge of being an apologist for the super-rich. I'm tempted to say that I dislike Elon Musk, Jeff Bezos, and Mark Zuckerberg as much as the next person (for the record, I don't drive a Tesla; I've never used Facebook, Instagram, or WhatsApp; and I shop on Amazon sparingly—I purchased $1,186.33 of goods, mainly books, in thirty-six orders from Amazon in 2021, and a similar amount in 2022). But somebody has to point out what is on the other side of the inequality coin and, in a book on money, it may as well be me. The question is not whether there is inequality, or whether it has been increasing over time. Rather, the question, in two parts, is (1) to what extent is this inequality a natural concomitant of the workings of a market-oriented economy, which brings manifest compensating benefits; and (2) will attempts to prevent it in the first place or redress it after the fact do more harm than good. It can be asked, too: Is the inequality egregious and reprehensible, or is it, in some sense, justifiable and more innocuous than it is made out to be? I lean toward the latter view.

LADY LUCK

The first thing to say about income and wealth inequality is that, like it or not, there being a certain amount of it is the natural state of the economy. There is no reason to expect that the distribution of income and wealth outcomes in a market-oriented economy at any given time would be anything like equal, and every reason to expect that it would not be. Pick any person at random and look at their income or wealth level. The person or their interlocutors likely won't see it this way, but the most important factor determining income or wealth will be luck: good, bad, or a complicated mixture. Any wealthy person, first and foremost, should thank their lucky stars: they, or their forebears, had enormously good fortune to be presented with the opportunities that the application of skill and effort helped to so greatly yield.[10] Luck, by definition, is highly unequal, as any trip to a casino will confirm.

Very wealthy people likely won't see it that way. Many have remarkable talent and worked extremely hard at turning that talent into highly lucrative skills. Somebody who worked their way to the top of the corporate ladder, entertainment industry, or sports world may not appreciate the suggestion that the biggest factor in their reaching that pinnacle was luck rather than their lifetime of sacrifice and effort. Yet, luck it was.

Good luck is a necessary, not a sufficient, condition for success. Some degree of innate talent and lots of hard work are usually required, too. Luck is invisible, easily taken for granted, and by definition out of your control; hard work and making constant sacrifices are a choice and loom large in your sense of self and in your memory.

NOTHING EQUAL ABOUT THE MARKET

Certain features of how an economy works are prone to generate considerable inequality. A market-oriented economy is a highly decentralized thing, resulting from markets coordinating the distributed decisions of myriad consumers, workers, producers, and investors. The US economy produced $25 trillion in output of goods and services in the most recent year (up until third quarter 2022): that's twenty-five with twelve zeros after it. Pockets of central planning were involved, but most of the economic activity occurred as a result of countless individuals making their own choices of what to buy and how much, where to work and how hard, and how to deploy their financial savings; and countless businesses making their own decisions about what to produce and offer for sale, how many people to employ and how to deploy them, and what capital investments to make for an uncertain future. All of them, whether consciously or not, reacted to the price signals that markets were providing and that they were collectively producing. The US economy produces all manner of goods and services, but the composition of GDP shifts over time, as technology and tastes change. There is nothing remotely "equal" about it.[11]

The stock market works similarly. The total market capitalization of the S&P 500 index as of December 2022 was $33.57 trillion. That represents the collective opinion of all the investors in the world of the total value of the five hundred companies comprising the index. Nobody is forcing anyone to hold any of the shares of these companies and their stock prices. Market capitalizations are therefore determined as a part of a decentralized process of voluntary exchange among countless investors. The outcome of this process is highly unequal. Although five hundred of the largest companies are in the index, the biggest five (as of December 5, 2022) made up about a fifth of the total market capitalization: Apple (6.6 percent), Microsoft (5.5 percent), Alphabet (a.k.a. Google; 3.4 percent), Amazon (2.4 percent), and Berkshire Hathaway (1.7 percent).

Every economy is a mixed one, comprising a private sector and a public sector, and each relies on markets (regulated to varying degrees) and the government to guide resource allocation. But the resulting output of the economy is largely the result of uncoordinated, decentralized decision-making and behavior. There is no reason to expect the economy to produce outcomes that are "equal" in any sense. Broadly speaking, we can think of the market and the private sector as being the drivers of prosperity, with both being disinterested in or agnostic about how income and wealth is distributed, and the government and the public sector as (among other things) being the vehicle for the collective action necessary for society to provide the infrastructure for markets to function and the vehicle for spreading the fruits of prosperity around. Government intervention to redistribute purchasing power, including by providing a social safety net, is society's way of undoing much of the effects of luck. Effort and hard work, often over many years, are also crucial ingredients in producing output, and it is impossible to undo the effects of good and bad luck without distorting incentives to exert effort and work hard in the process. Understanding this, and feeling some professional responsibility for helping society manage the trade-offs involved, is the albatross that economists wear around their necks, regardless of where they locate themselves along the "bleeding heart" (left) to "tough love" (right) spectrum.

STOCK MARKET WEALTH COMES FROM FUTURE SATISFIED CUSTOMERS

One of the problems with much of the hand-wringing about rising and extreme inequality, particularly wealth inequality, is that the issue is usually discussed out of context, notably that of how the extreme wealth came into existence and what sustains it.

Take Jeff Bezos as an example. Like many of the Big Tech über-rich, most of Bezos's net worth, and what gives it its eye-popping nature, is his ownership in the company he founded, Amazon. The market capitalization of Amazon represents the net present value of the company. As is the case with any listed company, investors want to hold Amazon's stock because of the flow of future dividends they expect to receive. Any specific investor doesn't necessarily envisage collecting all of those expected dividends by holding the stock way into the future; they can sell the stock at any time, and in that case its buyer will be purchasing the right to collect those dividends instead.

The dividends come out of future profits, and the future profits come out of future sales, and those sales will only happen if Amazon survives in a highly competitive and disruption-prone market and keeps satisfying its customers, to the point where they prefer to buy from Amazon than from any other firm.

What gives rise to Jeff Bezos's gargantuan wealth is the expecta-tion that the company he founded and continues to run as executive chairman will keep on satisfying its customers, enough to hold on to their business at least, and will attract new ones, many of whom have not even been born. Look at Jeff Bezos's net worth and feel indignation and disgust that one man could accumulate so much wealth; but look at the other side of the coin and see that most of that wealth exists only because some of the most hard-nosed analyti-cal people in the world—stock market investors—judge that Amazon will induce countless consumers to voluntarily and happily part with their money for as long as the eye can see.

WINNERS TAKE ALL

One of the things that leads certain successful people, be they entrepreneurs, movie stars, or sports starts, to accumulate huge fortunes is the winner-take-all nature of competition in many fields. "Winner-takes-all" is a slight misnomer; it is more often a case of winner-takes-most or winner-takes-a-disproportionate-amount. The winner of a gold medal at the Olympic Games may beat the silver medal winner by the slimmest of margins, due more to luck on the day than anything else, yet they will gain most of the fame and glory. Meanwhile, their fellow athlete, who slipped into fourth place on a twist of fate—perhaps having woken up out of sorts that day—and missed out on a medal, will be largely forgotten to history.

The winner-takes-all phenomenon smacks of unfairness, but is likely deeply rooted in human psychology. If the contest revolves around who can run fastest from the predator on the savanna, small differences in performance could have disproportionately significant outcomes, such as escaping versus being eaten. Humans use all kinds of heuristics or mental rules of thumb to simplify and guide their assessments and decisions.[12] Winner-takes-all is one.[13]

Inequality, by definition, is looked at in relative not absolute terms. Consider two kinds of situation. In one, everyone in society is getting richer over time but some people, perhaps a very small percentage, are doing much better than everyone else. Inequality is also increasing, which is deemed a bad thing, as far as that goes. In the other, a very unequal society becomes more equal by everyone becoming worse off, the very wealthy much more so than everyone else. Clearly, the former situation is far superior to the latter, even with increasing inequality.

Another subtle human behavioral bias seems to be lurking here, in the form of a "ratchet effect" in the perception of material progress. As technological progress drives increases in the standard of living over time, we quickly incorporate those innovations and improvements into a new baseline of what we expect and take for granted. Once that happens, absolute improvements in the standard of living—such as having a computer or smartphone providing constant, instant connectivity to the rest of the world—are taken for granted, but one's relative position in the societal wealth hierarchy retains much salience. As economist Robert Gordon and others have pointed out, even poor people today, in many ways, enjoy a higher standard of living than the royalty of medieval times.[14]

The size of the economic pie matters, not just its distribution. The problem is that the two processes—increasing the size of the pie and dividing it up—are inextricably linked. For any bigger pie, it would be nice to have a more equal distribution of it, but that may not be possible. Attempts to divide up the pie may end up making it smaller. Income and wealth redistribution policy should aim to do minimum damage to the pie-making, but this is far more difficult than many seem to think.

The winner-takes-all phenomenon is observed to varying degrees in many walks of economic life, wherever there are benefits to consumers. Those benefits often come from the supply side and are associated with increasing returns to scale. If firms can reduce their unit costs by producing more output, they can outcompete rivals and gain a larger market share, often becoming the dominant firm in the market. Small, seemingly random differences in "initial conditions" can determine which of many potentially dominant firms will ultimately prevail.

The winner-takes-all phenomenon has been accentuated dramatically by the hyperconnectivity of the modern information age and by globalization. Dominant platforms now reach a bigger potential market, making for outsized winner-takes-all profits.

TOP EXECUTIVE COMPENSATION

One contributor to extreme inequality of income and wealth at the top, particularly in the US, is top executive compensation. Median

CEO pay at S&P 500 companies in 2021 was reported to be $14.2 million.[15] The highest total compensation for a CEO was $247 million, for Discovery Inc.'s David Zaslav, followed by $213 million for Amazon's Andy Jassy. How much more top CEOs are paid than their shop-floor employees is often a major bone of contention, to the point that financial reform legislation passed after the Global Financial Crisis, known as Dodd-Frank, imposed a regulatory mandate on public companies to disclose as part of their annual filings the ratio of CEO pay to median worker pay. One 2018 study of the top 225 Fortune 500 companies found that this ratio averaged 339 to 1, from a low of 2 to 1 to a high of nearly 5,000 to 1.[16]

Supply and Demand

The basic workhorse model used by economists for analyzing the price of something is the model of supply and demand. The market price of something is likely to be roughly the price that equates supply and demand, or the price at which the (usually downward-sloping) demand curve intersects with the (usually upward-sloping) supply curve. A price above that market-determined price would result in more of the thing being supplied than was demanded at that price, putting downward pressure on the price, while a below-market price would result in less of the thing being supplied than was demanded at that price, putting upward pressure on the price.

This model goes a long way toward explaining the price of labor, that is, the wage rate. Of course, there are many kinds of labor, depending on the kind of work that needs to be done and the associated skill and experience level required. Labor markets differ in many ways from markets for goods and services, particularly those for highly standardized and traded commodities. Still, nuances and qualifications notwithstanding, economists would argue broadly that people are paid roughly what they are worth. In a competitive market economy, firms have to compete with one another to attract workers and retain them by paying them enough. On the other hand, firms will not want to pay their workers more than they have to or their competitors do because doing so would put them at a competitive disadvantage.

Although the numbers look implausibly high to be true, this basic model also can be applied to CEO compensation, with some important qualifications. Unquestionably, top executives of public corporations get paid very handsomely. Being such a CEO, even for a short time, almost certainly makes you financially set for life; being at or near the top of such a corporate hierarchy for many years—sometimes even decades—could make you a billionaire. Nobody is going to claim that top business executives, particularly of leading household-name companies, are underpaid for their talents and efforts. The question is whether they deserve to receive such generous-looking pay packages.

Most CEOs are not paid in the way that most salaried workers are. A typical CEO compensation package comprises a relatively small base salary ("relatively" being the operative word), a substantial amount of deferred compensation such as "restricted stock units" or "performance stock units" and stock options, and other perks and benefits (sometimes extending beyond their tenure with the company). Restricted stock units are promises to deliver the CEO a certain amount of company stock at preset future dates. Performance stock, while similar, is linked to preset performance targets of the company or division. Stock options are the opportunity to buy shares at some future date at a preset price (the "exercise price"). The idea is to tie most of the CEO's compensation to the subsequent fate of the company, which presumably will provide the CEO and other top executives strong incentives to make decisions that increase stock prices over time.

CEOs, by definition, are highly experienced individuals who have reached the top after what is typically a decades-long tournament of advancement. According to a 2019 study of the top one thousand US companies by revenue, the average age of a CEO was fifty-nine.[17] Nor is the job of a CEO a walk in the park. Their job is to oversee the day-to-day management of the company; to set medium- and long-term strategy; to select and lead a senior management team;

to communicate with investors, employees, the board of directors, regulators, and the public; and to be there to catch the buck when it comes around. A good CEO therefore needs a combination of skills. As well as having the requisite knowledge and experience, they need to be a strategic thinker, an inspirational leader, an effective operator, a person of sound judgment and integrity (no hotheads or crooks, please), a good communicator, and a hard worker. Such people don't come cheap!

Applying the supply-and-demand model suggests that top managers are probably being paid roughly what they need to be, given market forces. Suppose the CEO of a company were being underpaid. Presumably, they will make their opinion known to the board of directors and win the raise they seek. If they are unsuccessful, they will look for another CEO job. The fact that a CEO continues in their job is a good indication that they are not being underpaid. Economists use the logic of "revealed preference," better known as "actions speak louder than words," to arrive at conclusions like this. Wanting more money is one thing, but how can someone like a CEO be considered underpaid if they voluntarily keep turning up to work every day?

Can CEOs be overpaid? There are three main reasons for thinking they are not or, if they are, not grossly so. First, the market for CEOs is very competitive, and competition helps to keep costs down. For corporate managers, becoming a CEO is the ultimate career prize, and competition for these top slots is intense, even if the more cutthroat aspects of C-suites and corporate boardrooms lie behind a cloak of courtesy and collegiality. There are always plenty of contenders for the top job both inside and outside the company. This competitive pressure can be expected to provide a check on individual CEOs pricing themselves out of the market.

Shareholders provide a second check. They are often regarded and described as the "owners" of the company, particularly by economists and those influenced by them. While this is a useful shorthand, it is a bit of a misnomer. A company or corporation is a legal entity that serves as an organizational device for people to cooperate, directly and indirectly, in the production of goods and services. Shareholders do not "own" the firm; shareholders own securities issued by it, which convey certain rights and give shareholders a unique position among the various stakeholders in the firm. Shareholders bear much of the risk associated with the operations of the firm and can decide who will run it. These two things— risk-bearing and control—logically go together: it makes sense to let those who have the most at stake in a decision-making process have the most sway over it. In the modern governance framework of public corporations, the board of directors, whose members are chosen by the shareholders, owe them a fiduciary duty to manage the affairs of the corporation, importantly including choosing and overseeing the CEO.[18]

Every dollar that is overpaid to the CEO is a dollar less in profits to the shareholders. Shareholder pressure therefore can be expected to provide a check on CEO compensation and ensure that the CEO and other top management are not overpaid, at least not by too much. This shareholder pressure can manifest itself through various channels, including the board of directors, activist shareholders, equity analysts, ESG (environment, social, governance) ratings firms, and the business press (although some of these do so only as a by-product of their own self-motivated activities).

But how can such eye-popping compensation packages not be prima facie evidence of the recipients being grossly overpaid? A third reason for resisting leaping to that conclusion is that, in perceiving and judging CEO compensation from an outside observer's perspective, there is a "scale mismatch" or kind of "category error." Is a bread crumb big? Not to you, but to an ant or a fly it is, and it is gigantic to a dust mite. It is similar with shareholders. From the shareholders' perspective, a highly paid but good, let alone great, CEO is a bargain. A "good" CEO is one who looks after the interests of shareholders.

How to look at the interests of shareholders has become more complicated with the advent of ESG investing and the growing support for "stakeholder capitalism." Proponents of these ideas challenge the traditional notion that the firm should be run in the interests of shareholders and that the job of the CEO and top management is to maximize "shareholder value"—that is, to operate the firm so that its share price increases to the maximum extent possible over time. Instead, they stress the need for corporations to take into account the interests of all of its stakeholders, including customers, employees, suppliers, and local communities as well as shareholders, and to discharge their wider "corporate social responsibility," not just focus on making money.[19] The US Business Roundtable, an association representing the CEOs of America's leading corporations, attracted much attention in August 2019 when it released an updated statement on the purpose of the corporation touting its "moves away from shareholder primacy" to a "commitment to all stakeholders."[20]

Top Executive Pay and the Scale Mismatch

Let's stick with the traditional view for the moment. All shareholders are interested in the same thing: increasing shareholder value or the stock market capitalization of the firm. This is not quite the same thing as saying they want the stock price to be maximized, because the stock price depends on the number of shares issued. If the share price of a company is $100 and it implements a two-for-one stock split, the share price will drop to $50, but its stock market capitalization will be unchanged. For the purposes of analyzing the relationship between the shareholders and the CEO, whom they choose and control via the board of directors, we can treat the multitude of shareholders as if they were a single shareholder. If there are a thousand individual arms-length shareholders, or a million for that matter, and they all prefer more income to less, we can consider them a single shareholder who prefers more income to less.

Herein lies the scale mismatch. Outside observers, who are individuals like you and me, tend to look at the compensation of CEOs on the level or scale of an individual. That is precisely what the Dodd-Frank–imposed CEO/median worker pay ratio does. From that viewpoint, Jamie Dimon's $34.5 million annual compensation package looks exorbitant, to some people even "obscene." But the individual, representative shareholder is operating at a very different (and much larger) scale: that of the market capitalization of the company.

The market capitalization of JPMorgan at the time of writing (December 6, 2022) was $383.50 billion. Jamie Dimon's annual compensation amounts to 0.01 percent of that. As CEO and chairman of the board, Dimon is responsible for managing the massive market value of this enterprise—not just maintaining but increasing it as much as he legally and morally can. The single notional shareholder of JPMorgan paying him $34.5 million a year to motivate him to do so is like you or me having a $100 meal and leaving the waiter a one-cent tip! I'm not going to go as far as to say that the shareholders put Ebenezer Scrooge to shame, but you get the point.

For the sake of getting the best CEO talent money can buy and paying them enough to ensure that they put your interests ahead of those of everyone else—the principle on which a private-ownership, market-oriented economy is based—paying the kind of sums of money seen in CEO compensation packages, to shareholders, may seem like a pretty good deal.

How does this line of argument change when we adopt the stakeholder capitalism view of the firm? Not much. In this model, the interests of shareholders are still given considerable weight; to that extent, the foregoing argument applies. But here's a radical thought: perhaps top management should be paid *more* under the stakeholder capitalism model, given that they likely need even more knowledge and skill, and are subject to even more pressure and stress, than under the shareholder primacy model. In the stakeholder-oriented model, top management is supposed to take the interests of all stakeholders, including shareholders, into account. How exactly they are supposed to do so—specifically, what weight they are supposed to assign to each category of stakeholder and how they are supposed to manage the trade-offs between competing interests—is far from clear. It's an even more challenging task than just focusing on the profit bottom line.

WALL STREET WHEELERS AND DEALERS

Another category of the über-rich whose success contributes to widening wealth inequality is the hedge fund investor class.[21] Hedge funds are investment firms, usually operated by one or more founder figures, that manage their own money and that of other high-net worth individuals and institutional investors. They typically seek high returns, implying they also take a lot of risk, employ specialized investment strategies, and use considerable leverage to help boost their returns. A lot of hedge fund owners and traders begin their careers as traders with large **investment bank**s like Goldman Sachs or Morgan Stanley before branching out on their own, sometimes partly seeded by their former employer. Probably the most famous hedge fund manager is George Soros, who famously "broke the bank," forcing the United Kingdom to abandon its peg to other European currencies on September 16, 1992, under the European Exchange Rate Mechanism. Other notables include Steven Cohen (SAC Capital; said to be the inspiration for the protagonist of the hit TV series, *Billions*), Ray Dalio (Bridgewater Associates), Kenneth Griffin (Citadel), Julian Robertson (Tiger Management), David Shaw (D. E. Shaw & Co.), James Simons (Renaissance Technologies), and Paul Tudor Jones (Tudor Investment Corporation), among many others.

How exercised should we be about the huge fortunes that such hedge fund luminaries accumulate? Are those who make their fortunes "speculating" in the financial markets, as many contend, economic leeches and rent-seekers, people who contribute little or nothing productive to society but just skim off the top the riches produced by others—takers, not makers, as one financial journalist has put it?[22]

A standard defense, which has considerable merit, is that the sophisticated machinery of modern financial markets *is* part of the productive apparatus of the economy. Financial markets provide a range of functions that facilitate the economy's operation and the generation of wealth. These include notably guiding the allocation of scarce investment resources, facilitating large-scale investment projects, providing mechanisms to transfer wealth and purchasing power into the future, reducing and transferring risk, monitoring corporate management and keeping them on their toes, and providing mechanisms to shift control of productive assets between competing management teams. An important way in which financial markets accomplish this is by providing price signals, which contain information that is dispersed across the global economy and that is otherwise often costly to obtain, interpret, and act on.

Adam Smith's invisible hand is at work in financial markets, too. Hedge funds, traders, and other financial speculators make money by trying to be the first to spot which securities will increase in price and which will decrease, buying ("going long") the former and selling (or "going short") the latter. To do so, they invest resources to gather and analyze information, often vast amounts of it. Such attempts to exploit inefficiencies in financial markets helps make those markets highly efficient. Society benefits from these activities. The fact that some people make a lot of money in the process of delivering these societal benefits may be a price worth paying.

As with CEO compensation, there is a similar scale-mismatch effect in financial market transactions. Take investment banking, for example. Investment bankers help conceive, arrange, finance, and market various kinds of financing and restructuring deals for their corporate clients, such as issuing debt and equity securities and arranging mergers and acquisitions. The financial scale of these deals is often in the billions of dollars. The acquiring company may pay the shareholders of the target company in new stock, cash, or both. The largest reported M&A deal in 2021 was the acquisition by Canadian Pacific Railway of Kansas City Southern Railway for a reported $31 billion in stock and cash.[23] In January 2022, Microsoft, the king of acquisitions, announced a $68.7 billion all-cash acquisition of Activision Blizzard, a game development company.[24]

When such large amounts of money are at stake, the individual investment bankers, lawyers, and accountants who are involved in advising or representing the acquiring and acquired firms, respectively, may earn what ordinary people may consider exorbitant sums, in the hundreds of thousands or even millions of dollars. Judged in relation to the size of the deal, however, such fees appear much more reasonable. Suppose an investment bank receives a fee of 0.1 percent of the transaction value of a $10 billion corporate acquisition—on the low side for the M&A world. That translates into $10 million. A decent chunk of that fee will find its way into the annual compensation of the senior investment bankers involved (much less for the associates who work night and day on the pitch books, but their turn will come!).

Investment banking is a highly demanding but also highly lucrative field. And it is a competitive one, too. There is no shortage of investment bankers and M&A advisory firms eager to bid on advising these lucrative M&A deals, especially since both sides of the deal need their own advisors. Both the acquiring firm and the target firm have an interest in getting the best advice possible, given the potentially billions of dollars of value in play. Neither party has an interest in overpaying for the M&A advisory services, but neither do they have a financial interest in driving too hard a pricing bargain and getting stuck with inferior advice and service.

THE LIMITS OF SOAKING THE RICH

Governments often have the bright idea of paying for ambitious new spending programs by "taxing the rich." Unfortunately, this doesn't work. Society pays for new government programs via the opportunity cost of not being able to use the resources for other purposes.

I have debunked the notion that governments raise taxes or issue bonds in order to spend. Rather, governments use taxes to do three things: redistribute income, encourage or discourage certain activities, and modulate aggregate demand. They issue bonds to separate monetary and fiscal functions within the government, and create a check on their own money printing.

The problem with taxing the rich is that doing so does not garner anywhere nearly enough resources to launch or expand society-wide government programs. Relative to the size of the entire economy, there are too few rich for the money these programs require; the rich directly consume too few resources, and the amount of their consumption is insufficiently responsive to changes in their wealth, for this solution to be viable.

Let's concentrate on the über-rich, whose net worth runs into the billions if not tens of billions of dollars. Politicians are tempted to think that if they could just get their hands on a chunk of that money, they could fund such-and-such a program. But it is real economic resources—labor, capital, and ingenuity—that programs need, not money per se. The real resources that taxing the rich will directly free up are minimal: their marginal propensity to consume is zero or close to it. The über-rich are the worst candidates to be taxed if the purpose is to free up resources. If you give short shrift to "trickle-down economics," forget about "soaking the rich."

It is the same with corporations. Imposing higher taxes on corporations in a market economy will lead firms to try to recoup some of the lost profitability by raising prices and investing less, thus lowering share prices. Every first-year microeconomics student learns the important distinction between who a tax is imposed on and who ends up paying it, and that taxes impose a cost on society in foregone activity ("deadweight losses"). Again, not a great way to generate new resources.

Those who see taxing the rich as an easy way to pay for new government programs confuse paper wealth with real resources. Four of the top five stocks in the S&P 500 are Big Tech behemoths; several of their founders' net worth is in the tens of billions of dollars and that of a couple exceeds $100 billion. Yet, most of that wealth corresponds to the stock market valuation of the companies they own: the present discounted value of the companies' expected future earnings, which rest on the expectation of there being satisfied customers as far as the eye can see. This wealth, while representing one of the marvels of the free-enterprise capitalist system, does not represent resources that can be commandeered to produce more output today. Thus, there is no point in taxing it for that purpose.

Suppose the US federal government was able to wave a magic wand and get its hands on a trillion dollars of the stock market wealth of half a dozen Big Tech entrepreneurs in such a way that, unlikely as it would be, did not erode that wealth. Having that paper wealth would bring the government no resources per se and, given that it can produce dollars at will, grant it no more command over society's real resources than it already had. True, the government could sell the shares and use the proceeds to fund infrastructure projects and hire teachers, doctors, and nurses, but its ability to do so hinges on the availability of the resources, not the source of the money used to acquire them. If a government wants to launch or expand a clutch of spending programs, there are only three ways to "pay for" them.

One is to eat into any "economic slack" that there may be, as a result of the economy not operating at full capacity. A second is to call forth more resources, such as growing the workforce by immigration, raising the labor force participation rate, or boosting productivity by promoting technological innovation and high-powered market incentives. Both of these ways have limits and neither is helped by raising taxes; quite the reverse.

This leaves the third: divert resources from existing uses. Herein lies the underappreciated role of monetary policy and the aggregate-demand-management part of fiscal policy. Sooner or later the economy will reach full employment and start to overheat, and the government will need to take steps to rein it in. The central bank will need to tighten monetary policy by raising interest rates and shrinking its balance sheet if there is scope to do so, and the fiscal authorities will need to tighten fiscal policy by raising taxes and curbing expenditures.

It is the resources that become available when tighter monetary and fiscal policy suppress economic activity across the board that will "pay for" any new permanent spending programs, and very few of these will come from "the rich."

HELPING THE POOR

Suppose a society, or the government acting on its behalf, is concerned about the extreme inequalities that a market-oriented economic system is prone to produce, particularly at a time of highly popular, disruptive technologies being developed. What should such a society or its government do to remedy this? If income and wealth inequalities are largely a result of the economic system delivering prosperity, and if much of the über-rich's wealth is just the capitalized value of future satisfied customers, taking steps to stop such inequalities from arising in the first place would seem ill advised, a bit like throwing the baby out with the bathwater.

A more sensible approach would be for the government to ensure that the poorest in society have sufficient income to enjoy a decent standard of living. This is the basis of the welfare state or income redistribution policy. The sad fact of life is that there is no such thing as a free lunch: everything comes with some price tag or hidden cost, even if the ostensible cost is zero. A lunch, even if provided free to the recipient, costs society the resources that go into producing it. And there may be another more indirect and hidden cost: when people receive free lunches, some of them may be less inclined to work and earn the money to buy their own lunches.

The conundrum associated with social welfare and safety net programs is that it is impossible to provide welfare without reducing the incentives of the recipients to take the necessary steps to put themselves in a position where they no longer need that welfare. There is a trade-off for society between compassion and efficiency: provide too much compassion and society will be less productive and prosperous, but provide too little and society cannot live with itself. Consider two extremes. In one society, the government mandates that all citizens receive everything they need for free; in fact, they would receive next to nothing because everybody would be waiting for the goods and services to arrive, but nobody would be producing them. In the other, the government provides no social safety net and requires everyone to stand on their own feet, the consequences be damned. This would produce a lot of workers, eager to put food on the table, and private philanthropy would no doubt provide some social welfare, but many of the less fortunate and downright unlucky would live in misery, shaming the whole society. A good social welfare system tries to locate itself between those two extremes, expanding the size of the economic pie while ensuring that everyone gets a decent slice.

Suppose that it costs $100,000 to permanently house a homeless person, and assume there are 500,000 homeless people in the United States. A politician who is well-intentioned but unschooled in the economic literacy department has the bright idea of levying a one-time tax of $50 billion on Jeff Bezos to pay for this program to eliminate homelessness, in the form of $50 billion worth of Amazon stock (equivalent to about 5 percent of Amazon's total market capitalization, at the time of writing). The legality of such a scheme aside, the government confiscating that much of an individual's stock would probably trigger a big drop in Amazon's stock price (and weaken stock prices across the board). The base problem would be left unchanged, too: housing the current homeless population does not solve the complex underlying factors that lead people to become homeless in the first place. Does this scheme make sense? Would it work?

Let's assume the government carries off this seizure, then sells the Amazon stock and nets $50 billion of cash by doing so (unrealistically, because the act of selling such a big position in Amazon's stock would cause its price to fall). The government could now deploy that $50 billion to procure the housing and management services needed to house the half-million homeless people: land, buildings, building materials, furniture, energy, and lots of labor. Those resources have to come from somewhere, but they do not come from Jeff Bezos. Given that Bezos's net worth is about $113 billion and he still has about $63 billion after Uncle Sam dipped its hand into his pocket, it is safe to assume that he will not materially (excuse the pun) alter his consumption patterns as a result, certainly nowhere near enough to release $50 billion worth of resources.

The $50 billion of purchasing power that the government now has can be used to command those resources, but it is the process of countless individuals either exchanging their property for the government's money, or providing their labor services, directly or indirectly, for them that gets the job done of housing half a million homeless people. Jeff Bezos, other than being the original source of the dollars, has nothing to do with it.

The government is not short of dollars. There is no need for it to get the dollars required to solve the homeless problem from Jeff Bezos; it could just as easily conjure the dollars out of thin air by printing the money. The usual argument against it doing so is that it would cause inflation. But using the $50 billion from Jeff Bezos will be just as inflationary because the multibillionaire does not release any resources to speak of by having $50 billion shaved off his net worth. It is the government commandeering the resources that potentially produces the price pressure. The question then becomes: What needs to be done to dampen demand sufficiently to release the necessary resources so that commandeering them to end homelessness does not result in excessive inflation, and who should do it? The answer, of course, is some combination of monetary and fiscal policy tightening. The monetary tightening is done by the central bank and the fiscal tightening is done by the government in one of three ways: cutting spending on goods and services, making fewer income transfers, or raising taxes on somebody. The last one, raising taxes, has nothing to do with the government needing to raise money; it has everything to do with it needing to withdraw purchasing power and free up resources.

The government occasionally may realize that it needs to deploy fiscal policy to stimulate economic activity, but it does not usually think of using fiscal policy to cool down an overheating economy. That task falls principally upon the central bank. If the economy is at full employment when the government launches its program to end homelessness, the central bank will likely need to tighten monetary policy at least a bit, or bring forward the monetary tightening that was in the pipeline a bit, to dampen demand enough to divert the necessary resources from other uses.

A market economy is a highly decentralized mechanism. The people who are releasing the resources won't be aware that they are releasing them, let alone that they are doing so because the government is launching a homelessness-eradication program. Rather, they will be making decisions within their budget constraints about how much money to spend and what to spend it on. Nor does the central bank need to be particularly informed or concerned about where the price pressure is coming from. It just needs to know that price pressure is building and tighten its monetary knobs accordingly. The price mechanism of the market will take care of everything else.

I have argued in this chapter that income and wealth inequality is not the big economic problem that it is often made out to be. Much if not most of the inequality results from the market-oriented economy doing its job of producing prosperity, via technological innovation and entrepreneurs trying to produce goods and services that cause consumers to voluntarily part with their (generally) hard-earned money. It is difficult for people to get rich, legally at least, without doing something useful for society in the process. Adam Smith's invisible hand reaches into every corner of the economy.

From a purely economic perspective, it is hard to see that extreme wealth can do much damage. Most of the wealth of the über-rich represents claims on financial assets, notably shares in companies, and on real assets, such as houses and expensive cars, artwork, jewelry, and perhaps private jets, yachts, and even islands. Beyond the financial claims are underlying claims on real assets, such as office buildings, factories, warehouses, and intellectual property. Most of this wealth derives its value from providing goods and services to consumers. Some of the über-rich are prone to conspicuous and extravagant consumption. Stephen Schwarzman, founder of private equity firm Blackstone, is famously reported to have spent upwards of $5 million on his sixtieth-birthday bash at a Park Avenue, Manhattan, haunt in 2007. But it is hard for the über-rich to spend their money without benefiting a lot of people in the process: those employed in providing the goods and services the rich are so lavishly procuring.

One thing that many of the über-rich do with their money is give it away. If you can't take your money with you when you die, you might as well try to do some good with it while you are alive. Many billionaires (and multimillionaires) set up philanthropic foundations. As well as being a vehicle for doing good in the world, a foundation can be a tax-effective way for the rich to deploy part of their assets. Timely, accurate numbers are hard to come by, but according to one report, the endowments of nonprofit organizations in the US totaled $1.7 trillion as of the end of 2017.[25]

The real economic "damage" that the über-rich do is depriving others of resources through their extravagant consumption. A multibillionaire might have a string of houses across the major cities and upscale holiday spots of the world. Those properties will generate employment for a host of people who construct and maintain them, such as housekeepers, gardeners, guards, and maintenance and repair staff. Still, most of the properties will sit empty most of the time. Homeless people could be living in these properties or, more plausibly, in the houses vacated by the people at the bottom of the chain of affluence who, in this thought experiment, would move up to the next level were all the real estate in question to be utilized more efficiently and parsimoniously.

A similar argument can be used for the surplus cars, private jets, and magnificent yachts at the beck and call of the extravagant billionaire that sit idle most of the time. Suppose a benign social dictator was able to rearrange the resource allocation deckchairs to more efficiently deploy the resources monopolized by the über-rich, while still leaving them living in style. Because the number of über-rich is infinitesimally small compared to the world's total population, even to the numbers of the most needy, this would hardly yield a game-changing benefit to the human race. The limited benefits to be realized are a measure of the limited damage done. And, human nature and incentives being what they are, attempts by governments to expropriate the wealth of the über-rich may just result in less wealth being generated.

That does not mean that governments can do nothing about wealth inequality. But the focus of public policy should be on giving those at the lowest end of the income and wealth spectrum a helping hand to move up, rather than trying to drag those at the top down. To do whatever they deem is necessary, governments don't need the money of the rich—they can produce their own at will. Of course, by doing so, and deploying it for the benefit of the poor, resources will have to be garnered from somewhere. If the economy is at full capacity, as it should be, that somewhere has to be the rest of the population, which numerically is overwhelmingly the "middle class." Taxing the "rich" to help (i.e., give tax cuts to) the middle class, while having a nice political ring to it, is in economic terms a non sequitur.

MONEY IS POWER

None of this is to suggest that wealth inequality may not pose a problem for society. Extreme wealth can buy political power; economic power can seep into and corrupt the political sphere. Even the least well-off billionaire, one whose net worth is a mere billion dollars, would be hard pressed in normal times to spend enough on personal (and family) consumption to stop their wealth from growing, because of the investment returns they can expect to earn. Billionaires have access to high risk/high return investment opportunities, such as hedge fund and private equity investments. Even if this minimal billionaire earned just 5 percent on their investments, that would be $50 million before tax. It is hard to blow through that kind of money simply by spending on consumption, even after Uncle Sam has taken a slice.

There are reasons for society to be concerned about a small number of individuals accumulating vast financial wealth. Topping the list should be the ability and temptation to leverage that economic and financial power for political purposes. For at least some of the über-rich, deploying their financial wealth in the political realm to gain and deploy political power may be an attractive option. There is a fundamental difference between a billionaire spending their money on their own (or their family's) consumption or to amass more wealth—that is, spending it in the economic realm ("economic dollars")—and using it to amass and wield political power by spending it in the political realm ("political dollars").

The über-rich have long passed the point where, even living in luxurious style, they will ever be able to spend all their money (on consumption goods and services) in their lifetime or even have their children and grandchildren do so. Suppose a billionaire has four children, each of whom has four children. Including the kids' spouses, that makes twenty-four people to set up for life. Sidestepping the question of whether it makes moral or pastoral sense, establishing a $10 million trust fund for each person would cost $240 million—a doable task for a billionaire—each of which would yield (assuming a modest 5 percent annual return) a tidy income of $500,000 before tax. Earning ever more investment income increases the billionaire's net worth but can be expected to yield diminishing returns in terms of utility.

If the attraction of gaining power eclipses that of helping the world's needy, the billionaire may find the idea of using their financial wealth to achieve political objectives compelling. For some, the psychic value of being able to influence policy and political affairs, even the fate of a nation or the world, could far exceed that of adding zeroes in the net worth column of a spreadsheet. Using financial wealth to further political ends can take various forms, including making political donations on a large and wide scale, financing think tanks and other nonprofit organizations to promote particular policy or political issues and viewpoints,[26] or buying influential media assets.

A key concept in economics is that of diminishing marginal returns in consumption or production. When it comes to material consumption, the über-rich are deep in marginal-diminishing-returns territory; their marginal utility from additional wealth can safely be assumed to be in the vicinity of zero. However, the marginal returns to political consumption, to exerting political influence and control over society, may be very high.

The purchase by Jeff Bezos of the *Washington Post* newspaper in 2013 for a reported $250 million is a good example. The price tag represented about 1 percent of Bezos's reported net worth at the time[27] (now more like more like 0.2 percent)—pocket change for such an influential platform. Elon Musk's acquisition of social media platform Twitter for $44 billion in October 2022 is another example of the uber-rich deploying their wealth in ways that could yield outsized political and societal influence. In Musk's case, the relative price tag is considerably higher, at about 24 percent of his reported net worth.

From a purely economic perspective, the Adam Smith logic may apply: billionaires find it hard to deploy their wealth without benefiting society in the process, in this case by keeping a venerable newspaper afloat even as many have sunk in the digital age, and an army of reporters and staff employed; in Elon Musk and Twitter's case, by striking a blow against "cancel culture" and in favor of free speech. But many may question whether success in the economic realm should be so easily leveraged in the political realm, a thorny issue that requires much more societal attention.

So far in this book, we have considered money largely in a positive light, as an ingenious human invention and social construct—fashioned into its modern incarnation over centuries of innovation—and as a driving force of economic prosperity. But there is another, darker side to money: as centuries of financial crises attest, money can wreak havoc on economies and societies, too. We turn now to a consideration of how and why that happens, and what can be done to mitigate the adverse consequences.

6

THE POWER OF MONEY TO WREAK HAVOC

I wake up every single night thinking what could I have done differently.

Richard ("Dick") Fuld, chairman and
CEO of Lehman Brothers, 2008[1]

Money helps the economic world go around, but sometimes it helps to bring it crashing down. The history of money, banking, and finance is also a history of monetary, banking, and financial crises. Harvard economists Carmen Reinhart and Kenneth Rogoff's impishly titled 2009 book *This Time Is Different* chronicled, as the subtitle stated, "eight centuries of financial folly"; Charles Kindleberger's classic *Manias, Panics, and Crashes: A History of Financial Crises* is going strong after eight editions.[2] The memories of the Global Financial Crisis of 2007–2009, when the world's financial system almost collapsed over one fateful weekend, are still vivid to many, including me. The weekend was September 13–14, 2008, at the tail end of which Lehman Brothers, the fourth-largest US investment bank, filed for bankruptcy; for my sins, I was global chief economist of Lehman at the time.

What causes financial crises? Can they be prevented? If so, what is the best way to do so? If not, what is the best way to handle the crisis? Is money a cause or cure for financial crises, or perhaps a bit of both? Let's try to answer these and related questions.

FINANCIAL CRISES GALORE

Financial crises come in all shapes and sizes; no two crises follow exactly the same course.

First, there are banking crises, such as Japan's in the 1990s or the more recent Global Financial Crisis, often called the "subprime crisis." In a banking crisis like Japan's, commercial banks finance overinvestment in risky assets, usually real estate, helping to feed a bubble in those assets. When the bubble bursts, the banks' capital is eroded and depositors rush to withdraw their money, forcing banks to close or the government to bail them out. The Global Financial Crisis of 2007–2009 combined elements of a conventional banking crisis with a "shadow banking" or capital markets crisis: the capital of commercial banks like Bank of America and Citibank was eroded by a collapse in the value of their bubble-inflated assets, while such capital market products as mortgaged-backed securities, collateralized debt obligations, and credit default swaps turned out to be much riskier than envisaged. In this combined crisis, short-term capital market funding froze as perceived counterparty risk went through the roof, bringing down investment banks like Bear Stearns and Lehman Brothers and, in the case of credit default swaps being called in, almost dooming the giant insurance company AIG.[3]

There are also stock market crashes like the Wall Street Crash of 1929, which predated and likely helped trigger the Great Depression of the 1930s; and the bursting of the information technology/Nasdaq bubble (a.k.a., the "dot-com crash") at the start of the 2000s. In a typical stock market crash, "irrational exuberance," or excessive investor optimism about the future, pushes stock prices into bubble territory, and investors who have borrowed money to finance ever-more expensive stock purchases get wiped out when the bubble bursts, often bringing down the economy with them. Japan's "bubble economy" of the 1980s involved both stock market and real estate bubbles, the bursting of both in the 1990s leading to the country's decade-plus banking crisis (Japanese banks historically had big shareholdings in the companies that borrowed from them, so the simultaneous collapse of stock prices and land prices delivered a one-two punch to their capital).

In addition, there are balance of payments crises, like those experienced by Indonesia, South Korea, and Thailand in the 1997 Asian financial crisis. In a typical balance of payments crisis, businesses in countries that peg their exchange rate to the US dollar borrow too much in those dollars to finance domestic investments. If the projects and the economy sour, pressure builds on the currency peg to give way. When it does, the domestic currency depreciates sharply, driving up the real value (in domestic currency) of the debt of banks and businesses that had borrowed in foreign currency and pushing many into insolvency.

A variant of a balance of payments crisis is the **sovereign debt** crisis, such as the Latin American debt crisis of the early 1980s. In a typical sovereign debt crisis, a country's government ends up borrowing too much in foreign currencies, usually the US dollar, or assuming the debts of domestic banks and companies, but finds itself unable to generate enough income to pay its debts back. A government should never have to default on debts denominated in its own currency because, push come to shove, it can always create money at will, but it cannot run another country's printing press. The euro area sovereign debt crisis of 2010–2015 is an interesting variant, which we will look at in the next chapter.

Financial crises share a common element: an inherent liquidity mismatch between the monetary economy and the real economy. Financial claims are inherently more liquid than the underlying assets to which they lay claim. Financial crises happen when lenders demand their money back faster than borrowers can liquidate their assets to supply it. But financial crises don't happen in a vacuum. Something triggers the loss in confidence that causes investors and bank depositors to want their money back.

THE INHERENT LIQUIDITY MISMATCH

The human invention of money, and a monetary economy paralleling, mirroring, and facilitating the real economy, is a marvel of human civilizational development and has helped to generate endless prosperity. But it has a blind spot: the liquidity it creates and that is so central to its operation is fragile and rests on collective confidence being maintained. The financial system creates a liquid overlay on an illiquid real economy, but the liquidity is largely a mirage and can evaporate. When it does, we call it a financial crisis.

"Liquidity" is a slippery word. It is one of those words that people toss around as if everyone understands it, yet seldom stop to define, even though it is not often clear exactly what they intend by the word. To economists, "liquidity" has three distinct meanings or usages.

The first meaning captures how "money-like" a financial asset is, in the sense of how close it is to being usable as a medium of exchange, to buy things (goods and services or assets) or to settle debts. Financial wealth in the form of real estate is not very liquid, and money in a term or savings deposit is less liquid than money in a checking or demand deposit account. If you have a lot of liquid assets, you have a lot of assets that are either conventionally classified as money (such as bank deposits) or assets that can readily be turned into money (such as Treasuries or blue chip stocks). Highly liquid assets may not be regarded as money, but there are a lot of people who have money and will readily accept the assets in exchange. Liquidity is a measure of how easy it is to turn an asset into money.

A second meaning of liquidity is as a synonym for reserves or central bank money. Central banks "injecting liquidity into the market" in the sense of them increasing the amount of reserves in the banking system (or deposits in the banking system), often to calm down jittery markets, is common financial market parlance. Supplying "liquidity" to the market is one of the main jobs of central banks.

A third is liquidity in the sense of how easy it is to buy or sell an asset without affecting the asset's price. This is usually termed "market liquidity." An asset is said to be highly liquid if there are lots of potential buyers and sellers and they can transact in reasonably big amounts without influencing the price much. The US Treasury market is the quintessential liquid market. That doesn't mean that market prices don't move; they constantly do, as new information comes to the attention of the market. But it is the new information that moves the market, not the desire of individual holders to convert part of their Treasury holdings into a more liquid form.

The liquidity mismatch between the monetary and real sides of the economy is intrinsic and unavoidable. The real side of the economy is inherently illiquid: it is a world of physical capital, embodied in infrastructure, residential and commercial buildings, computers, and factories and warehouses. It is a world of human capital, embodied in the skills and knowledge that workers, managers, technologists, and scientists have acquired through years of education, training, and experience. It is also a world of institutional, social, and cultural capital, embodied in the laws, norms, and rules that underpin the operation of society. This accumulated stock of capital is what enables the world to produce the massive amount of goods and services that are either consumed or used to replenish and augment the capital stock every year.

The financial system creates liquid claims: that is, claims on the capital stock that can be readily converted into other claims or into money. Take the banking system. Ultimately, the banking system holds claims on wealth-producing assets in the real economy, such as ports, factories, airplanes, telecommunication networks, and houses, and even the skills people acquire through their education (think "student loans"). The banking system translates the claims on these inherently illiquid assets into liquid ones in two stages, corresponding to the two sides of its balance sheet.

On the asset side of the banking system's balance sheet are loans, bonds, stocks, and other financial securities. Financial markets make these claims more liquid for those who hold them than the underlying assets. Financial assets can be illiquid, too; how liquid they are depends on whether there is a market in which they can be traded and how "deep" and active that market is. A deep market is one with many active buyers and sellers. In recent decades, a trend toward increasing securitization of assets developed, although the Global Financial Crisis presented a roadblock. Financial markets and securitization go hand in hand. When assets are securitized, they can be more easily traded in financial markets.

On the liability side of its balance sheet are mainly deposits, classified as a form of money. Money, in the form of deposits in the banking system, is a highly liquid asset, but the ultimate assets from which it derives value are illiquid. The financial system liquefies the claims on the productive assets of the economy, but this doesn't change the illiquid nature of the underlying assets.

The marvel of the financial system is that it creates liquidity out of illiquidity. But the liquidity so created is fragile and depends on collective trust and confidence in the system to sustain it. Liquidity is endogenous—arising from inside the economic system—not exogenous, or coming from outside of it. An asset is liquid because many people are willing to acquire it in exchange for money, but a major reason they are so willing is because they expect that other people will be prepared to buy the asset when they decide to sell it. My contribution to making an asset liquid is dependent on me believing that everyone else, or at least enough people, will make their contribution, too. In that sense, liquidity involves network effects: just as the value of a network increases the more people use it, the more willing people are to buy an asset, the more liquid it becomes.

LIQUIDITY VERSUS SOLVENCY

In times of financial stress or crisis, a sharp distinction is often drawn between problems of liquidity and solvency. In fact, the distinction is not as sharp as supposed; the line between the two is quite blurry. A borrower is said to have a "liquidity problem" if it does not have enough liquid assets on hand to meet its obligations when they come due. It is said to have a "solvency problem," or be "insolvent," when its assets are not sufficient to cover its liabilities—that is, when it has negative net equity. Liquidity is akin to a flow, solvency to a stock.

A borrower that is solvent (i.e., has positive net worth) but is facing a liquidity problem should in principle be able to get out of its jam. If the value of its assets exceeds its liabilities and the only problem is a shortage of cash on hand, it should be able to borrow the money to tide itself over. If it is a bank, it should be able to borrow from the central bank. One of the key functions of the central bank is to act as **"lender of last resort"**; more on this below.

The question of whether a firm or individual with debts is solvent is less clear cut than it seems. The difference between solvency and insolvency often hinges on whether the firm or individual is able to solve its liquidity problem. A firm experiencing a liquidity problem that can solve it by securing the necessary cash in the short term is likely to remain solvent; the issue may not even come up. But if the same firm struggles to solve its liquidity problem and has to sell off some of its assets for the money to meet its obligations, it may become insolvent. Solvency or insolvency becomes a self-fulfilling phenomenon, depending on how actual or potential lenders assess the situation. This is because illiquid assets that have to be sold at short notice to raise cash generally must be sold at a big discount, perhaps well below their book value (their value as assessed and recorded on the balance sheet). The danger of a liquidity problem bleeding into a solvency problem can become severe during a financial panic when many people are trying to sell at the same time and potential buyers at prevailing prices are few. A negative feedback loop may become a downward spiral as buyers or lenders holding back induce others to do so. In a financial panic, it is said, "no one wants to catch a falling knife."

The very fact that a monetary economy exists, as a kind of virtual economy alongside the real economy, creates a liquidity mismatch between the two. Usually, the creation of liquid assets out of illiquid ones that the financial system engineers is a blessing. But it rests on a fallacy of composition: what appears to be true for individuals is not true at the level of the entire society or economy.

An individual who has, say, $100,000 in a checking or demand deposit may regard that asset as highly liquid, believing that they can draw on it any time they like. And this is true for an individual because a bank always has enough reserves on hand at the central bank to accommodate a withdrawal of that size. But if every depositor (or enough of them) tried to withdraw their money at the same time, the bank would not have enough reserves, because, if the bank is doing its job, most of its assets will be claims on illiquid real-economy assets.

There are two lines of defense against a rush for liquidity overwhelming the system and exposing the liquidity mismatch or the fallacy of composition. One is the modern institution of deposit insurance, introduced in the US in 1933 after widespread bank failures helped provoke the Great Depression.

DEPOSIT INSURANCE

In most advanced countries, the government operates a bank deposit insurance scheme for "small-lot" deposits, or those up to a certain size: in the US, currently $250,000 per depositor per bank. Deposit insurance works like any insurance in that banks pay premiums to the government deposit insurance agency—in the US, the Federal Deposit Insurance Corporation—and if a bank fails, the agency guarantees deposits up to the insured limit. In the unlikely event that the deposit insurance agency does not have enough premiums in the kitty to cover losses at a certain point, the government stands behind it, guaranteeing any borrowing it may need to smooth its cash flow requirements. Because the government operates and stands behind the deposit insurance scheme, the incentive of most individual depositors (i.e., those whose deposits are fully insured) to withdraw their deposits in a bank panic is drastically reduced if not completely eliminated.

But deposit insurance covers only banks (depository institutions) and does not cover all deposits: large-lot depositors, wealthy individuals, and small and large businesses still stand to lose money in a bank failure. This is where the second line of defense comes in.

THE CENTRAL BANK AS LENDER OF LAST RESORT

Both to deter a bank or financial panic from happening and to manage it if one does happen, the central bank acts as lender of last resort—"lender" and "last resort" being the two key terms. The central bank is supposed to provide liquidity (that is, reserves) to tide the financial system over, not to cover financial losses; if the latter happens, it is supposed to be the responsibility of the fiscal authorities and politicians, who are beholden to taxpayers and voters, and only when the private sector is unable or unwilling to act.

The central bank is the only entity in the economy that can produce money at will by buying assets or lending to banks against the collateral they offer. Suppose a bank finds itself with rising bad loans and starts to lose deposits, and counterparties in the interbank market start to get leery of lending to the bank. In the first instance, a dollar of deposits leaving a bank reduces the bank's reserves at the central bank by a dollar. If the deposits just move to another bank, as is likely to be the case when depositors move money on perceived-safety grounds, the level of reserves in the banking system will be unchanged, and the bank that lost the deposits should be able to fill the shortfall by borrowing the reserves from the bank that received the deposits. But if the receiving bank perceives there to be counterparty risk—that is, risk that the borrowing bank may not repay its loan—it may decide to hoard the reserves.

In such a case, the struggling bank could restore its reserves at the central bank by selling assets in the market. During a financial panic, however, this could lead to contagion, as financial problems spread from one firm to another.

The mechanics of the central bank acting as a lender of last resort are straightforward, even if the policymaking and the politics of such "bailouts" are not. The central bank simply lends reserves to banks against collateral that borrowers provide, creating the loaned money out of thin air. Imagine a bank needs $100 of reserves, because it is bleeding deposits and is unable to secure reserves from other banks. The central bank credits the bank's reserve account (a liability for the central bank) for $100, recording a loan to the bank of the same amount, this loan being secured by some agreed-upon assets held by the bank. The bank now has $100 of reserves on the asset side of its balance sheet and $100 of borrowing from the central bank on the liability side.

There are three main ways in which a central bank typically acts as a lender of last resort.

Bank Funding Squeeze

The first way is when one or more banks are experiencing a funding squeeze on reserves. In normal times, a central bank doesn't need to be concerned about the distribution of reserves in the banking system across banks; it only needs to ensure the banking system in aggregate has enough reserves. If the central bank is supplying enough reserves, which it will be, and if all banks are in sound financial condition, which they should be, then a bank finding itself at any point in time with too many reserves will lend its surplus reserves in the interbank market to a bank with too few.

However, banks are highly sensitive to the financial conditions of their counterparties. If economic and financial conditions deteriorate sufficiently, they may expose a weak link in the system, such as a Bear Stearns in March 2008 or a Lehman Brothers in September 2008: one or more banks whose asset quality becomes questionable and starts to find it difficult if not impossible to roll over its short-term funding. Rather than the central bank relying on the reserves finding their way to the problematic bank—which, as the situation deteriorates, they won't—it can lend directly to the questionable bank. Walter Bagehot, a noted nineteenth-century British economist, famously captured this idea in a dictum usually summarized as, "[To] avert panic, central banks should lend early and freely (ie, without limit), to solvent firms, against good collateral, and at 'high rates.'"[4] The assumption is that the borrowers are solvent but are experiencing liquidity problems, with the cure for a liquidity problem being, unsurprisingly, liquidity.

Keeping the Wheels Turning

A second way is when key market segments freeze up and central banks try to get them functioning smoothly again by acting as a stopgap liquidity provider. Such actions came to the fore in the Global Financial Crisis, when the Fed in particular launched a number of emergency lending programs that became known as **credit easing**." Like many so-called unconventional monetary policies, credit easing was pioneered in the modern era by the Bank of Japan. In April 2003, two years into its pioneering QE experiment, the BOJ launched an asset-backed securities purchase program aimed at "[paving] the way to providing SMEs [small- and medium-sized enterprises] with a new financing channel, contributing to strengthening the transmission mechanism of monetary easing."[5] The BOJ's scheme was very small scale and hardly registers in the annals of modern monetary policymaking history.

Later that decade, the Fed's actions during the **Great Recession** aimed to keep the wheels of the financial markets turning in such areas as commercial paper, money market funds, and asset-backed securities. Its actions included lending to participants in these markets, using the assets in question as collateral, or buying the assets indirectly through a special-purpose vehicle, usually with some form of indemnity by the US Treasury against potential losses. Such tactics made a second and even more dramatic appearance during the COVID-19 pandemic, with newly launched facilities being aimed at buoying municipal bond markets, corporate bond markets, "Main Street" lending, and lending under the government's Paycheck Protection Program.

Credit easing is similar to quantitative easing in that the central bank acquires assets (usually by making loans) financed by creating reserves, resulting in the central bank's balance sheet getting bigger than it normally would. The idea behind credit easing is that the measures are aimed explicitly at improving the transmission of monetary policy through credit and other financial markets. Recall that a central bank sets the monetary-policy ball rolling, but most of the work of stimulating or restraining economic activity, as needed, is done by financial markets. If the financial system remains unstable or, worse, threatens to implode, not only could the implications for the real economy be dire, but the effectiveness of monetary policy is likely to be stymied, too. With two major global shocks in fifteen years forcing most major central banks to operate at the effective lower bound on interest rates, credit easing is becoming a part of the standard monetary policymaking toolkit.

Too Big to Fail

The third, and most controversial, aspect of the central bank acting as a lender of last resort involves rescuing or "bailing out" individual banks or other financial institutions that are deemed "**too big to fail**." Institutions are so deemed if their failure would wreak so much havoc, via financial contagion and associated harm to the economy, that it is less costly to bail them out. Bailing out an institution that is "too big to fail" sounds inherently unfair, inimical to the principles of a market economy, and a recipe for **moral hazard**, but those side effects can be mitigated variously. For example, the central bank can require top management to be relieved of their duties, and the government can take a large ownership stake in the bailed-out firm, thus diluting the interests of existing shareholders.

Central bank rescue operations can take various forms. Most conventionally, the central bank would keep an otherwise failing bank afloat with emergency financing until the cavalry arrived, in the form of a stronger bank to take it over, often with some arm-twisting by the authorities. In other cases, the central bank might finance a carve-out of nonperforming assets. Central banks are usually at pains to point out in such situations that it is not the institutions themselves they are bailing out, but rather, by sparing them disruption and losses, the financial system, wider economy, and therefore Main Street and the general public.

THE FED'S SECTION 13(3) LENDER OF LAST RESORT AUTHORITY

A central bank's lender-of-last-resort role, by its nature, takes that bank into treacherous waters by exposing it to risk and intervening in the market, potentially benefiting some firms over others. Both of these are no-no's in conventional monetary-policy thinking, particularly to those of a more conservative persuasion. Not surprisingly, this lender-of-last-resort role is carefully circumscribed by legislation.

In the Fed's case, the key rule is Section 13(3) of the Federal Reserve Act, known as the "unusual and exigent circumstances" section. The version that existed at the time of the Global Financial Crisis read as follows:

> In unusual and exigent circumstances, the Board of Governors of the Federal Reserve System . . . may authorize any Federal reserve bank . . . to discount for any individual, partnership, or corporation, notes, drafts, and bills of exchange . . . [that are] . . . secured to the satisfaction of the Federal reserve bank: Provided . . . that such individual, partnership, or corporation is unable to secure adequate credit accommodations from other banking institutions. All such discounts for individuals, partnerships, or corporations shall be subject to such limitations, restrictions, and regulations as the Board of Governors of the Federal Reserve System may prescribe.

Section 13(3) is regarded as the "lender of the last resort" clause of the Federal Reserve Act, although that term is not used in the act. It had its inception in the Great Depression but largely lay dormant until the 2008 financial crisis, when the Fed invoked it numerous times.[6] It did so first when it brokered a rescue merger of the troubled investment bank, Bear Stearns, by banking behemoth, JPMorgan Chase. Controversially, this deal involved the Fed, ahead of the rescue merger, purchasing (via a Special Purpose Vehicle) $30 billion of Bear Stearns's problematic assets, with JPMorgan taking the first billion dollars of losses. The Fed also invoked its Section 13(3) authority to set up six credit facilities: the Term Securities Lending Facility, the Primary Dealer Credit Facility, the Commercial Paper Funding Facility, the Money Market Investor Funding Facility, the Term Asset-Backed Securities Loan Facility, and—the biggest mouthful of all—the Asset-Backed Commercial Paper Money Market Mutual Fund Liquidity Facility.[7]

Short as it is, the legislative wording of Section 13(3) has some interesting aspects, bordering on internal contradictions, which might evoke differing reactions and interpretations among economists versus among lawyers. The section is silent on what the purpose of the Fed invoking it is—that is, on what problem the Fed should be trying to solve or what outcome it is trying to achieve. The equivalent article in the Bank of Japan Act makes clear its purpose: "The maintenance of [an] orderly financial system." The wording of Section 13(3) may be coy and arcane, but there is little mystery about its purpose: to give the Fed the authority to take emergency actions to maintain the stability of the financial system when required. This can also be inferred from the fact that Section 13(3) gives the Fed the power to lend to any individual, partnership, or corporation, rather than to its normal counterparties: those member banks of the Federal Reserve System able to maintain reserve accounts with it.

This being the case, there is a natural interpretation of Section 13(3): that the Fed is empowered to take actions if it is satisfied that it needs to do so in order to maintain financial stability. There is a key word in Section 13(3) and a key condition that need to be read together. The key condition is that the borrower is unable to obtain finance from any other source; turning to the Fed has to be a last resort.

The key word is that the lending has to be secured to the "satisfaction" of the Fed. A commonsense reading, in the overall context of the section, would be that this imposes a relatively low bar on the Fed. The Fed does not run a private sector moneymaking operation; it is charged with fulfilling certain governmental functions in the public interest, including (notably in the context of Section 13(3)) preserving the stability of the financial system. This certainly includes taking whatever actions it can to prevent that system from melting down or crashing. The Fed being "satisfied" with the security it obtains in making loans under Section 13(3) should not mean that it will make loans only if it is fully assured of getting its money back. There is a point of logical consistency here: If the only circumstance under which the Fed is authorized to make a Section 13(3) loan is when the borrower cannot obtain finance from any banking institution, how could the Fed be able to make a fully-secured loan? Presumably other banks could demand the same collateral as the Fed could.

The only way to square the circle is to envisage circumstances in which there is total panic and financial markets have ceased functioning to the extent that solvent borrowers are unable to obtain funding to roll over or refinance their existing commitments as they come due. But here we start to enter the realm of financial tautology. Would borrowers really be solvent in such dire circumstances, circumstances in which the only willing lender is the Fed?

This thought experiment highlights a critical difference between the central bank and other banks and private entities. As the monopoly supplier of base money (reserves and banknotes) and the operator of monetary policy, the central bank, unlike any private bank, does not have to—indeed, is not supposed to—accept the condition of the economy and its future prospects as given. Rather, it is required to keep the economy at full employment and on an even, noninflationary keel and to maintain financial stability.

This has an important implication, in the nature of a chicken-and-egg problem: whether a systemically important bank is deemed solvent or not, and therefore eligible to receive central bank lender-of-last-resort financing, may depend on whether that central bank provides the support. In other words, it is easy to conceive of situations in which a big bank needing help from the central bank would be insolvent if it could not get the help but would be solvent if it could, because the actions of the central bank itself change conditions in the economy and the outcome for the bank in question. It would not make much sense for the central bank to deny lender-of-last-resort funding to a bank on the grounds that it is insolvent if the bank's condition of insolvency reflects a very poor state of the economy that the central bank is obligated to try to ameliorate—and that, if so ameliorated, would result in the bank being solvent again. Ultimately, the solvency of banks, particularly big "systemically important" ones, depends on the conditions in the economy. The Fed is on the hook for them.

Should the Fed Have Rescued Lehman?

This line of reasoning is relevant to the debate over whether the Fed, coordinating with the Treasury and other arms of the US government, should have "bailed out" Lehman Brothers, Bear Stearns–style, rather than allowing it (or, in some interpretations, forcing it) to declare Chapter 11 bankruptcy on September 15, 2008. In considering this issue, my intention as an economic analyst, as always, is to be impartial and objective. However, I have to declare an interest, as I was global chief economist of Lehman at the time and lost a significant amount of money as a result of Lehman's failure. Not that I would expect or seek any sympathy over that: people who work on Wall Street are generally talented and hard working, but also exceedingly well compensated and in many ways lucky, so they should be toward the back of the line when it comes to receiving the world's sympathy for falling on hard times.

Judging in hindsight, and viewing the crisis through an economic lens, my view is that the Fed, with the backing of the Treasury and the administration—the dying days of the Bush administration—could and should have engineered a Bear Stearns–like operation to rescue Lehman. Lehman was about four times bigger than Bear Stearns, but a Fed–Treasury rescue operation could have followed a similar template: the Fed taking over a portfolio of problematic assets with a certain proportion of first losses to be taken by the rescue bank, or a consortium of major banks, including itself; and a merger with that rescue bank on very dilutive terms for Lehman shareholders.

Some snippets from the FOMC meeting the day after Lehman Brothers filed for Chapter 11 bankruptcy hint that the Fed saw itself as having made a conscious decision in the preceding days not to use emergency lender-of-last-resort facilities to keep Lehman afloat or help to broker some kind of rescue operation along Bear Stearns lines.[8] A couple of comments suggest that a desire to curb moral hazard was a factor. Federal Reserve Bank of Richmond President Jeffrey Lacker stated that: "By denying funding to Lehman suitors, the Fed has begun to reestablish the idea that markets should not expect help at each difficult juncture."[9] Federal Reserve Bank of Kansas City President Thomas Hoenig said: "I think what we did with Lehman was the right thing because we did have a market beginning to play the Treasury and us, and that has some pretty negative consequences as well, which we are now coming to grips with."[10] Federal Reserve Bank of Boston President Eric Rosengren was less comfortable: "I think it's too soon to know whether what we did with Lehman is right. Given that the Treasury didn't want to put money in, what happened was that we had no choice. But we took a calculated bet."[11]

The Fed's failure to rescue Lehman triggered an acute financial crisis and severe recession (at the time, the worst since the Great Depression), which imposed huge costs on the economy and the financial system.[12] Real GDP fell in the next two quarters (from October 2008 to March 2009) by 3.3 percent in the US, 4.9 percent in the euro area, and 7.1 percent in Japan. The unemployment rate in the

US rose from 6.1 percent in August 2008 to a peak of 10.0 percent in October 2009, in the euro area from 7.7 percent to 10.3 percent (February 2020), and in Japan from 4.1 percent to 5.5 percent (July 2009).

The cardiac arrest that the financial system suffered after the Lehman collapse sent shock waves through the global financial system and pushed most major economies into recession. After some initial complacency, the Fed scrambled to cut interest rates (from 2 percent to close to zero by December 2008) and roll out a swath of credit and quantitative easing measures. The financial meltdown galvanized Congress, after some angst-filled hiccups, to pass legislation, establishing a euphemistically named Troubled Asset Relief Program, popularly known as the TARP. This created a $700 billion fund to recapitalize banks, which was quickly and effectively deployed.

It is impossible to be definitive about what would have happened to the economy had Lehman been rescued. The recession triggered by the housing bubble bursting is dated as having already started in December 2007, and the Fed had started cutting interest rates from 5.25 percent in August 2007 to 2.0 percent by the time of the Lehman failure. However, it is highly likely that the economic and financial-system fallout from the housing bubble being unwound and the subprime crisis would have been much less severe, able to be significantly absorbed and offset with the right mix of monetary, fiscal, housing, and banking system policies. Lehman's failure came amid rapidly escalating financial stress on the heels of the government bailout of Fannie Mae and Freddie Mac (the two federally sponsored housing-finance giants[13]). In the end, for various reasons—mainly political but possibly also reflecting institutional failure—the Fed rescuing Lehman in a Bear Stearns–style operation proved to be a bridge too far.

The Fed's defense was it did not have the authority under Section 13(3) to rescue Lehman because Lehman did not have sufficient good collateral. In his first public speech after the Lehman failure, Fed chairman Ben Bernanke laid out the Fed's argument for why it rescued Bear Stearns and the giant insurance company AIG but not Lehman. It is worth quoting Bernanke at some length:

Attempts to organize a consortium of private firms to purchase or recapitalize Lehman were unsuccessful. With respect to public-sector solutions, we determined that either facilitating a sale of Lehman or maintaining the company as a free-standing entity would have required a very sizable injection of public funds—much larger than in the case of Bear Stearns—and would have involved the assumption by taxpayers of billions of dollars of expected losses. Even if assuming these costs could be justified on public policy grounds, neither the Treasury nor the Federal Reserve had the authority to commit public money in that way; in particular, the Federal Reserve's loans must be sufficiently secured to provide reasonable assurance that the loan will be fully repaid. Such collateral was not available in this case . . . In the case of AIG, the Federal Reserve and the Treasury judged that a disorderly failure of AIG would have severely threatened global financial stability and the performance of the US economy . . . To avoid the default of AIG, the Federal Reserve was able to provide emergency credit that was judged to be adequately secured by the assets of the company.[14]

Bernanke's argument hinges on the questionable assertion that the Fed's hands were tied because any loan would have to be "fully repaid." As I have argued, this reason appears specious. The issue was not how confident the Fed was of getting all of its money back, but rather how necessary and feasible a rescue package for financial stability and economic health might be. From that angle, a rescue was justifiable both ex ante as well as ex post.

Chairman Bernanke's synopsis of the Fed's conundrum at the time given at the October 28–29, 2008, FOMC meeting is worth reproducing here: "I never took this [the criticism that we have no business interfering with the market process. We should let them fail. The market will take care of it] seriously. I just don't believe that you can allow systemically critical institutions to fail in the middle of financial crises and expect it to be not a problem."[15] But this is precisely what happened with Lehman. He goes on to state that: "The Fed and the Treasury simply had no tools to address both Lehman and the other companies that were under stress at that time." True, the Treasury did not yet have a TARP-like fiscal capacity, but the Fed had Section 13(3) and used it repeatedly, both before and in the wake of the Lehman bankruptcy. Was it really the case that the Fed could not "secure" its advances to its "satisfaction," which would seem to be a fairly low bar for using a lender-of-last-resort facility whose other sole criterion is that the borrower be "unable to secure adequate credit accommodations from other banking institutions"? Or, in the absence of a TARP-like fiscal capacity, was a Bear Stearns-like Lehman rescue operation a political or a moral hazard bridge too far for the Fed, as hinted by the chairman's observation that: "There is a political economy overlay. You have to get to the point that it is not only the right policy to induce fiscal support but also that it is politically possible"?[16]

There was a catch-22 aspect to the failure to prevent the Lehman failure. The weekend of September 13–14, 2008, was a frenetic one for all parties concerned as Henry Paulson, the secretary of the Treasury, and Timothy Geithner, the president of the New York Federal Reserve, led the charge in Manhattan to broker a Wall Street rescue of Lehman and stave off a feared US and global financial system collapse—ultimately unsuccessfully. Efforts centered on corralling a consortium of Wall Street banks to finance a carve-out of Lehman's most problematic assets that would smooth the way for a major bank to rescue Lehman, much as JPMorgan had saved Bear Stearns six months earlier. Barclays Bank of the United Kingdom was the favored arm-twisted suitor after Bank of America demurred.

As is clear from Secretary Paulson's account in his memoirs and other such histories, the catch-22 was that, close as a deal appeared to be, the Wall Street banks would not step up without the Fed joining

in, with moral support from the Treasury and the Bush administration, but the Fed would not contemplate *that* without the Wall
Street banks stepping up, including the prospective rescue bank. To
quote Paulson, "Unlike with Bear Stearns, the Fed's hands were tied
because we had no buyer," but it is as clear as day that there was no
buyer or supporting Wall Street consortium because there was no
Fed! As Paulson explained to President George W. Bush at 3:30 PM on
Sunday, September 14, regarding why Lehman was different from
Bear Stearns, "There was just no way to save Lehman. We couldn't
find a buyer even with the other private firms' help."[17] Catch-22: no
rescue buyer, no Fed support; no Fed support, no rescue buyer.

Section 13(3) Reformed

The Fed's Section 13(3) authority was modified after the financial crisis, as part of a comprehensive regulatory overhaul of the financial
system in the form of the Dodd-Frank Wall Street Reform and Con
sumer Protection Act, more commonly known as just Dodd-Frank.[18]
As well as adding considerable reporting requirements, Dodd-Frank
restricted the Fed's authority under Section 13(3) in three ways:
henceforth the Fed would need the approval of the secretary of the
Treasury to invoke the authority; Section 13(3) programs or facilities
would need to be ones with "broad-based eligibility," not ones aimed
at individual financial institutions; and any participating borrowers
would have to be solvent, as certified under procedures established
by the Fed.

The Fed invoked its Section 13(3) authority again during the recession triggered by the COVID-19 pandemic, resurrecting four of the
earlier programs (the Commercial Paper Funding Facility, the Primary Dealer Credit Facility, the Money Market Mutual Fund Liquidity Facility, and the Term Asset-Backed Securities Loan Facility) and
adding five new ones: the Primary Market Corporate Credit Facil
ity, the Secondary Market Corporate Credit Facility, the Main Street
Lending Program, the Municipal Liquidity Facility, and the Paycheck
Protection Program Liquidity Facility.

Another important Dodd-Frank reform was the introduction of a new framework for handling the failure of large, systemically important financial institutions—that is, ones that are deemed "too big to fail." At the time of the Lehman Brothers failure, the only alternatives to a Fed-led bailout, along the lines of the Bear Stearns or AIG ones, were Chapter 7 (liquidation) or Chapter 11 (reorganization) bankruptcy. Lehman filed for Chapter 11 bankruptcy in the US, which triggered analogous legal bankruptcy proceedings in national jurisdictions around the world. Title II of Dodd-Frank established an alternative to bankruptcy and to (now disallowed) Fed-led bailouts for large complex financial institutions, called "Orderly Liquidation Authority," under which the FDIC could be appointed to manage the wind-up of the entity. As of the time of writing, this has yet to be invoked, an ounce of prevention—in the form of much stricter banking-system oversight and capital adequacy requirements—being worth a pound of cure.

RISK AND MORAL HAZARD

Another fallacy of composition becomes manifest in financial crises, one relating to risk. The future is inherently uncertain and entails risk.[19] When a farmer plants next season's crop, they don't know what the size and quality of the harvest will be, nor do they know, for any given outcome, what it will fetch at market. A major function of the financial system, dating back to antiquity, is to provide incentives for risky investments to be undertaken and to distribute and diversify the associated risk. Because risk can be shifted from one party to another, financial instruments can be devised that turn inherently risky investments into very safe ones, or safe-looking ones, for individual investors or groups of them. The risk of the underlying investment has not changed, but much or most of the risk has been channeled to investors who happily accept it—for a price, of course. Higher risk means higher expected return, while low or nearly no risk means low expected returns.

Corporate equity and debt is a prototypical example: debt holders are "promised" a "safe" return—interest payments and the return of the principal upon maturity of the debt—but they also know (or they should) that in the unlikely event that the company goes belly up, they may only get back pennies on the dollar. Equity holders, on the other hand, are happy to shield debt holders from losses when times are tough because they get a bigger share of the gains in good times (but the times can't be too tough, because then they will just walk away from the firm, handing it over to the creditors).

The fallacy of composition is that, while avoiding risk is possible at the individual level, it is not possible at the societal level. Society as a whole cannot avoid being exposed to the risks that exist in aggregate. If a massive earthquake destroys much of the infrastructure of a major city, individual property holders may take some solace in their earthquake insurance contracts, but all the earthquake insurance in the world doesn't undo the damage.

The combination of financial claims being both more liquid than the ultimate assets that back them and being designed to shift risk to other parties can make them particularly susceptible to being instrumental in a financial crisis. Deposits run, bond markets crash, repo markets freeze, capital flees. Central banks play a useful social role when they provide liquidity in a financial panic: they bridge the liquidity mismatch and limit the damage from too many people seeking to shield themselves from losses, running for the door at once, and causing more damage in the process. But the central bank acting as lender of last resort raises the vexed issue of moral hazard.

"Moral hazard" is a term from the insurance world that refers to the distortive effect that insurance has on behavior, specifically the tendency of an insured person to be less inclined to take costly actions to reduce the likelihood of that event happening. Moral hazard is an unfortunate term because it suggests that morality is at the heart of the matter, rather than human nature. An economist would just say that "incentives matter."[20] The closest thing to a law of gravity that economics has is the Law of Demand: a demand curve slopes downward, meaning that more of something is demanded when its price goes down. If the price of not taking care goes down, you get more of that—that is, less care—too. No moral judgment involved, just economics (read: human nature).

Many economists and financial market participants worry that central banks acting as lenders of last resort, or even just operating monetary policy, induces moral hazard. Bailing out banks invites them to take more risks, which leads them to need more bailouts in the future. Heads, things go well—the banks and other investors win. Tails, things go south—taxpayers lose. There is something to this, but the solution is not for policymakers to take the moral hazard high ground in the middle of a financial crisis. The fire brigade doesn't let houses burn down, let alone entire neighborhoods, to teach careless homeowners a lesson. Policymakers shouldn't be in the business of protecting private businesses and investors from the consequences of their bad decisions. But neither should they stand back and let both the financial system and the economy collapse if they have the tools to help prevent it.

The central bank's lender-of-last-resort role is complementary to monetary and fiscal policy; and they should all be deployed in tandem. If a financial crisis erupts and the central bank holds back as lender of last resort, it may need to be even more aggressive in easing monetary policy, and the government in implementing fiscal stimulus, to counter the resulting economic fallout.

MONEY AND ASSET PRICE BUBBLES

Financial crises happen for a reason. Many are preceded by a credit-driven asset price bubble. When the bubble bursts, the crisis ensues. To understand financial crises, it pays to understand asset price bubbles.

Like "liquidity," "bubble" is another term that people tend to toss around loosely. Asset prices rise over time because the amount of economic activity does, too, and assets are a claim on economic output. The fact that asset prices are rising, possibly quite strongly, does not necessarily mean there is a bubble. It might just mean future economic prospects have gotten much brighter, perhaps because of the advent of new transformative technologies such as home computers, the internet, and smartphones.

To economists, an asset price bubble has a very specific meaning. Asset price bubbles occur when asset prices become untethered from underlying "fundamentals" and rise to levels that these fundamentals cannot justify. In a bubble, investor expectations drive prices higher, making the bubble a self-fulfilling process. Asset prices keep rising further into bubble territory because investors expect them to and buy the assets on that basis. This optimistic buying pushes prices higher, validating the price rises, pushing asset prices further away from a level justifiable by the underlying fundamentals, and further fueling the fire. This process can go on for a long time as asset valuations become more extreme. Most famously, it was said that at the peak of Japan's bubble, the grounds of the Imperial Palace in the center of Tokyo were worth more than the whole state of California.[21]

The tricky thing is that, while an asset price bubble has to be judged relative to "the fundamentals," those fundamentals are not directly observable but have to be inferred. What the fundamentals are is largely a matter of investor opinion. Certain objective aspects of the asset in question, the overall economy, and the state of the world might be relatively easy to ascertain, but an asset's fundamentals are determined largely by what happens in the future. That's what an asset price does: discount future prospects into a single value in the present. Life is full of surprises. Because the future hasn't happened yet, it might turn out differently from the past.

The only sure thing about a bubble is that it will eventually burst—until it does, it cannot be proved that it is a bubble. There is also the infamous "while the music plays" effect to contend with. Even if most investors judge there to be a bubble, nobody knows how long it will last, and lots of money can be made while it does. Former Citi CEO and President Chuck Prince famously quipped in a July 2007 *Financial Times* interview that "as long as the music is playing, you've got to get up and dance." His words before that were just as instructive: "When the music stops, in terms of liquidity, things will be complicated."[22]

The indexing problem exacerbates matters. A lot of money is invested in index funds: funds that track a stock market or other index, such as the S&P 500 or MSCI World Index. There is a lot of sense and sound finance theory behind people investing in an index, but it means that indices, or particular stocks within an index, that are experiencing bubbles will attract more inflows from so-called passive investors who are buying the index. This problem exists even for active investors, those who are actively managing funds aimed at outperforming a chosen index. Many funds designed for active investors will still be managed against an index, meaning that managers will be obliged to keep within certain risk limits of the index, denoted by "tracking error." Once a stock gets to be a certain percentage of the overall index, it becomes very hard for many investment managers not to hold at least some proportion of their portfolio in the stock, no matter how overvalued or in bubble territory they judge it to be. Otherwise the portfolio they are managing will deviate too much from the index, violating the risk limits imposed by their clients (the investment manager having sold their services to the client on the basis that they will control this risk).

Bubble narratives invariably drive investor sentiment. In Japan's asset price bubble in the second half of the 1980s, there was a widespread belief that real estate prices would continue to rise because they had never fallen in the postwar period and the Japanese economy appeared to be a "miracle economy," about to take over the world.[23] In the Nasdaq stock bubble of the late 1990s, as market valuations went through the roof, the predominant narrative was that traditional valuation metrics, such as price-to-book and price-to-earnings ratios, were no longer relevant in the internet age and could be ignored. In the mid-2000s US housing bubble, a common narrative was that financial innovation, centering on securitization of mortgages, had raised the capacity of even low-income households to own their own homes and had permanently raised the share of residential investment in GDP.

A bubble cannot go on forever, however. The only way to settle the question of whether a run-up in asset prices constitutes a bubble or a true change in future prospects and fundamentals that the future has yet to reveal is to wait for it to burst. By definition, bubbles burst; if they don't, they weren't a bubble. This fact itself can exacerbate a bubble: the longer a bubble goes on the more that the bubble believers can point to the fact that it has not burst as evidence that it is not a bubble!

Asset price bubbles typically collapse under the weight of their internal contradictions. The same profit-seeking motive that fueled the bubble becomes its undoing. The longer a bubble persists, the smaller the pool of remaining investors likely to be drawn into it, and the larger the profits that earlier investors can lock in by selling the asset. This is a perilous combination. As sellers eager to take profits overwhelm buyers who are leery of buying at the top, asset prices are prone to plummet, confirming that this indeed was a bubble. Like a soufflé, a bubble rarely rises twice, and the market is left to pick up the pieces and figure a reasonable valuation for the asset or assets in question.

Japan's Land Price Bubble

Asset price bubbles are most dangerous, and most prone to lead to financial crises, when the run-up in asset prices is fueled by bank credit—that is, by money creation. Asset price bubbles financed by new bank lending create a mismatch in the perception of risk between the asset and liability side of the banking system's balance sheet. Take Japan's 1980s real estate bubble.[24] Real estate prices skyrocketed, particularly in major urban areas, fueled by a dramatic increase in bank lending; stock prices soared in tandem (figure 6.1). Both crashed in the early 1990s, triggering a banking crisis that lasted a decade and ushering in Japan's notorious "lost decades."

As the decade of the 1980s progressed, banks in Japan rapidly expanded their direct and indirect lending to finance real estate purchases, creating real estate loans on the asset side of the banking system balance sheet and deposits on the liability side. Because Japan was experiencing what turned out to be a real estate (and stock market) bubble, the loans were quite risky, although they were not perceived as such at the time. The longer the bubble went on, the riskier new real estate loans became, because the real estate whose purchase was being financed was increasingly becoming overpriced and destined later to experience correspondingly deep price falls.

On the other hand, bank deposits are regarded as safe assets for those who hold them. Indeed, no bank depositor in Japan had lost money in the postwar period, and Japan's Deposit Insurance Corporation, the government entity established in 1971 to guarantee "small-lot" deposits (those up to ¥10 million, about $80,000 as of the early 1990s), until the bubble started to burst in the early 1990s had never been called upon to pay out a penny to make deposits whole in a bank failure.

FIGURE 6.1 JAPANESE RESIDENTIAL PROPERTY PRICES AND M2 MONEY STOCK, 1980–2022

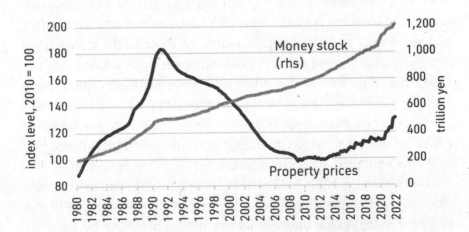

Bank for International Settlements (property prices) and International Monetary Fund (money stock, until 2006), retrieved from FRED, Federal Reserve Bank of St. Louis, and Bank of Japan (money stock, from 2007); quarterly data.

As banks continued to lend to finance real estate purchases, they helped to push real estate prices ever higher. The deposits created by this lending moved from the bank borrower to the seller of the real estate. From the seller's point of view, often an individual farmer or landowner, the real estate price bubble was allowing them to switch out of an increasingly inflated and risky asset into a safe one.

When the bubble burst, real estate prices fell dramatically: in the case of the index for commercial land prices in the six major urban areas, 87 percent from peak to trough. Once that happened, the underlying value of the asset side of the banking system's balance sheet also plunged, leaving many banks insolvent on a mark-to-market basis, that is, with negative equity were they to be forced to recognize the true value of their assets. Negative equity means that the value of the banks' assets would not be sufficient to fully cover the claims of creditors and depositors.

The Japanese government handled the country's banking crisis by implementing a policy of forbearance, rather than tackle the problems head-on by marking assets to market, aggressively restructuring bad assets, and massively recapitalizing the banks. On the asset side of the banking system's balance sheet, the banking authorities allowed banks to hide the true extent of their latent losses from bad loans and dispose of them gradually over time, hoping that the banks would be able to stay afloat and replenish their capital using a steady flow of operating profits; on the liability side of the banking system's balance sheet, the government muted the pressures on banks by issuing a blanket guarantee on all deposits, initially for five years but extended, for some noninsured deposits, for a decade.

Given the size of the hidden hole in the banking system's balance sheet and the deflationary forces unleashed by the bursting of the bubble, this approach outlived its usefulness and, one by one, the weakest banks started to fail. Eventually, the government had to bite the bullet and inject public funds to recapitalize the banks. In financial crises, the logic of balance sheet arithmetic eventually prevails.

The euro area sovereign debt crisis, which lasted from 2010 to 2015, was yet another kind of financial crisis. It began with the Greek sovereign debt crisis in April 2010, and the groundwork for ending it was laid by Mario Draghi, then president of the ECB, by a few words in a July 2015 speech in London. Why it started and how it ended tell us a lot about money, and how society getting the monetary rules of the game wrong can cause a lot of economic hardship. We turn to that story next.

7

THE FOLLY OF THE EURO

Within our mandate, the ECB is ready to do whatever
it takes to preserve the euro. And believe me, it will
be enough.

Mario Draghi, president of the
European Central Bank, July 26, 2012[1]

The euro, as a currency, was born in 1999 when eleven countries, all members of the then-fourteen-member European
Union (EU), adopted the euro as their common currency. But
the euro is more than just a currency: particularly with the United
Kingdom having left the EU, the now-twenty-member euro area (or
eurozone, as it is sometimes called) forms the cornerstone of the
twenty-seven-member EU. It is a very shaky cornerstone, however.
Why that is so revolves around money.

The euro area is a "monetary union," but it is a deeply flawed one, because it is not also a fiscal union, or at least not a full one. In most countries, particularly developed ones, even though the central bank has operational independence from the rest of the government, it is still part of the government. Even if monetary and fiscal policy are separate and operate largely independently of one another, they are two parts of one government, and, if the need arises, they can act as one.

That is not the case with the European Central Bank, the central bank for the euro.[2] The ECB is not the central bank of a single sovereign nation. Nor does the ECB form part of a consolidated government, or all of the government's component parts viewed together. The ECB does not have one treasury with which it can coordinate or one government to which it is accountable. Rather, the ECB is a supranational institution sitting above or alongside the twenty member states that form the "euro group" (the member states of the EU that have adopted the euro as their currency). Its fiscal and political counterparts are the twenty treasuries of the euro area governments and those national governments, as well as EU-level institutions such as the European Commission, the European Council, the European Parliament, and the European Court of Justice.

Herein lies the source of the euro's dysfunction. To work properly, a monetary union needs also to be a fiscal union: not too much space should be allowed between the monetary and fiscal arenas of macroeconomic policy or sand thrown into the cogs that connect them. And fiscal union cannot happen without political union, because fiscal affairs invariably involve or impinge upon political issues. The euro has an even bigger flaw, however: the failure to recognize that monetary union—the pooling of national monetary sovereignty—is an inherently political act, not, as it is too often treated, just a technocratic one. Monetary and fiscal affairs are two sides of the same sovereign coin: to separate them too widely is to court economic danger.

THE HALF-BUILT HOUSE OF THE EUROPEAN UNION

The EU is a complicated political entity, and how the euro area and the ECB are situated and operate within it is also complicated. The euro, and its deep flaws, cannot really be understood without putting it in the context of the EU.

The EU came into being in November 1993, when the Maastricht Treaty took effect, but had its antecedents in earlier agreements and treaties dating back to the days following World War II. What eventually become the EU started as a project to increase economic cooperation and trade. The European Coal and Steel Community (established by the 1951 Treaty of Paris) evolved into the European Economic Community (established by the 1957 Treaty of Rome) with its emphasis on a "common market," which became, with the 1992 Maastricht Treaty, the European Union. The Maastricht Treaty laid the groundwork for the introduction of a monetary union based on the euro, which was introduced electronically in January 1999 and as circulating notes and coins in January 2002.

The EU now comprises twenty-seven countries or "member states," Germany, France, Italy, Spain, and the Netherlands being the biggest ones, in declining order. As a political entity, the EU stands somewhere along a spectrum between a collection of cooperating but independent countries, such as those in a trading bloc like the United States–Mexico–Canada Agreement, or a military alliance like the North Atlantic Treaty Organization, and a federation of states forming a single nation, such as the United States of America, the Commonwealth of Australia, the Federal Republic of Germany, or the Russian Federation.

The EU occupies this in-between status because member nation states have pooled certain aspects of their sovereignty and transferred them to the EU level while retaining others at the national level. Regarding those pooled aspects of sovereignty, the EU functions as if it were a single nation state, such as for monetary policy (for those member states in the euro area), freedom of movement, trade policy, and customs. The EU even has a parliament (of sorts), a flag, and an anthem, all familiar trappings of a nation state.

When it comes to individually retained aspects of sovereignty, however, the EU functions more like a collection of cooperating nation states. For instance, member states retain responsibility for their fiscal policy decisions (although subject to EU constraints—more on that below), foreign policy (although the EU now has a High Representative of the Union for Foreign Affairs and Security Policy, who plays a coordinating role in this area), military defense (although most EU member states are members of NATO), and protecting their external borders (although the EU has a Border and Coast Guard Agency that provides some support and is being beefed up). And many have different languages and distinct national and regional characters and cultures.

The EU is also a work in progress. It is widely believed that the EU's "founding fathers"[3] intended the building blocks of a fully functional economic, monetary, and political union to be put in place one by one, starting with the easier, obvious ones and relying on the fact that one thing would lead to another. They presumed that over years and decades, the EU would gradually develop in the direction of becoming a more federated nation-state model resembling a United States of Europe, and this has happened. This slow but steady process of pooling national sovereignty at the EU level has progressed as a result of successive treaty changes and, more recently, in response to economic, financial, immigration, pandemic, and, most recently, geopolitical crises.

The euro sovereign debt crisis triggered a debate, which continues to this day, about the need to strengthen or, more ambitiously, complete the Economic and Monetary Union by making it also a "banking union," a "capital markets union," and a "fiscal union," although not necessarily a "fiscal transfer union." These ideas were laid out in such high-level political documents as the June 2012 "Four Presidents' Report," the June 2015 "Five Presidents' Report," and the March 2015 European Commission White Paper on the Future of Europe. (The four presidents were the presidents of the European

Council, the European Commission, the Euro Group, and the European Central Bank; the fifth president, who tellingly got in the act only later, was the president of the European Parliament.)

During the debt crisis, many actions were taken and new institutions crafted to compensate for the deficiencies of the euro framework, including the establishment of "bailout" funds and mechanisms (the European Financial Stabilisation Mechanism, the European Financial Stability Facility, and later the European Stability Mechanism); the introduction of a banking union (a Single Supervisory Mechanism, a Single Resolution Mechanism, and plans for a common deposit insurance system); the overhaul of the fiscal rules framework (a new Fiscal Compact and system of fiscal surveillance); and actions by the ECB (the Securities Market Programme, the Outright Monetary Transactions framework, and several Asset Purchase Programmes).

The exit of the United Kingdom from the EU on January 31, 2020, following the passing of a referendum in June 2016 to do so, was the first major reversal of the treaty-based aspiration of "ever-closer union," and a seismic one at that. The UK's nominal GDP was a bit more than the combined total of the smallest eighteen EU member states, so the UK's exit was equivalent, in terms of economic weight, to the number of member states going from twenty-eight to ten.

THE LOGIC OF THE EURO

The euro, in principle, is the currency of the European Union, although member states have to satisfy certain "convergence criteria" in order to be able to adopt the euro as their currency. So far, twenty EU member states have done so, the latest one being Croatia, on January 1, 2023. Adopting the euro is supposed to be a one-way street; there is no mechanism in the European Union treaties for a country to leave the euro area after admission, although there is a procedure for countries to leave the EU. The UK left the EU, but it had not adopted the euro and had been under no obligation to do so.[4]

The euro is an odd currency, one unlike any other major currency. Most countries have a national currency that serves as the unit of account in that country and therefore the medium of exchange and store of value. Having its own currency is a key element of national sovereignty in the Westphalian system of international relations that has existed in the world for more than three centuries.[5] As an element of what it means to be a nation, having a national currency goes along with such things as having a border, a military, and a system of laws and justice. A nation having a currency is a deeply sovereign act not just because it helps to bind its people together in commerce and provide a common sense of identity like a language, flag, or anthem; it also allows the government to exist and function. A Leviathan needs a printing press.

When it was formed, the euro embodied an implicit deal between two subsets of countries; call them the "frugal north" (countries like Germany, the Netherlands, and Finland) and the "profligate south" (countries like Italy, Spain, and Portugal). The "frugal north" had monetary credibility and, usually, low inflation and stronger currencies, while the "profligate south" lacked monetary credibility and tended to have higher inflation and weaker currencies. The euro was essentially a device for countries like Italy, Spain, Portugal, and later Greece to commit to importing Bundesbank-like monetary credibility and discipline from the frugal north. In return, the profligate south committed credibly (because the euro was supposed to be irreversible) to stop seeking competitive advantage by depreciating their currencies. By accepting the strictures of the Stability and Growth Pact, the profligate south agreed not to free-ride fiscally on the monetary credibility of the ECB, which was largely "imported" from the Bundesbank.

Because the euro area was envisioned, initially at least, as a monetary union but not a fiscal union, it was thought necessary to impose fiscal constraints on national governments. Otherwise, it was believed, some member states might exploit the euro's monetary credibility by running too loose a fiscal policy. The ECB sets monetary policy for the euro area as a whole, not for any individual country in it. EU planners thought that individual countries, unless fiscally shackled, would be prone to run a looser fiscal policy than they otherwise would, because any inflationary impact of doing so would be "diluted" by that country being only one part of a monetary union to whose overall monetary conditions the ECB would react. But if every country ran their own loosened fiscal policy, it would loosen policy too much across the whole euro area, and the ECB would have to offset it by tightening policy more than they otherwise would have. Better to curb those fiscal impulses with strict fiscal rules, planners reasoned, and give the ECB the latitude to operate monetary policy unconstrained by fiscal policy.

The Maastricht Treaty's Stability and Growth Pact was designed to do just that. In principle, countries were supposed to keep their budget deficits to within 3 percent of GDP and their (government) debt-to-GDP ratios below 60 percent, and the European Commission was tasked with monitoring compliance with the fiscal rules and enforcing them as needed. This was all well and good until the Global Financial Crisis and Great Recession, which set the stage for the euro area to be plunged into an existential "sovereign debt crisis," starting in 2010 with the weakest link, Greece.

THE FOLLY OF SPLITTING MONETARY AND FISCAL SOVEREIGNTY

For most of its first decade, the euro appeared to have gone swimmingly from the viewpoint of monetary policy. In the euro's first eight years, monthly CPI inflation had averaged 2.1 percent year-on-year, a tad above the ECB's stated inflation target of "close to but below 2 percent."

Establishing the euro as a shared currency meant that there was no longer any foreign exchange risk involved in moving money between member countries. With inflation under control, borrowing costs dropped, and with exchange rate risk eliminated, funds flowed liberally. Current account imbalances within the euro area started to form, but, driven as they were by housing bubbles and private sector borrowing, there was little check on this. Meanwhile, in financial markets, investors were treating the sovereign debt of euro area members as more or less equivalent in terms of risk, and sovereign spreads against German bunds narrowed to the point of almost disappearing. Such narrow sovereign spreads could be taken as evidence of the success of the Economic and Monetary Union, resting on a single currency and strict fiscal rules.

Yet, this arrangement had a flaw: by becoming a monetary union but not simultaneously a fiscal union, the euro area created a situation that was tantamount to requiring member governments to borrow in a foreign currency. By adopting the euro, governments handed over the keys to their printing press to the European Central Bank, newly formed in Frankfurt, without also combining their fiscal functions into a single euro area treasury, which would be responsible for union-wide budgetary matters like spending, taxing, and borrowing.

Why was this omission a problem? When it comes to monetary affairs, the member countries of the euro area are akin to states in a federal system like the United States. They use the currency of their country, but they do not have the ability to create their own currency at will. The ability to create euros out of thin air, with a tap on a computer keyboard, resides with the ECB, not with individual national central banks or the national governments of which they are a part. This statement requires some qualification. Under a framework known as Emergency Liquidity Assistance, in certain situations the national central banks can provide central bank money (euros) to financial institutions in their bailiwick (but not directly to their government), subject to a two-thirds majority vote of the ECB Governing Council.

Forming a monetary union but not a fiscal union had appeal in terms of its symbolism and convenience for citizens, particularly mobile ones, but it was deeply misguided. Fiscal or budgetary matters are righly regarded as political ones that lie at the heart of what it means for a country to be a sovereign nation. The twelve countries that first entered into the Maastricht Treaty, which laid the groundwork for the euro's 1999 adoption, had no intention of pooling their sovereignty to that extent. That would have been a giant constitutional step for Europeans, analogous to the separate member nations of the loosely knit European Economic Community becoming a "United States of Europe." What the EU's founders did not realize (or, if they did, they did not sing from the rooftops) was that forming a monetary union represented just as much a pooling of sovereignty as forming a fiscal union would have.

After several years of smooth fiscal sailing, the Global Financial Crisis and Great Recession hit, which then morphed into the euro area sovereign debt crisis. In that recession, GDP in the euro area fell by 5.7 percent from peak to trough over one year and, not surprisingly, budget deficits started to rise and government debt levels started to mount.

The sovereign debt crisis erupted in early 2010 amid deepening fiscal red ink and news that Greece had fiddled with its economic statistics. Sovereign debt yields of southern European countries and Ireland started to shoot up both in absolute terms and relative to yields on bunds (German government bonds). The crisis was essentially a process of financial markets starting to realize that the architecture of the euro area was badly flawed and that, in a severe economic downturn, countries were deeply hamstrung in their ability to use macroeconomic policy tools to jump-start an economic recovery, which in turn could force them out of the euro and into default.

The Macroeconomic Straitjacket of the Euro

Suppose you gave an economist the following challenge: come up with a suggestion for an institutional framework for a collection of largely contiguous countries that, when hit by a large adverse shock, would give individual countries the least macroeconomic room for maneuver. It would not be surprising if the economist came up with a macroeconomic design that closely resembled the one governing how the euro area operated at the time of the Global Financial Crisis and ensuing sovereign debt crisis.

Here is why. A framework giving individual countries the maximum macroeconomic-policy flexibility would work along the following lines. Each country would have its own currency and monetary policy independent of other countries; a flexible fiscal policy framework able to respond to negative shocks to aggregate demand or financial system stability; the ability and inclination to coordinate monetary and fiscal policy responses; a flexible, floating exchange rate whose market-driven movements would insulate the domestic economy from shocks; and the ability to print its own currency.

Now compare the preceding framework with that governing an individual country in the euro area. It does not have its own monetary policy but rather has to accept the monetary policy stance set by the ECB, reflecting the body's judgment of economic conditions in the euro area as a whole. It lacks the ability to operate a strongly countercyclical fiscal policy and is constrained by the fiscal rules and contractionary fiscal policy (i.e., austerity) bias of the euro area. It has very little if any ability to coordinate its fiscal policy stance with the monetary policy stance of the ECB or with the fiscal policy stances of other member countries. Its exchange rate is in effect permanently fixed against its major trading partners (that is, members of the euro area) and it enjoys exchange rate flexibility only versus the non–euro area rest of the world. Last, it cannot print its own currency (other than under the strict constraints of the Emergency Liquidity Assistance framework).

Figure 7.1 highlights how damaging this lack of macroeconomic policy flexibility can be for individual countries that are hit by a big negative economic shock. As of second quarter 2022, the level of real GDP in Greece was a staggering 24.0 percent below its pre-crisis peak (reached in second quarter 2007); even that of Italy, the euro area's third-largest economy, was 3.9 percent below its peak level (first quarter 2008). Meanwhile, the level of real GDP in Germany, until now commonly reckoned to be the strongest euro area economy, was 14.0 percent above its pre-crisis peak (first quarter 2008). By way of comparison, the level of real GDP in the US (as of second quarter 2022) was 26.0 percent above its pre-crisis peak (second quarter 2008) and that of the UK was 16.2 percent above (first quarter 2008).

FIGURE 7.1 REAL GDP INDEXED TO PRE-FINANCIAL CRISIS PEAK: GERMANY, ITALY, GREECE

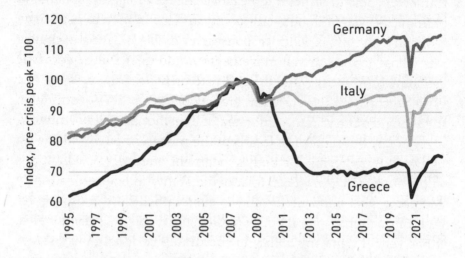

Eurostat, retrieved from Federal Reserve Bank of St. Louis; quarterly data.

Germany's better growth outcome partly reflects its enjoying a lower exchange rate than otherwise for being part of the euro area. In principle, the euro foreign-exchange rate should reflect a weighted average of the stand-alone exchange rates of its twenty member countries. Given the superior export competitiveness of the German economy and its historically strong currency (the Deutschmark), Germany's stand-alone exchange rate should be stronger than that of most other euro area members and therefore of the euro itself. To see the point another way, consider the mental experiment of Germany leaving the euro area now. Would its exchange rate have appreciated after doing so? Most observers judge that it would, which implies that it enjoys a weaker exchange rate by being part of the euro.

Normally, a country struck by a severe economic downturn can deploy several tools to stimulate economic activity and recovery. It can shift monetary policy; the central bank can cut interest rates and, if it exhausts its conventional interest rate ammunition, do QE. It can mobilize fiscal policy, running a big budget deficit by increasing spending and income transfers and by cutting taxes. Its exchange rate is likely to weaken against its major trading partners, which will boost competitiveness and stimulate exports and domestic production. If its banking system gets into trouble, it can mobilize public funds to clean it up and make sure it is adequately capitalized. And investors know that, in a pinch, the central bank, even if ostensibly independent, will stand behind its government's credit; they know that government cannot "run out of money." Deteriorating public finances do not necessarily constrain fiscal policy and do not lead to much tighter financial conditions across the board due to heightened perceived government default risk. Exhibit A in this regard is Japan: it has the worst fiscal metrics of any advanced economy and has for years; yet the central bank is both willing and able to keep ten-year government bond yields around zero percent (a policy the Bank of Japan has implemented since September 2016).

Here's the rub. Every one of these tools is constrained or problematic in the euro area. Consider an individual country like Italy, the area's third-largest economy. During the Global Financial Crisis, Italy's real GDP fell by 5.4 percent over five quarters; its GDP started to recover but then fell again during the sovereign debt crisis. By the first quarter of 2013 its GDP was 9.5 percent below its pre-crisis peak. Being a part of the euro area, Italy did not have its own monetary policy, which its central bank could have calibrated to its situation. The country did benefit from the monetary easing of the ECB, but the ECB sets monetary policy for the euro area as a whole, not for any individual country in it. By the first quarter of 2013, for instance, real GDP in Germany, the largest economy in the euro area, and therefore the one exerting the most influence on ECB policy, was 1.2 percent above its pre-crisis level.

When it came to fiscal policy, Italy had the worst of both worlds. Being subject to the fiscal rules of the Maastricht Treaty, Italy's ability to implement a countercyclical fiscal policy was heavily constrained. On the other hand, unlike Italy's relation to monetary policy, it could not benefit from a euro area–wide fiscal expansion: because the euro area is not a fiscal union, there was no area-wide fiscal authority ready to implement a countercyclical fiscal policy. The EU and the euro area gradually have been developing some such fiscal capacity, but it is still quite limited and far from nimble.

Nor could Italy depreciate its currency against its major trading partners—other euro area countries—because it shared the same currency. Countries in the euro area effectively have permanently pegged their currency against the Deutschmark, the former currency of the most competitive member country. Of course, the euro itself is a floating currency and has weakened against the US dollar, both on occasion and on a broad trend since the financial crisis, but again, Italy has to accept the average exchange-rate effect of all euro area member countries rather than having an exchange rate reflecting just its own conditions (and those of individual countries against which its rate would be moving).

Countries like Italy faced one more problem with the construction of the euro. When Italy's currency was the lira, there was no question over the government's ability to repay its lira debts in nominal terms. The Central Bank of Italy, a part of the Italian government, could produce lira with the tap of a keystroke—so why would it refuse to do so, if that was required for the government to make good on its bonds? Investors might have worried about unexpectedly high inflation eroding the real value of their holdings of Italian government bonds, but they could rest assured that the Italian government would always be able to credit their bank accounts when the time came.

Italy having the euro for its currency was another matter. Control of the euro printing press lies with the ECB, not with the Central Bank of Italy. The Maastricht Treaty prohibited the ECB from financing governments of member states: no overdrafts, no lending, and no direct buying of bonds. A national central bank and a national government finding a way around such prohibitions is one thing, but would the ECB back governments in a crisis? This was uncharted territory for financial markets, and it took a multiyear process of learning by doing for markets to get the answer: yes, the ECB would.

Governments doing all of their borrowing in a foreign currency that they ultimately do not have the ability to create is dangerous. Yet, by design, this is how the euro area works. It imposes market discipline on member governments because it represents a credible commitment not to print money. But the flip side of that discipline is market chaos—a sovereign debt crisis—when market participants conclude that governments may not be able to refinance their maturing debt and may be forced to default.

This is what happened in the euro area in 2010 as the Greek debt crisis unfolded and infected the rest of the euro area "periphery" (countries such as Ireland, Portugal, and Spain): sovereign spreads (against bunds) started to blow out (figure 7.2). Investors began factoring in the possibility that one or more of these countries might decide (or be forced) to leave the euro area and revive their national currency. Such an action almost certainly would lead to a sharp depreciation of the new currency against the euro and either a forced

FIGURE 7.2 GREEK-GERMAN TEN-YEAR GOVERNMENT BOND YIELD SPREAD, 1997–2022

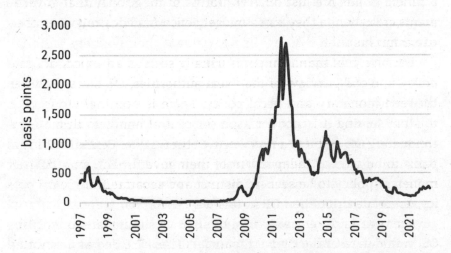

Organization for Economic Co-operation and Development, retrieved from FRED, Federal Reserve Bank of St. Louis; daily data.

redenomination of euro sovereign debt into the new domestic currency or an outright default on the debt.

The sovereign debt crisis was quelled when the ECB president, Mario Draghi, his back to the wall, sent a very strong signal that the ECB would do whatever it took to ensure that the euro area would not start to break up. His key words in a July 2012 speech in London were, "Within our mandate, the ECB is ready to do whatever it takes to preserve the euro. And believe me, it will be enough." This stance was codified in the Outright Monetary Transactions framework that the ECB established that September (but has never had to disburse even one euro under). Spreads collapsed as market participants were reassured that periphery countries would not decide to leave the euro area and default on their debt as a result.

WHY THE ECB'S QUANTITATIVE EASING IS DIFFERENT

As argued in chapter four, QE by a central bank, when it involves the purchase of government debt securities, can be viewed as a debt refinancing operation of the consolidated government. This way of looking at QE highlights the fact that central bank reserves and government bonds are just different forms of the money that governments create when they run a budget deficit (and destroy when they run a surplus).

Because debt management is usually seen as an aspect of fiscal policy and the purview of the fiscal authorities, QE blurs the lines between monetary and fiscal policy. There is nothing wrong with this per se, and it is not a reason for central banks to desist from conducting QE, but it is a noteworthy observation. Central banks, at pains to be seen as independent of their government, and for their monetary policy to be seen as distinct and separate from fiscal policy, do not describe their QE in this way.

Among major central banks, the ECB was quite late to embrace QE in the wake of the Global Financial Crisis. The Fed announced a QE-like policy shift in December 2008, the Bank of England declared it was launching QE in March 2009, and the Bank of Japan announced a QE-like policy in October 2010 and then began an aggressive QE program in April 2013 under the incoming governor, Haruhiko Kuroda. It was not until January 2015 that the ECB launched QE, after signaling its intent in September 2014. To underscore how late the ECB was to embrace QE, it came after the ECB had implemented a negative interest rate policy (June 2014), arguably a more radical monetary policy tool and one certainly challenging to explain to the public.

The ECB's QE is different from that of other central banks in one key respect, and this doubtless was a major factor behind the ECB dragging its heels in adopting QE: the ECB's QE cannot be viewed as a debt refinancing operation of the consolidated government because, in the euro area's case, there is no consolidated government. Rather, the ECB buys the bonds of twenty governments.

This makes the ECB's QE intrinsically more fiscal in nature. The ECB is always at pains to emphasize the "singleness" of its monetary policy. Its QE removes a member government's bonds from the market and replaces them with ECB money (reserves). ECB money is not the same thing as a euro bond, but in some respects resembles one. The ECB's QE can be viewed as mutualizing the sovereign risk of member countries, providing a kind of backdoor or shadow fiscal union. Complicating this interpretation a bit is the curious policy adopted by the ECB in announcing its public sector asset-purchase program: any losses on 80 percent of the asset purchases would accrue to the respective national central banks, and the ECB would be liable for the remaining 20 percent.

WAITING FOR THE LAST CHAPTER TO BE WRITTEN

At the time of writing, the EU, and the euro area within it, while still dealing with the aftermath of the COVID-19 pandemic, is being hit badly by another negative economic shock: the knock-on effects of the economic sanctions it imposed on Russia after its February 2022 invasion of Ukraine. Now, alongside the various other "unions," the need for the EU to become an "energy union" has moved front and center. It is not clear what the final resting place of the EU and the euro area will be. What is clear is that the current configuration is not sustainable. Either the economic and monetary union will be bolstered and completed by also making it a fiscal union, or pressures on the euro to break up will eventually become overwhelming.

Supporters of the EU often claim that, at its heart, the EU is a political project, not an economic one per se. They point out that the impetus for the EU came from a yearning for peace among the peoples of Europe, traumatized by two devastating world wars in half a century. They are no doubt correct.

But there is a paradox in all of this. When pressed on why the EU's political leaders make such heavy weather of taking the next logical step—as urged in the June 2012 Four Presidents' Report—of bolstering the euro area by making it into a proper fiscal union, too, a common refrain from European interlocutors is that there is not the political will to do so. The contradiction is stark: political will drove the nations of Europe to band together, but the lack of political will prevents them from doing so in a truly viable way.

There is a further contradiction, which at some point must be resolved. There is a tendency among European commentators and policymakers to see fiscal union, because it inevitably entails monetary transfers between member states, as being a political act and therefore as being (at least right now) a bridge too far when it comes to reforming the EU and pursuing "ever-closer union." What they miss is that pooling monetary sovereignty is no less a political act. The right of a nation state to create and control its own money is a core aspect of sovereignty, not to be surrendered lightly and certainly not on merely technocratic or convenience terms. If the EU political class cannot explain to their electorates that monetary union is just as deeply political in nature as fiscal union and garner the necessary consent to complete the economic and monetary union, the days of the euro may be numbered.

Among the major currencies, the euro is unique for being the currency of a large (and growing) group of countries, rather than just one. Euro area countries have tied themselves together monetarily, as if they have all permanently pegged (or fixed the value of) their currencies to one another.[6] But, how do the various moneys or currencies of the wider world—the dollar, the yen, the pound, the renminbi,[7] as well as the euro—fit together in the international world of finance? That is a subject we turn to now.

8

THE POWER OF INTERNATIONAL MONEY

The dollar is our currency, but your problem.
John Connally, United States Secretary of the Treasury,
to G-10 meeting, Rome, November 1971[1]

Each country (or, in the euro's case, group of countries) generally has its own unique currency: the US dollar, the Japanese yen, the British pound, the Chinese renminbi, and so on. Each country having its own currency solves a coordination problem within that country: everyone is using the same monetary standard and the economic wheels turn smoothly (most of the time). But economic and financial activity does not stop at the national border—far from it in our highly interconnected, "globalized" world.[2] How do these myriad domestic monetary systems fit together? How do international trade and the international monetary system relate to each other? How does one country's monetary policy affect the economy and the monetary policy of another? How does government "intervention" in foreign exchange markets work? What does it mean for a currency to be a **"reserve currency,"** and what are the advantages and disadvantages of being one? One cannot understand money fully without understanding its international aspects.

A key thing to bear in mind when considering international monetary issues is that money is created in domestic economies, in the ways identified in earlier chapters. It is exchanged in international transactions, but it is not created in them. Grasping this essential fact helps cut through a lot of international monetary fog.

MONEY DOESN'T REALLY FLOW

The language of international finance can be confusing. Economists cloud their conceptual insights in such jargon as balance of payments, current account deficits and surpluses, capital flows, sterilized and unsterilized **foreign exchange intervention**, fixed versus floating exchange rates, reserve currencies, and so on. Let's try to demystify this.

There are two main reasons for money to move between countries. One is as part of international trade in goods and services: exporters need to be paid and importers need to pay them. The other is as part of international investment: investors and traders in one country want to hold investments in other countries, for periods ranging from a few seconds in the case of foreign exchange (or even milliseconds in the case of so-called high-frequency traders) to years in the case of long-term investors. In terms of frequency and volume, financial transactions swamp transactions related to international trade and drive short-term fluctuations in exchange rates.

The foreign exchange market, the market in which one country's currency is traded for another's, plays a central role in the international monetary system. Think of this market as being the vehicle for moving money from a bank account in one country, denominated in that country's currency, to a bank account in another, denominated in the destination country's currency. Suppose I want to send a hundred dollars in my US bank account to my own bank account in Japan. That hundred dollars goes through the foreign exchange market. Abstracting from the role of intermediaries and all the computer terminals and optical fibers involved, I am swapping my hundred-dollar bank deposit with someone in Japan who has a bank deposit of 13,500 yen (using the approximate exchange rate at the time of writing and ignoring transaction costs). Before I sent the hundred dollars to Japan, I had a hundred-dollar deposit in my US bank account; afterward, I have a 13,500-yen deposit in my bank account in Japan. But that means someone else who had a 13,500-yen deposit in a bank account in Japan does not have that anymore and has a hundred-dollar deposit in a bank account in the US instead.

Economists and market participants talk in terms of money or capital "flowing" from one country to another. In this example, it would be as if my hundred dollars got up and transported itself over to Japan. That is a misleading metaphor, however. Goods and services *do* flow in the sense that they start in one place, where they are produced, and travel to another, where they are consumed. For goods this is obvious; for some kinds of services it is less so, particularly for flows of information (since information is infinitely replicable and can be in more than one place at the same time).

But money is different. Money does not *flow* between countries, at least not in the sense the term conjures up; it is *exchanged* between countries. If you want to think in terms of money flowing, consider it a two-way process, a flow in one direction necessarily being matched by a flow in the other. These "flows" are really credit and debit entries in ledgers. Money moving between two countries doesn't change the amount of money (bank deposits) in each country; it changes who owns the money.

What is true for my hundred-dollar money transfer from the US to Japan is true for any kind of money payment. When I buy a toy made in China at Walmart, I pay for it in US dollars, but the firm that made the toy in China gets paid in renminbi. What happens in between? Essentially the same process I just described. Again, abstract from the intricacies of the foreign exchange market, which is a complicated network of computer terminals, foreign exchange traders, and back-office settlement processes. In short, the Chinese firm has the renminbi equivalent of an extra hundred dollars in its bank account, and some other Chinese entity has a hundred dollars more in their US account, the hundred dollars that I used to have. The monetary transactions behind the Chinese export of goods to the US involves a change in ownership of both US dollars and Chinese renminbi in US and Chinese bank accounts, respectively.

Take another example. A London-based hedge fund, which is managing pound sterling funds, increases its asset allocation to South Korean equities (on an unhedged basis—that is, taking on the associated foreign exchange risk). What happens in simplified step-by-step form? The fund converts part of its pound bank deposits into a bank deposit in South Korean won; that means someone in South Korea traded their won bank deposit for an equivalent amount of pound sterling deposit. The fund buys South Korean equities, the seller now having more won deposits in their bank account. The net effect is no change in the amount of pound sterling or won bank deposits, but more British ownership of South Korean equities and more South Korean ownership of British bank deposits.

Economists and financial market participants would describe the investment by the London-based hedge fund in South Korean equities as a "capital flow," but this is misleading. "Capital" is another one of those economic terms that is used in many different senses and whose usage can confuse as much as it clarifies. The capital stock of a nation includes the factories and warehouses, the transportation and communications infrastructure, the computers and telecommunications equipment, and the residential and commercial real estate (buildings) that are used to help generate its output of goods and services, and that exists by virtue of the cumulative investments made in prior periods. This capital does not usually "flow"; it tends to be quite immobile, often bolted onto the ground. If it does flow, it does so as part of international trade, not as part of what economists call "capital flows." When economists use that term, they are referring to the kinds of changes in the ownership of financial assets and the associated distribution of risk described in the previous examples. If something monetary is flowing, it is more likely to be crisscrossing computer messages traveling close to the speed of light than suitcases full of greenbacks (although that happens, too).

What economists routinely call capital flows often facilitate *actual* capital flows. Suppose a developing country plans to build a modern factory full of capital equipment. It may secure a US dollar loan from a US bank to finance the project. The owner of the factory in the developing country uses the dollar deposits to purchase the capital equipment from overseas manufacturers. The dollars move around the US and perhaps the international banking system, and the capital equipment is shipped to the developing country. The capital equipment is the real capital that "flows," not the dollars circulating in the banking system. What causes the capital to flow is the ability of the borrower to deploy the dollar loan.

Let's return to the example of my buying a Chinese toy at Walmart. No money flows, because my purchase of renminbi with US dollars is also a purchase of US dollars with renminbi by somebody in China. However, to focus on this transaction, I use the renminbi to buy the toy, so I end up with fewer dollars and a toy, whereas someone in China now has my dollars; they also have fewer renminbi, but somebody else in China (the factory owner and workers) has that person's renminbi. Dollars move around the US banking system and renminbi move around the Chinese banking system, but the net result is that a toy moves from China to the US and someone in China ends up with some more dollars. It is this net result that makes it look like dollars are flowing to China. They are not; you might as well say that Chinese credit is flowing to the US.

The example I started out with presupposes that my desire to move one hundred dollars into 13,500 yen is exactly matched by there being someone who wants to move their 13,500 yen in Japan into one hundred dollars in the US. At the level of an individual transaction, that should be no problem, because there are countless transactions between major economies going on every second of the day; finding someone who wants to send the same amount of money in the other direction should be no problem. My hundred dollars is just a drop in the bucket compared to the foreign-exchange-market ocean.

But what happens if, when all the transactions are taken into account, there is an imbalance in one direction or the other? Imagine that after all the transactions match and, in a sense, cancel one another out, I am left wanting to send one hundred dollars to Japan, and there is nobody in Japan who wants to send 13,500 yen to the US. Think of it as my having a hundred dollars while trying to buy a 13,500-yen bank deposit in Japan, but there are no sellers of yen (or buyers of dollars) at that rate.

Enter the notion of a flexible exchange rate, sometimes called a floating exchange rate (as opposed to fixed). The exchange rate of the yen will strengthen just enough to induce someone to sell their yen and buy my dollars because they are now a bit cheaper (say 134.99 yen to buy one dollar, instead of 135 before). A flexible exchange rate means that the exchange rate between the yen and the US dollar will always adjust in one direction or the other to ensure there are parties on both sides willing to swap their currencies. No wonder foreign exchange rates are in constant flux.

THE IMPOSSIBLE TRINITY

There is a remarkable insight having to do with international monetary affairs known as Mundell's impossible trinity, named after the famous Canadian economist Robert Mundell, who won a Nobel Prize in Economics for this and other insights.[3] He stated that a country cannot have all the following three things at the same time: the free movement of money in and out of the country (known as an "open capital account"); the ability to control domestic monetary policy; and a fixed exchange rate—that is, an exchange rate pegged against another major currency, usually the US dollar. It can have only two.

If a country wants to allow money to move freely in and out and keep control over its domestic monetary policy, then it cannot fix its exchange rate. If a country wants to allow money to move freely in and out and maintain a fixed exchange rate, then it cannot maintain control over its domestic monetary policy. If a country wants to keep control over its domestic monetary policy and maintain a fixed exchange rate, then it cannot allow money to move freely in and out.

Suppose a country (call it country A) that allows money to move freely in and out and wants to keep control over its domestic monetary policy attempts to fix its exchange rate. If its central bank sets its policy interest rate at a higher level than that of the country against which it pegs its currency (call it country B), foreign exchange traders will have an incentive to sell country B's currency and buy country A's in unlimited amounts to make money on the interest rate differential. To keep its exchange rate from appreciating, country A's central bank will have to supply the foreign exchange traders with an unlimited amount of its currency, which it can do by simply creating it (electronically printing it). In other words, the attempt by country A to set its interest rate at a higher level than country B's, while simultaneously maintaining its exchange rate peg to country B's, forces it to engage in an unlimited monetary expansion, losing control of its monetary policy.

Suppose country A's central bank sets its policy rate at a lower level than that of country B. Then, foreign exchange traders will have an incentive to sell country A's currency and buy country B's in unlimited amounts to make money on the interest rate differential. To keep its exchange rate from depreciating, country A's central bank will have to supply to the foreign exchange traders an unlimited amount of country B's currency, which it cannot do because it cannot create country B's currency at will. It may have previously accumulated reserves of country B's currency that it can sell, but sooner or later it will run out, at which point it will have to abandon the peg.

To keep either of these things from happening, a central bank that allows money to move in and out freely and wants to maintain domestic monetary control will have to let its currency float. The exchange rate will adjust in such a way as to offset the interest rate differential. The exchange rate of the country with the higher interest rate will be expected to weaken over the period during which it is expected to have a higher interest rate. This exchange rate "disad-vantage" will exactly offset its interest rate differential advantage. How does an exchange rate get to a level from which it is expected to weaken? First, by strengthening. Again, no wonder foreign rates are in constant flux. They will experience pressure to move—in two different directions!—every time investors revise their expectations of future interest rate differentials between the two countries.

Suppose country A allows money to move freely in and out and fixes its exchange rate, but also tries to keep control over its domestic monetary policy. It will find that to maintain the peg while allowing money to flow freely, it will have to keep its interest rate in line with that of the country against which it pegs its currency, thus removing the incentives to move money just to exploit an interest rate differen-tial. In effect, it loses control of its domestic monetary policy, ceding it to the country against which it pegs its currency (usually the US).

Now, suppose country A wants to keep control over its domes-tic monetary policy and peg its currency, and at the same time let money move freely in and out. It will find that the only way it can accomplish both goals is to limit the movement of money in and out. By doing so, it can prevent the profit-seeking forces of interest rate arbitrage that would otherwise make interest rate differentials impossible to sustain.

FOREIGN EXCHANGE INTERVENTION AND RESERVE CURRENCIES

What does foreign exchange intervention mean? Does some army march on the foreign exchange market? Fortunately not; it is much more prosaic than that. Suppose a less developed country is peg-ging or at least managing its currency against the US dollar, and economic conditions are pressuring its currency to appreciate. The country might be pursuing an export-led development strategy and not want its currency to appreciate too far, too fast, because this would dent the competitiveness of exporters. To prevent this out-come, the central bank occasionally would have to intervene in the foreign exchange market by selling its currency and buying US dollars. Depending on the institutional setup in the country concerned and who has responsibility for making foreign exchange intervention decisions, the central bank might intervene on its own account or on behalf, and at the direction, of the ministry of finance. The dollars that the central bank accumulates as a result are called "foreign exchange reserves."

Here is another pitfall for the unwary: foreign exchange reserves are different from and are not to be confused with reserves of the banking system, the money that banks have in their deposit accounts at the central bank. The "Reserve" in the Federal Reserve System, the Reserve Bank of Australia, or the Reserve Bank of India is the second kind of reserves, not the first. In fact, foreign exchange reserves, if they are held by the central bank rather than by another entity in the government such as the ministry of finance or a sovereign wealth fund, are on the asset side of the central bank's balance sheet, whereas reserves of the banking system are on the liability side.

But there is a connection between the two kinds of reserves. When a central bank conducts foreign exchange intervention, it acquires the foreign exchange reserves by creating reserves in the banking system, the money of one country being created to buy that of another.

Economics textbooks strongly distinguish between whether foreign exchange intervention is sterilized or unsterilized, meaning whether or not the central bank offsets the impact of the intervention on the domestic "money supply" (reserves) by selling bonds. In most cases, as a matter of operational procedure, such interventions are sterilized. In cases where the treasury or finance ministry is responsible for foreign exchange intervention, it will usually issue financing bills, whose reserve-draining effect offsets the reserve-creating effect of the intervention. In cases where the central bank intervenes on its account, it will implement some reserve-draining operation to offset the reserve-creating effect of its intervention. An exception would be if the central bank was doing QE, in which case it could use the foreign exchange intervention as one means of doing so.

In any case, the effect of foreign exchange intervention is to lead governments to accumulate foreign exchange reserves. The currencies that make up these reserves, not surprisingly, are called "reserve currencies." Only a few of the roughly 180 national currencies worldwide[4] are considered reserve currencies. As of the second quarter of 2022, world foreign exchange reserves in US dollar terms totaled $12.04 trillion. Not all foreign exchange reserves are held in US dollars, but the US dollar has by far the biggest share, 59.5 percent, followed by the euro (19.8 percent), the Japanese yen (5.2 percent), the British pound sterling (4.9 percent), the Chinese renminbi (2.9 percent), the Canadian dollar (2.5 percent), and the Australian dollar (1.9 percent).[5]

The five countries with the largest amount of foreign exchange reserves are China (US dollar equivalent of $3.22 trillion), Japan ($1.20 trillion), Switzerland ($883 billion), Russia ($568 billion), and Taiwan ($552 billion).[6] That these countries have such large foreign exchange reserves reflects the fact that, over the years, they have conducted a lot of foreign exchange intervention. The more a country resists upward pressure on its currency versus another currency and intervenes by selling its currency to buy the other one, the more foreign exchange reserves it will amass. Governments typically like to hold most or all of their foreign exchange reserves in government bonds, these being the safest and most liquid assets available. In recent years, some governments have shifted some of their reserves to so-called sovereign wealth funds, which seek higher returns by making riskier and less liquid investments.

Although there is no world currency, and no world government creating one, reserve currencies play a role in the global economy analogous to that played by domestic currencies in their nations' economies. Reserve currencies, particularly the dominant one, the US dollar, solve a coordination problem and fulfill the three functions of money: unit of account, medium of exchange, and store of value. The US dollar plays a particularly outsized role in international trade and finance.[7] Much international trade is priced and invoiced (unit of account) and settled (medium of exchange) in US dollars (and, to a lesser extent, other reserve currencies), and the US dollar serves as an important store of value for countries holding foreign exchange reserves and for investors holding treasures and other US dollar securities in their financial portfolios. Foreign and international investors hold almost one-third of total US Treasuries in the hands of the public (including those held by the Federal Reserve).[8]

Consider two companies in two countries, one selling to the other—say a mining company in Australia supplying iron ore to a steel mill in Japan. The two countries could price and settle the ore sales in Australian dollars or Japanese yen, but they may prefer to do so in US dollars, particularly if many or most other firms operating in the global iron ore market are, too. In international markets for standardized products such as agricultural, mineral, and processed commodities, there is an important network and "winner takes all" (or most) effect: markets become bigger, and more liquid and efficient, the more that buyers and sellers all use the same currency, and the easier it is to compare prices and market conditions across a range of commodities—and, if you are a commodities trader, arbitrage across them. Not surprisingly, most global commodities are quoted and traded in US dollars.

There is also a big incumbency advantage to being a dominant reserve currency. For its currency to achieve this status, a country has to establish itself as a major global economic and probably military power; but, once established, a dominant reserve currency is likely to maintain its status even if the country's relative power declines.

QUOTING VERSUS DETERMINING COMMODITY PRICES

The fact that many international commodities are quoted and traded in US dollars does not mean that their prices are set or determined in only that currency; others still factor in.

Take oil, for instance. The spot price of oil fluctuates from day to day and is one of the most closely watched global economic indicators. Oil prices are quoted, and most transactions executed in, US dollars. This obscures the fact that all currencies are entering into the process by which the price of oil is set. That is because the US dollar demand and supply curves, which intersect to determine the spot price of oil (or any other similar global commodity), move when the dollar exchange rate moves. The global demand curve for oil represents the demand of all the consumers in the world, who ultimately purchase the oil in their own domestic currencies.

Take that part of the oil demand curve coming from Japan, and assume that this demand curve is fixed, but that the Japanese yen appreciates against the US dollar. Now, for any dollar price of oil, the price in yen is lower than it was before. A demand curve slopes downward in price-quantity space[9]—that is, at a lower price, more is demanded—so Japanese consumers (or the companies that buy on their behalf) will demand more oil at any given dollar price than they did before: the US dollar demand curve will shift to the right.

Assume for the moment that the supply curve does not shift, and bear in mind that a supply curve slopes upwards (or in the very short term is vertical) in price-quantity space; when the yen strengthens (and the dollar weakens), the oil price in dollars will rise and output will increase. Assuming no change in supply, global oil prices rise when the dollar weakens (and vice versa: oil prices fall when the dollar strengthens). The price in dollars has to rise because demand for oil in Japan has increased, and to meet that demand a combination of two things happens: more oil is supplied and some of the demand of US consumers has to be suppressed.

A similar logic applies to movements in the supply curve. Global oil supply comes from dozens of countries around the world. Oil producers in each face an oil price denominated and traded in US dollars, but they incur many of their costs in their domestic currency. The global price of oil is determined by the intersection of dollar-denominated supply and demand curves, but the global supply curve comprises all the supply curves of all the oil-producing countries, which strongly reflect their respective domestic costs.

Japan doesn't produce any oil to speak of, so take that part of the global supply curve associated with Canadian oil production and assume that this Canadian supply curve is fixed, but that the

Canadian dollar appreciates against the US dollar. Now, for any US dollar price of oil, the price in Canadian dollars is lower than it was before. A supply curve being upward sloping in price-quantity space—that is, at a lower price, less is supplied—Canadian producers (or the companies that sell on their behalf) will supply less oil at any given dollar price than they did before: the US dollar supply curve will shift to the left.

To simplify the explanation, assuming that the demand curve does not shift, and bearing in mind that a demand curve slopes downwards in price-quantity space, when the Canadian dollar strengthens (the US dollar weakens), the oil price in dollars will rise and output will decline. Assuming no change in demand, global oil prices rise when the dollar weakens, and vice versa: oil prices fall when the dollar strengthens. The price in US dollars has to rise because the supply of oil from Canada has decreased, and to absorb that fall in supply a combination of two things happens: demand for oil slackens, and Canadian producers have to be coaxed to produce a bit more.

I simplified this explanation to bring out the point that, although reserve currencies like the US dollar exist and appear to simplify international commodity markets and international trade and finance, this is partly illusory. Economic activity takes place in national currencies, of which there is a multitude, and using one currency (or a small number of them) as international currencies shifts the inherent complexity of multiple national moneys existing to another, less visible, level.

In reality, exchange rate movements—movements in the value and purchasing power of one currency relative to another—move both the demand and supply curves of dollar-denominated commodity markets, causing dollar prices to fluctuate. And it is not just one pair of exchange rates but a multitude of them that are constantly in flux. Trying to untangle all of these effects would be a daunting task, but fortunately it is an unnecessary one. The decentralized activity of the market takes care of things, the associated price signals summarizing the bottom line for all to see.

"RECYCLING" PETRODOLLARS

Speaking of oil markets, much is made of "petrodollars," the US dollars that Saudi Arabia and other Middle Eastern oil-producing countries receive for their oil sales and that purportedly are "recycled" back into the US financial system. This arrangement, we are led to believe, has its roots in some kind of special deal that the US and Saudi Arabia struck back in the mists of time, as if they had any other meaningful choice in the matter. To a significant extent, they didn't.

The national accounting identity we encountered in chapter two yields the insight that a country's current account surplus (deficit) in a given period (say, a month, quarter, or year) represents the increase (decrease) in its financial claims on the rest of the world during that period. A country's current account is in surplus if it is receiving more from the rest of the world as a result of its trade in goods and services, investment income, and unilateral transfers (such as foreign aid and worker remittances) than it is paying to the rest of the world because of those items. If the reverse is true—that is, it is receiving less in net terms—it is in deficit.

Take Japan, for example. Japan has been running a current account surplus of close to 3 percent of GDP on average for the past four decades, because it generally has been exporting more than it imports and earning more on its accumulated overseas investments than it is paying to foreigners on account of their investments in Japan. The rest of the world, in aggregate (that is, netting everything out), has been racking up debts to Japan. This is often captured by noting that Japan is the world's largest net creditor to the rest of the world, a status it has enjoyed reportedly since 1990.[10]

Japan's claim on the rest of the world is a claim on dollar and other non-yen assets. The rest of the world does not produce yen assets. Japan, or any country that runs a current account surplus and is a net creditor to the rest of the world, can only accumulate claims on foreign assets in foreign currency terms. When Japan comes to the stage of cashing in these foreign claims by running a current account deficit, presumably when the country's population has aged sufficiently, it will be paying out more dollars and other foreign assets than it is taking in, and that difference will come from the foreign assets it had been accumulating.

Saudi Arabia and other oil-exporting countries that have been running decades of big current account surpluses are in the same boat. Given that their exports of oil were so substantial relative to the size of their economies and their capacity to absorb imports, they run large current account surpluses. Because the US has been the biggest economy in the world, and for a long time by far, and has imported a lot of oil, it was inevitable that these small, oil-rich, oil-exporting countries would accumulate large financial claims on the US and the advanced economies more generally. In Saudi Arabia's case, "recycling" didn't really come into it, other than being the other side of the current account coin.

EXORBITANT PRIVILEGE

It is often said that the US benefits from its status as the world's dominant reserve currency. France's finance minister, Valéry Giscard d'Estaing, famously termed this America's "exorbitant privilege,"[11] describing its ability to conduct trade and borrow internationally in its own currency. If the bulk of international trade and financial transactions is denominated in US dollars, US persons making these trades and transactions are essentially operating in their domestic economy. They needn't worry about converting US dollars into foreign currencies either for assessing terms or conducting business. That is not just convenient; it means that the other parties have to incur the (often substantial) transaction costs of converting currencies while bearing the foreign exchange risks—or the costs of hedging them.

This may be convenient for a country with the dominant reserve currency, but for the world at large, it may be inefficient and inequitable, which is the source of frustration and resentment inherent in the "exorbitant privilege" critique. Nobody legislates to become a reserve currency; rather, market behavior grants that status. The US dollar emerged as the top reserve currency in the twentieth century, particularly after World War II, because the US was the overwhelmingly dominant economic and military power. As long as countries have different currencies and engage in international trade and investment, and exchange rates fluctuate (as they do in much of the world), foreign exchange risk will arise. The only question is who will bear that risk. Generally speaking, larger and richer countries are better able to bear risks than smaller and poorer ones; yet it is the largest and richest country that gets to shift the risks to other countries. Those countries least able to bear foreign exchange risks and costs are the ones upon whom they are most foisted.

This exorbitant privilege may have some downsides for the country enjoying it. Having a dominant reserve currency means that the country possessing it has to supply enough dollars to the rest of the world to satisfy demand, which is likely to be large and continuous. Because we are talking about the US and the rest of the world here, the dollars that the US needs to supply are dollars in net terms—that is, after all the flows of money in and out of the country have been aggregated and netted out. The way that a country supplies its currency to the rest of the world in net terms is to run a current account deficit, because that means the country is paying out more in its own currency than it is taking in.[12]

Over the past fifty years, the US current account deficit has averaged 2.2 percent of GDP; over the past quarter century, it has averaged 3.3 percent. That is a lot of dollar claims the rest of the world is accumulating against the US. Still, if the US dollar is going to be the dominant reserve currency of the rest of the world, year in, year out for decades on end, the rest of the world will have a thirst for a lot of dollars and the US will have to supply them.

THE FED: CENTRAL BANKER TO THE WORLD

Another potential downside of the US being the world's dominant reserve currency is that it places a special onus on the Federal Reserve, which many look to as the world's central bank. The Fed's mandate is to look after the US economy, not the rest of the world's.

The Fed can always finesse this issue by claiming that it would only take actions on account of the dollar's global role if those actions were also in the interests of the US and consistent with its mandate. That can still put the Fed in some uncomfortable places.

One such occasion was during the Global Financial Crisis. Because of the importance of dollars in the world financial system, the escalation of perceived counterparty risk among banks after Lehman failed in September 2008 resulted in banks globally hoarding their dollars and an ensuing squeeze in global dollar-funding markets. The Fed responded by ramping up its central bank dollar-swap lines and expanding the number of foreign central banks with which it had these arrangements. In dollar swaps, the Fed provides dollars to the global market through foreign central banks.

These dollar swaps were a major driver of the expansion of the Fed's balance sheet during the financial crisis and again, to a lesser extent, during the COVID-19 pandemic (figure 8.1). Between the Lehman failure on September 15, 2008, and the time when the Fed's

FIGURE 8.1 FEDERAL RESERVE DOLLAR SWAPS, 2002–2022

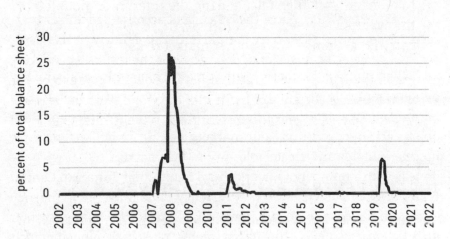

Board of Governors of the Federal Reserve System, retrieved from FRED, Federal Reserve Bank of St. Louis; weekly data.

balance sheet initially reached its peak size (December 17, 2008), the Fed's balance sheet increased by $1.329 trillion or 144 percent; central bank dollar swaps were responsible for 39 percent of that increase (56 percentage points).

The Fed's explanation of how these swaps work makes it sound like it just swaps dollars it has with the currency of the foreign central bank, with the swaps being reversed at a set future date at the exchange rate at which they were made. The Fed likes to stress that it is shielded from any exchange rate or credit risk, the Fed's counterparty being the foreign central bank, not the banks to whom that central bank lends the dollars. Here's how the Fed explains things:

> The Federal Reserve provides US dollars to a foreign central bank. At the same time, the foreign central bank provides the equivalent amount of funds in its currency to the Federal Reserve, based on the market exchange rate at the time of the transaction. The parties agreed to swap back these quantities of their two currencies at a specified future date, be it the next day or as much as three months, using the same exchange rate as in the first transaction. Because the terms of this second transaction are set in advance, fluctuations in exchange rates during the interim do not alter the eventual payments. Accordingly, these swap operations carry no exchange rate or other market risks.[13]

When quizzed on these operations in congressional testimony by Representative Alan Grayson on July 9, 2009, Fed chairman Ben Bernanke explained them this way: "Many foreign banks are short dollars and they come into our markets looking for dollars and force up interest rates and create volatility in our markets. What we have done is with a number of major central banks, that European Central Bank for example, we swap our currency dollars for their currency euros. They take the dollars, lend it [sic] out to the banks in their jurisdiction, that helps bring down interest rates in the global market for dollars."[14]

The reality is that the Fed creates new dollars, which show up as reserves on its balance sheet (the corresponding asset being the swap), and uses the foreign central banks as conduits to supply these dollars to the international markets. The Fed really is the central banker to the world.

We have traversed a lot of monetary territory in this book, but it has all involved the interconnected territory of the modern sovereign-based monetary system: the world of central banks, government treasuries, commercial and investment banks, national currencies, and the various forms of money that grease the wheels of commerce and economic activity over space and through time. Since 2009, in the aftermath of the Global Financial Crisis, however, befitting the disruptive information and digital age in which we live, a completely new form of money has burst onto the scene, that of cryptocurrencies. No book on money can be written today without explaining cryptocurrencies and assessing their potential to upend the monetary system. That we do next.

9

THE DISRUPTIVE POWER OF CRYPTOCURRENCIES

A specter is haunting the modern world, the specter
of crypto anarchy . . . Arise, you have nothing to lose
but your barbed wire fences!

Timothy C. May, The Crypto
Anarchist Manifesto, *1988*[1]

The subtitle of this book pointedly does not include "computers" or "computer algorithms" alongside "governments" and
"banks." The explosive rise of, and interest in, **Bitcoin**, Ethereum, and other cryptocurrencies since the early 2010s begs the
question of why not. Cryptocurrencies are an incredible, technologically driven, twenty-first century monetary innovation that will
likely have a permanent place in the financial ecosystem. Contrary
to the hopes of some crypto-evangelists and crypto-anarchists,

however, it is very unlikely that they will seriously challenge, let alone displace, sovereign (and sovereign-controlled) money.

Cryptocurrencies are currencies that exist on computer networks solely in digital form, the management and transfer of which relies on cryptographic technology and does not involve any central authority or intermediary. The history of cryptocurrencies can be traced to October 31, 2008, when a certain (and to this day mysterious) person using the name Satoshi Nakamoto published a nine-page online white paper, titled "Bitcoin: A Peer-to-Peer Electronic Cash System."[2] The approach Nakamoto laid out was used to launch the first **cryptocurrency**, Bitcoin, in early 2009. At the time of writing, there are about 21,961 cryptocurrencies in the world, with a combined market capitalization, in US dollars, of $856 billion.[3] That sounds like a lot of money, but it is equivalent to only about one percent of total global (M2) money supply.

There are at least four reasons for taking cryptocurrencies seriously. The main one concerns the insurgent ethos of the cryptocurrency world. Many of the developers, users, and promoters of cryptocurrencies espouse a strong distrust of and aversion to the government-controlled monetary system and pine for a world where the production and use of money requires no central authority or intermediary. It is likely no coincidence that Satoshi Nakamoto launched Bitcoin when "he" did: in the middle of the Global Financial Crisis, as governments and central banks, copious amounts of egg on their faces, were working desperately to stave off a collapse of the global financial system. The Bitcoin inventor marked the cryptocurrency's first transaction on January 9, 2009, with the following message for posterity: "The Times 03/Jan/2009 Chancellor on brink of second bailout for banks," referring impishly to the headline of a story in the British newspaper *The Times* of January 3, 2009.[4]

A second reason has to do with the arc of history: the world is undergoing rapid technological innovation with the explosion of the internet and the digitalization of everything. Who knows how cryptocurrencies will evolve in coming years and decades? The horse and buggy looked pretty entrenched as a mode of transportation when the first automobiles appeared in the late nineteenth century.[5] Third, and apropos of that point, the arrival of cryptocurrencies on the millennia-spanning monetary scene has pressured central banks and governments to innovate, as explored later in the chapter. Last, even if cryptocurrencies don't seriously displace the sovereign-led monetary system, they are likely to endure in some form.

Cryptocurrencies, as the name suggests, developed out of the computer science and cryptography world. It's an extremely nerdy world and very different from the buttoned-up one of bankers, central bankers, and treasury officials. The subject matter can get very technical and very confusing, very fast. I'll attempt to keep it simple here.

CRYPTO BASICS

Bitcoin, Ethereum, and other cryptocurrencies exist solely digitally, but being digital is not what makes them special. After all, most money these days exists in digital form, as entries in digital ledgers maintained by banks, central banks, and other financial institutions. As of November 2022, there was $2.30 trillion of physical money—coins and banknotes—circulating in the US, equivalent to about 10 percent of M2 money supply. Household financial assets totaled $108.70 trillion as of the second quarter of 2022, so physical money represented only about 2 percent of that. Across the entire modern world, money is overwhelmingly electronic—not surprising for a phenomenon that keeps economic tally and facilitates economic activity in an increasingly digital world.

The differences that make cryptocurrencies special are the digital technology they use and their underlying philosophy. Satoshi Nakamoto's innovation, on which subsequent cryptocurrencies have been built, was to use cryptography to solve the "double-spending" problem in a system without any central authority or gatekeepers. The double-spending problem refers to the need to ensure that the same piece of digital money is not spent two or more times. When you send an email and the recipient receives it, you still have the email you sent, and you could send it again to another person, or to many people for that matter. Unlike normal economic goods, information is almost infinitely replicable at very low cost; its consumption by one person doesn't preclude its consumption by others. If digital money were like an email message, it would not work: everybody would be a potential money printer. Trust—the reassurance that the digital money you received was not being sent to hordes of other people, too—would break down.

The conventional financial system solves this double-spending problem by centralizing parts of the distributed, economy-wide payments system and having a relatively small number of financial intermediaries—notably central and commercial banks, credit and debit card companies, payment services operators, clearing houses, and stock exchanges—mediate and validate transactions. When I pay my monthly electricity bill, something like the following happens. The electricity company sends a request to my bank to pay the (let's say) $200 bill. Because I gave the bank prior standing authorization to do so, it does this by debiting my bank account by $200 and crediting the bank account of the electricity company for the same amount. As far as I'm concerned, that $200 is gone—I can't spend it again—because trusted, regulated intermediaries like banks maintain ledgers that record how money is moving around the banking system.

Things are a little bit more complicated when I use my credit card to pay for restaurant meals, groceries, and online purchases, but the same principle of trusted, regulated intermediaries tallying flows between digital financial ledgers obtains. In this case, my credit card company pays on my behalf, debiting its bank account and crediting the bank accounts of those who provide the goods and services to me, and once a month my bank debits my bank account for the grand total and credits the bank account of my credit card company. The credit card company itself has a line of credit from its bank or other source of low-cost working capital, so it is able to bridge the gap between when it pays the merchants and when it receives payment from the credit card holder. By doing so, it earns a tidy spread on the interest differential for those credit card holders who actually use their card as a credit card rather than, like me, a pseudo debit card.

Cryptocurrencies radically break with this system of "trust through centralized intermediation and regulation" by using **blockchain** or "distributed ledger" technology to eliminate intermediaries. The cryptographic details, not to mention crypto market jargon, can be bamboozling, and there are many variations on the crypto theme, but boiled down, the Bitcoin blockchain works like this.[6] Information on who owns which Bitcoins, and the details of the associated transactions leading up to the current ownership configuration, reside in identical files (blocks) on many different computers spread around the world (computer "nodes"). People transacting in Bitcoin do so using their own virtual wallet, which is accessed using two keys: one public, visible to all; one private, known only to each Bitcoin owner.

Let's say I want to send to you one Bitcoin (or fraction thereof) that I own in exchange for something (goods, services, an asset, or US dollars) you provide to me. The instruction for transferring ownership of my Bitcoin to you will go into a new block of transactions, which will be added onto the existing block, like the last link in a chain, if and only if someone (more on who soon) solves a highly complex cryptographic problem. Once someone succeeds in doing that—and it will be obvious when they do—the result will be broadcast to the computer network, and the new block, validating the transactions contained in it, will be accepted and added to the chain of blocks—the blockchain.

This ingenious, decentralized system has no central authority or gatekeepers per se. Once it is set up and is running, the system relies on cryptographic problems generated autonomously within the system being solved. The solution being found and broadcast around the network is the cue for the new block of transactions to be accepted as valid and to be added by each node to the blockchain. As a result, even though each node exists independently in a decentralized network, they end up having exactly the same blockchain—that is, exactly the same information about who owns what and what transactions have taken place.

But why should the decentralized network accept or, in a sense, "trust" that the block of transactions has been validated? The answer is because the person who solves the cryptographic puzzle has demonstrated convincingly that they have "done the work," that they are legitimate, good-faith actors, not some high-tech fraudster out to scam the system (and try to double-spend). To be more accurate, it is the computers the person owns, not they themselves, that solve these cryptographic brain-twisters, which requires the expenditure of enormous amounts of computational power.

But why do people set up computers and expend the enormous resources necessary just to validate blocks of code? After all, once Satoshi Nakamoto launched the original Bitcoin blockchain, no central authority was needed to hire people to set up computer banks that would solve the necessary cryptographic puzzles and keep things running. The answer reveals another ingenious aspect of Bitcoin and its progeny cryptocurrencies. The people who put in the work and solve the computational puzzles are rewarded by receiving newly "minted" Bitcoin. For this reason, they are known as "miners." Just like frontier prospectors of old, no one tells them what to do; the profit motive spurs them into action. In this way, new Bitcoin gets into circulation via miners validating blocks of transactions.

Bitcoin has several other intriguing features, not all of which are shared with its imitators. One is that the total number of Bitcoin that will ever be mined is preset at 21 million coins, with the last one expected to be mined in 2141. A second is that the computational difficulty of solving the necessary cryptographic puzzle to validate new blocks and add them to the blockchain, and thereby obtain the reward of new Bitcoins, increases over time. Yet a third is that the amount of Bitcoin awarded to miners for validating a block, which happens once every ten minutes, halves every four years. Because more than 18 million Bitcoins have already been mined, it will be slim pickings from here on in.

These features of Bitcoin mimic the role that gold has played in global monetary affairs, harking back to the gold-standard days of the nineteenth and early twentieth century and the gold-exchange standard of the post–World War II Bretton Woods system. The latter ended in August 1971 when President Richard Nixon announced suddenly that the US was severing the link between the value of the dollar and the price of gold, a decision that ushered in the era of floating exchange rates.[7] The amount of gold in the world is presumably fixed (not so known reserves, of course) and, in principle, should be harder to find and extract over time, technological advances in mineral exploitation aside.

Bitcoin's features also evoke a famous dictum of Milton Friedman's, that the monetary authorities should aim to increase the money supply at a fixed rate, in line with nominal economic growth, and should eschew attempts to pursue an activist monetary policy.[8] But that is more apparent than real: the annual growth rate of Bitcoin in circulation has steadily declined and will continue to do so.

Satoshi Nakamoto's ingenious but convoluted mechanism kills three birds with one stone: Bitcoin transactions get validated, miners get new Bitcoin for doing so, and that new Bitcoin enters circulation. But it gives rise to a potential fatal flaw: mining Bitcoin and other cryptocurrencies that use a similar "proof-of-work" protocol uses an inordinate amount of electricity. One study estimates that Bitcoin mining consumes about 0.55 percent of worldwide electricity production.[9] That's not a good look in an age of climate change concerns.

In cryptocurrency land, however, or Silicon Valley more generally, one person's stumbling block is another's opportunity to innovate. A different method of validating blocks has been developed that does not need anywhere near as much electricity, called "proof of stake." The idea is that block validators must have a certain amount of the cryptocurrency in question in order to ply their trade. Both proof-of-stake and proof-of-work protocols aim to achieve the same effect: make it virtually unthinkable that a miner could or would engage in fraud and alter the blockchain history, spread as it is over multiple separate computer nodes.

So far, we have focused mainly on the original cryptocurrency, Bitcoin, and similar subsequent cryptocurrencies. Since Bitcoin's 2009 launch, however, there have been numerous head-spinning innovations and developments. Thousands of cryptocurrencies and approaching $1 trillion in market capitalization testifies to this rapid evolution.

For instance, some cryptocurrencies, like Ethereum, the most popular cryptocurrency after Bitcoin, allow "smart contracts" to be written and executed. Such contracts are fulfilled and discharged in cryptocurrency payments automatically without any human intervention, depending on certain specified conditions being met. "Tokens" are cryptocurrencies that sit "on top of" an existing block-chain that can be used for various transactional purposes on that network, such as settling a smart contract. Ethereum's token is called Ether, one of which went for about $1,265 at the time of writing (December 6, 2022). One innovative type of token is the "non-fungible token," a digital asset stored on a blockchain. There are also "stable-coins," like Tether, that aim to peg the value of a cryptocurrency to a fiat currency, usually the US dollar, by supposedly "fully" backing the cryptocurrency with a reserve of the fiat currency. This is reminiscent of the "narrow banking" idea of yesteryear that resurfaces occasionally.[10] Cryptocurrencies have become a source of new (fiat money) funding for crypto-asset and other online business-model ventures through the vehicle of "initial coin offerings."

THE CRYPTO CHALLENGE

Cryptocurrencies are not just about monetary technological innovation in the digital age, as head-spinning as that storyline is. There is also, to adapt Samuel Huntington's famous phrase, a defining "clash of world views" aspect to the cryptocurrency movement.[11] Many if not most crypto-evangelists reject the idea of centralized control over the monetary system by the government, the central bank, and big banks. Rather, they aspire to a world of decentralized, democratized money and finance, where "we the people," not government technocrats and fat-cat capitalists, control monetary affairs. To these crypto enthusiasts, the blockchain, free of central authority, is not just a neat technological innovation tailor made for the online digital age; it is a radical technology that empowers the citizenry to throw off the shackles of an oppressive and extractive bureaucratic/financial elite and reclaim their monetary autonomy. For the cryptocurrency community, there was and is a straight line between the perceived failings of the traditional monetary system and its unpopular bank "bailouts," and the need for a revolutionary, new, people-oriented approach.

In evaluating the potential for cryptocurrencies to disrupt or even displace the traditional monetary system, it is useful to distinguish the underlying technology—blockchain—from its most famous application: cryptocurrencies. The commercial world has been embracing blockchain and exploring use cases and applications of its distributed-ledger aspect in such areas as information sharing, record keeping, database management, and logistics, and in such sectors as finance, healthcare, transportation, and real estate. The irony here is that it is the distributed-ledger nature of blockchain, which allows for efficient information sharing and record keeping, not the lack of a central authority or gatekeepers, that is often the main attraction. Most applications of blockchain in the business world involve private or "permissioned" blockchains, not public or open ones requiring a convoluted "mining" incentive structure. In a permissioned blockchain, the blockchain owner controls who has access to it and who is able to enter new blocks.

Blockchain technology appears innovative and transformative, likely to join the pantheon of significant computer and digital technologies of the modern information age that we often take for granted, including barcodes, QR codes, smart phones, and the technologies underpinning the World Wide Web. The ability of cryptocurrencies to rival sovereign money, however, let alone dominate the monetary landscape, appears to be much more limited.

HOW CRYPTOCURRENCIES MEASURE UP

A good prism through which to evaluate cryptocurrencies is the workhorse three-aspect model of money: unit of account, medium of exchange, and store of value. On none of these do cryptocurrencies measure up as a formidable challenger to sovereign-based money.

Cryptocurrencies, even the dominant ones like Bitcoin and Ethereum, are not used in any meaningful sense as a unit of account, other than possibly within some niche crypto communities and in some murky corners of the dark web. That is, the prices of goods, services, and assets are not quoted and compared in Bitcoin or other cryptocurrencies. Even when cryptocurrencies are used to transact goods, services, and assets, chances are that their prices are being quoted and recorded in US dollars.

Nor have cryptocurrencies made many inroads as a medium of exchange—that is, as a way to transfer monetary value across space or between people, outside of the black market at least. Cryptocurrency transaction volume is reported to have reached $15.8 trillion in 2021, but most of this involves trading cryptocurrencies for other cryptocurrencies or fiat currencies on crypto exchanges. Speculation, not transactions, drives the demand for cryptocurrencies. There is not much point to using cryptocurrencies as mediums of exchange when they are not used as units of account, unless they are somehow superior as a payments system, and sufficiently so to more than offset the transaction costs of transferring out of and into fiat currencies at both ends of the exchange.

Much of the interest from potential cryptocurrency users has come from dissatisfaction with the slowness and high cost of transferring money or making remittances, particularly across national borders, in traditional bank-mediated systems. This is the key idea behind stablecoins: most track the USD but provide the ability to transfer money using blockchain instead of the traditional interbank remittance system (which relies on such twentieth-century infrastructure and protocols as the BIC/SWIFT messaging system and ABA bank routing numbers). In 2019, Facebook unveiled, to great fanfare, plans to launch a stablecoin, Libra (later Diem), aimed at dramatically increasing the access of people around the world to payment systems, but the plan eventually petered out. Establishing a new national (let alone global) payments infrastructure is easier conceptualized than implemented.

How do Bitcoin and other cryptocurrencies fare as stores of value? There is a lot of confusion about this point. The US dollar being a good store of value means that it should maintain its purchasing power reasonably well over time—in other words, the inflation rate should not be too high. For various reasons, as reviewed in chapter three, most central banks have alighted on a 2 percent inflation rate as the best one to aim for. This means that a person holding money in banknotes would experience an erosion of purchasing power of 2 percent in a year; 98 percent of their purchasing power would be preserved, and likely more than that if they put the money in a bank term deposit or a money market mutual fund.

Many crypto enthusiasts point to the fact that the US dollar price of Bitcoin has risen dramatically over time as evidence that it is an excellent store of value (figure 9.1). They assert that the limited supply of Bitcoin and the expectation that it will gain more users and fans over time virtually guarantee that its dollar price will continue to rise in trend terms over time. What figure 9.1 really shows, however, is the price of a risky dollar asset, akin to the price of an individual stock or a foreign exchange rate.

Risky assets are used to transfer purchasing power through time; thus they can be regarded as stores of value. However, *single* risky assets (as opposed to a highly diversified portfolio of them) are not usually regarded as *good* stores of value, because being risky means that the price can just as easily go down as up. At the time of writing, the price of Bitcoin was $17,052; someone who bought one Bitcoin on the first trading day of 2020 (when the price was $7,735) and continued to hold it might claim that Bitcoin is an excellent store of value, but someone who did likewise on November 8, 2020 (when the price peaked at $67,510), having since lost some 75 percent of their investment, would likely beg to differ. The bankruptcy of the

FIGURE 9.1 US DOLLAR PRICE OF BITCOIN, 2015-2022

Coinbase, retrieved from FRED, Federal Reserve Bank of St. Louis; daily data.

Bahamas-based cryptocurrency exchange FTX in November 2022 has further highlighted how risky crypto assets can be.

But there is a more subtle and substantive point. Because Bitcoin hardly functions as a unit of account or medium of exchange, to the extent that it is a (risky) store of value, it is a (risky) store of value for the *US dollar*, not for *itself*; likewise for all other cryptocurrencies.

A major part of a central bank's job is to deliver price stability—to keep the overall purchasing power of the currency they manage relatively steady. Paradoxically, the very thing that makes Bitcoin and other cryptocurrencies attractive to many—doing away with a central authority—is its downfall when it comes to being a good store of value: there is no central authority or government responsible for maintaining the purchasing power of Bitcoin or other cryptocurrencies over time. There is a rate of change in the dollar price of Bitcoin, making it a highly risky dollar asset, but there is no Bitcoin inflation rate and there is certainly no government or central bank to control it.

Bitcoin and cryptocurrencies are likely to become a permanent (if niche) part of the financial ecosystem and investment landscape. On the one hand, they may come to play a role in the online digital economy as part of payments mechanisms involving cryptocurrency/asset trading, smart contracts, tokens, initial coin offerings, non-fungible tokens, and other crypto innovations. As people spend more time online and as more economic activity migrates there to join them, it would not be surprising if, either because of convenience or the associated cachet, they used Bitcoin or other cryptocurrencies as a means of payment or even localized (with an application or among a set of related ones) store of value, in the same way that mileage or loyalty points are often used. But cryptocurrency, as with point incentives, will be connected to the fiat monetary system, always governed by an exchange rate (for that is what a cryptocurrency price is) against the fiat currency.

On the other hand, they are likely to function more as crypto-*assets* than as crypto*currencies*, sometimes likened to "digital gold." The crypto genie cannot be put back in the bottle, nor should it. Even if cryptocurrencies exhibit some features of a classic Ponzi scheme,[12] there may be enough "true believers" and sufficient inherent uncertainty about the future of the monetary system to generate a healthy amount of speculative demand. Cryptocurrencies, or at least the ones that survive the fierce Darwinian race currently underway, may take a permanent place among such assets as collectible artwork, antique furniture, rare stamps and coins, fine wine, and the paraphernalia of yesteryear's luminaries as stores of fiat currency value.

The biggest impact of cryptocurrencies, however, may well be the disruptive effect (using the term in a Schumpeterian, good sense) they have on the sovereign-controlled monetary system.

CENTRAL BANK DIGITAL CURRENCIES

The arrival on the scene of Bitcoin and other cryptocurrencies has been a classic disrupting event for, and wake-up call to, central banks worldwide.

The ascent of cryptocurrencies challenges central banks in three ways. One is by providing a direct alternative to the traditional

banking-system-based payments regime. Central banks are responsible for overseeing and, to a degree, operating an economy's payments system. As we saw in chapter three, transaction settlements
are ultimately made in central bank money, either banknotes or,
more often but hidden from view, reserves. If I hand over a ten-
dollar banknote to my local bakery for a coffee and donut, a liability
of the central bank changes hands; if a hedge funds buys a million
dollars' worth of shares, money moves between the bank accounts
of the hedge fund and the sellers of the shares and, to the extent that
different banks are involved, between the reserve accounts of the
banks at the central bank. Behind the scenes, central banks provide
and operate some of the most foundational infrastructure for all this
monetary activity and the associated commerce to take place. Cryptocurrencies threaten to usurp this function.

A second challenge is the potential disruption of central banks'
conduct of monetary policy and maintenance of financial stability,
both core mandates in the banks' mission statements. By design, no
central authority, certainly not a central bank, controls the cryptocurrency "money supply." The supply of Bitcoin is capped at 21 million,
but the supply of Ethereum and many other cryptocurrencies is not
(there are some annual supply limits on Ethereum). Given the blockchain and "mining" technology underlying cryptocurrencies, and
assuming sufficient proliferation of existing new cryptocurrencies—
perhaps the ultimate winner has not even been invented yet!—the
cryptocurrency money supply could grow dramatically, all outside
the control of central banks.

This could raise concerns for financial stability. Excessive growth
of money often accompanies financial instability, potentially creating bubbles and financial crises in the cryptocurrency ecosystem.
Even if cryptocurrencies don't displace the traditional monetary
system but just flourish and coexist alongside it, there would be
scope for spillover effects or contagion from one to the other, given
that they are joined at the monetary hip (a consequence of cryptocurrency prices being quoted in US dollars). Or think of some kind of

future "Y2K problem meets crypto" phenomenon that we can't even imagine yet.

Cryptocurrencies' third challenge to central banks is more philosophical and existential. Hardcore crypto folks view central banks and banks as "the enemy" and would like to see them put out of business. Cryptocurrencies are not just their shiny new digital toys, another modern technological innovation to add to the ever-expanding list; rather, they are a long-awaited solution to a deep-seated structural feature of capitalism: control over the economy and exploitation of little people by Big Government, Big Banks, and Big Wigs.[13]

Perhaps not surprisingly, central banks, being slow-moving, conservative, bureaucratic organizations, were hesitant in responding to crypto's arrival on the financial scene. Among central banks, the premier one, the Federal Reserve, was particularly cautious in its approach. For the first few years of cryptocurrency, central banks, absorbed as they were dealing with the aftermath of the Global Financial Crisis and navigating the uncharted territory of quantitative easing, credit easing, **forward guidance**, sovereign debt crises, negative interest rates, and **yield curve control**, as needed, did little more than watch cryptocurrency developments out of the corners of their eyes.

Since then, central banks have paid closer attention. Virtually every significant central bank, and related international institutions like the Bank of International Settlements, the International Monetary Fund, and the World Bank, have launched efforts to study cryptocurrencies and consider how they should respond.[14] By and large, central banks have adopted a kind of "if you can't beat 'em, join 'em" kind of attitude. They have recognized the technology underlying cryptocurrencies is transformative and that, as guardians of the payments system and the wider monetary and financial system, they need to help foster, shape, and partially adopt the innovations that drive it.

Central banks are picking up the gauntlet thrown down by the crypto world by studying and, in some cases, moving to introduce "central bank digital currencies" (CBDCs).[15] Central banks are seriously asking themselves two questions: (1) Given the technological and market developments surrounding cryptocurrencies, how should we be responding? (2) Specifically, should we plan to introduce a new form of digital currency ourselves? One set of issues revolves around technical questions relating to the feasibility, desirability, and practicalities of central banks adopting crypto technologies such as blockchain, digital tokens, and smart contracts. If nothing else, answering these questions affords the central banking community an opportunity to build up much-needed technical and operational expertise in these emerging and evolving technologies. But what this endeavor really boils down to is the question of whether, with the declining relative importance of cash in the economy, central banks should consider issuing a digital form of their currency to the general public as a digital alternative to paper and coin money.

Although central banks haven't gotten there yet, their issuing digital currency directly to the public makes a lot of sense. Banknotes are a direct liability of the central bank and are exchangeable at par with bank deposit money. Joe or Jane Public can change a (digital) liability of a bank into a (paper) liability of the central bank at will (and vice versa)—by withdrawing or depositing money via a teller or ATM—but they cannot change a paper liability of a central bank into a digital or electronic one. Only banks and other authorized financial institutions have that privilege via their (digital) reserve accounts.

The private sector now offers all manner of electronic payment systems that allow the public to use digital money in daily commerce: not just credit and debit cards but also various mobile payment services and digital wallets. If the technology exists—and cryptocurrency developments suggest it now does—for central banks to create a digital version of banknotes, such as an e-dollar, an e-euro, or an e-renminbi, then there is a compelling case for doing so. Indeed, several central banks have launched CBDC pilot schemes, most notably China, Ecuador, and Sweden, and the Bahamas introduced a CBDC, appropriately named the Sand Dollar, in October 2020, which, as with most such initial efforts, is operated by authorized banks.[16]

The case becomes even more compelling given that US Treasuries—the other form of government liability held by the public, at least in the US—are now issued and held only in digital or electronic form, the last paper Treasuries bowing out in 2016.

Getting CBDC into Circulation

If central banks issued their own digital currency to the public, not just to banks, how would this work? Where would the CBDC get into circulation? There are four possibilities: the public could exchange banknotes for CBDC; they could convert bank deposits into CBDC; the government could fund its budget deficit using CBDC (a form of "monetization" of the deficit or, depending on how it was done, "helicopter money"); or the central bank could buy assets or do QE by issuing CBDC (see Technical Handout for details).

The first is the prima facie reason for CBDC: making digital what is currently paper. The second would be a natural consequence of introducing CBDC, since the public holds and uses a portion of its bank deposits for payments purposes. Central banks worry that the existence of CBDC would make bank runs more likely in a financial crisis, although that argues more for not allowing crises to develop than eschewing CBDC, and central banks could limit how much CBDC they issue. The third would raise the specter of "fiscal dominance" and so would be anathema to supporters of central bank independence, but could come in handy when disinflation, deflation, or secular stagnation was the prevailing macroeconomic threat, and central banks had spent all their interest rate ammunition. That kind of condition, variants of which prevailed for more than a decade after the Global Financial Crisis, has been superseded by the return of high inflation in most countries, thanks to the pandemic and the policy reaction to it, but it could well return again in the future. The fourth would give central banks another string to their balance sheet bow and, through bypassing the banking system, could be a form of "People's QE," a term coined by Jeremy Corbyn, former leader of the UK Labour Party, in the context of his policy proposals.

The introduction of CBDC opens up even more radical possibilities that involve the use of **"programmable money."**[17] Imagine a future in which CBDC is not just a digital entry in a computer-based ledger, but is also imbued with smart contract-like functions that can respond to economic circumstances and government policy decisions. One possibility would be to allow the CBDC to bear an interest rate that could be used as a monetary policy variable; this would grant central banks the option of imposing negative interest rates without having to worry as much about a possible flight to banknotes, as it could restrict such swaps or even eliminate banknotes altogether.[18] Another possibility would be the government using CBDC as an instrument of (expansionary or contractionary) fiscal policy. More dystopian possibilities include the government using programmable money to restrict or promote certain kinds of expenditures and therefore social behaviors, deploying these in the service of the "surveillance state."[19]

Slow out of the gate, central banks are now actively responding to cryptocurrencies under the guise of exploring the launch of CBDCs. They are being cautious and conservative, acting wholly within the guardrails of the existing macroeconomic policy framework that preserves the conceptual distinction between, and operational separation of, monetary and fiscal policy—in that, they are backed by their finance ministries and governments. It is very unlikely that cryptocurrencies will seriously challenge, let alone displace, the monopoly position that central banks and governments occupy when it comes to creating and regulating money. What is more likely is that the disruptive forces unleashed by cryptocurrency innovation will, with time, be instrumental in reshaping the system of sovereign money in a way that not so much blurs the boundary between monetary and fiscal policy, as renders it moot.

CONCLUDING THOUGHTS

All this time the Guard was looking at her, first
through a telescope, then through a microscope, and
then through an opera-glass. At last, he said, "You're
travelling the wrong way," and shut up the window
and went away.

Lewis Carroll, 1871[1]

I close this book on the power of money with five reflections.

The first has to do with the inconsistency and inadequacy of the current policy framework for managing the demand side of the economy, and the need for its reform. As explained in chapter three, this framework rests on a strict conceptual and operational separation of monetary and fiscal policy, and the assignment to monetary policy of the primary responsibility for managing aggregate demand, to ensure price stability and full employment. The government gives the central bank the "independence" to make the necessary monetary policy decisions.

This framework has several problems. There is an important aggregate-demand management component to fiscal policy. When trying to rein in demand to bring down inflation, raising taxes is to fiscal policy what raising interest rates is to monetary policy. Why is one component of aggregate-demand management assigned to a technocratic entity, independent of the political arena, while another is left in the hands of politicians? Two answers are usually given: one, that monetary policy alone can always control inflation—in particular, that it can always offset any expansionary or inflationary effects of fiscal policy—and, two, that fiscal policy inherently involves distributional issues and inevitably has differential sectoral impacts, so must be left in the political realm.

The first assertion is looking increasingly shaky in light of recent historical experience: Japan's chronic deflation and pre-pandemic concerns in the US and elsewhere about "secular stagnation" suggest that monetary policy needs help from fiscal policy when its gets near the zero interest rate bound. Also, the surge in developed-world inflation in the post-pandemic recovery calls into question the notion of leaving inflation fighting to monetary policy. The second assertion is suspect, too, because monetary policy also has distributional and sectoral impacts, including likely leading to a bloated financial sector.[2] Independent central bankers may want to ignore these impacts, but that doesn't mean the government should.

Whether the goal is managing aggregate demand or finessing distributional issues, closer coordination and joint deployment of monetary and fiscal policy is needed. The problem is that the current operational and conceptual framework doesn't facilitate that: monetary-fiscal coordination, let alone joint action, borders on anathema to devotees of central bank independence. Consideration should be given to restructuring the policy framework to clearly make aggregate-demand management a joint responsibility of monetary and fiscal policy, and to more explicitly recognize the distributional and sectoral impacts of monetary policy.[3]

The second reflection is that the time has come to overhaul how we talk and therefore think about money and related economic policy matters. Our current terminology reflects the existing institutional framework and received thinking. That is fine as far as it goes, but it results in confused reasoning on many key issues, which is not conducive to sound policymaking. I don't have the linguistic answers, but I can list a few problems.

First, we need a better way of talking about what we currently call "monetary policy" and "fiscal policy." Fiscal policy is quite *monetary* in nature. As we saw in chapter two, the government cannot target the size of its budget deficit, as this is determined simultaneously via countless decentralized economic decisions by individuals and businesses, domestically and overseas. But, just like the central bank, the government can influence demand by adjusting how much net purchasing power it injects into the economy by way of sending out checks and changing tax rates.

In this context, we need to be clearer about the meaning of "government *spending*" or "government *expenditure*." These terms are often used to encompass two very different activities: government spending on consumption and investment that directly enters GDP; and money that the government hands over to the private sector, either as part of social welfare payments (called "entitlement" programs in the US) or as discretionary transfers. In 2020, as a result of the pandemic and its attendant policies, the US federal budget deficit increased by $2.15 trillion compared to 2019, but direct government spending into GDP (in nominal terms) increased by just $169 billion. Most of the increase in the deficit arose from the government creating and providing money to keep businesses and households afloat—a very *monetary* policy.

It might be better to call what central banks do when managing aggregate demand "financial conditions policy," as a shorthand for "credit and financial conditions policy." Central banks could focus their communications, in light of their assessment of demand in the economy (relative to supply) and the outlook for inflation, on whether they deem that financial conditions need to be tightened, eased, or kept as is in order to restrain, buoy, or maintain demand, respectively. They could decide on the requisite policy actions—adjusting the short-term interest rate or the size and asset composition of their balance sheets—independently, but in close consultation with the fiscal authorities, taking into account the discretionary spending plans and other growth-impacting policies of the government.

Government "debt" is another term overdue for retirement. We shouldn't think of government bonds as debt that needs to be repaid—as opposed to rolled over—any more than we do reserves and banknotes. Adding in reserves and banknotes and netting out the government bonds held by the central bank, we should just call it (the stock of) "government-created money" and stop worrying about the putative nightmare the government—that is, us—will face one day having to repay it. The amount of government-created money might well prove to be excessive if it is deployed as purchasing power into the economy beyond the economy's capacity to absorb it and triggers inflation. In this scenario, restraining inflation is the reason to worry and change policy—not national solvency.

In a last point on language, when it comes to new or expanding government programs, we need to stop worrying about how we are going to pay for them (that is, where the money is going to come from) and start talking, or at least thinking, in terms of where the *resources* are going to come from—and, importantly, which parts of the economy are going to have to release their resources to help generate the new ones needed. Reducing all of this complex activity to monetary terms is very convenient—and is part of the power of money—but it should not deceive us about what the relevant economic restraint is: not money, but real resources, and how productively they can be used.

A third reflection concerns the nature of commercial banks. There is a tendency to draw a bright line between the public and private sectors, or between the government or state and the market, and to locate banks clearly on the private sector/market side of that divide. The reality is more complex. As we saw particularly in chapter one, commercial banks are joined at the hip with the central bank and with the government in the production and circulation of money. Banks create money and help finance economic activity, and in the process help transmit monetary policy. Their balance sheets are connected to that of the central bank and intertwined with the fiscal operations of the government and its money creation, and banks are often at the epicenter of financial crises. No wonder banks are heavily regulated.

Banks are often described as "financial intermediaries," portrayed as hoovering up the savings of households and channeling them to business firms so as to finance their production and investment. In this reckoning, banks "take in" deposits and then "lend them out." As I have shown in this book, and as some (but by no means all) economists understand, the reality is quite different. The important role that banks play in lending to businesses to build factories, or to individuals to build houses, is to provide those parties the necessary purchasing power to command needed resources. This money the banks conjure from thin air; the resulting investment, as an addition to society's capital stock, is itself the economic act of saving. By the time the assembly line worker or bricklayer sees their paycheck land in their bank account, the associated investment and saving has already taken place; the changes in bank ledger entries are just the post-event record of that. Commercial banks are often described as deposit-taking institutions, but more accurately they might be called loan-making and deposit-safeguarding ones.

Why is this important? Partly for the intellectual satisfaction of understanding a mysterious and complex phenomenon, but also to underscore that banks are not your run-of-the-mill capitalist business enterprise. Granted the privilege of being at the center of the sovereign-based monetary system, and heavily regulated as a result, banks straddle the public and private sectors and blur the line between them. Top executives of global banks often bridle at the regulatory burden imposed on them and want freer rein, particularly regarding capital adequacy requirements.[4] Much of that regulation may or may not be sensible or effective, but nobody should doubt that banks are in a special class and need to be closely regulated.

My fourth point is to flag, with concern, recent developments impinging on the heretofore dominant reserve-currency status of the US dollar. In response to Russia's February 2022 invasion of Ukraine, the US, along with other G7 nations and the EU, imposed unprecedented financial and other sanctions on Russia, aimed partly at cutting Russian financial institutions and its central bank off from the US and global banking system. These measures included freezing Russia's foreign exchange reserves and denying Russia's major banks access to SWIFT, the global messaging system that allows banks to transfer funds around the world.[5] The US government has frozen the foreign exchange reserves and other assets of adversaries before, most recently Afghanistan's in the wake of the 2021 takeover of the country by the Taliban, and also those of Iran, Syria, and Venezuela. To do so against Russia—the sixth-largest economy in the world (on a purchasing-power parity basis);[6] a close ally of China, the world's largest economy (on the same basis); a member of the G20; and a permanent member of the UN Security Council—dramatically ups the financial-sanctions ante. Longer term, it risks undermining the dominant reserve currency status of the US dollar, discussed in chapter eight, and stands to accelerate the tectonic economic and financial shifts underway in the world, most notably those associated with the rise of China and its clear intent, in its perception, not to have its fate held hostage to Western hegemony.[7]

It is the dominance of dollar-based trade and finance that gives the US and its G7/EU partners such clout. But this dominance and preeminence is neither set in stone nor something that the US can dictate or take for granted. Rather, it derives from enough countries willingly using the dollar and doing so because of the net benefits it brings to them, and US actions affect that calculus. Strong incumbency advantages notwithstanding, US actions that raise the costs or risks associated with relying on the dollar, if they become an established pattern of behavior, put its reserve currency at risk. As tempting as it may be for the US and the G7/EU to wield their financial power in the service of geopolitical objectives, such actions are shortsighted and, in the long run, may undermine the international role of the US dollar and provide powerful incentives to China, Russia, and other countries to reduce their reliance on the dollar in international trade, finance, and banking, instead developing their own competing infrastructure and institutions. The US cannot have it both ways: enjoying the "exorbitant privilege," to use Giscard d'Estaing's famous phrase, of being the dominant international reserve currency and using that status as a geopolitical weapon against its adversaries.

My final reflection is to observe that the twin economies—the monetary economy and the real economy—are inexorably converging, as both become more digital. As long ago as 1999, Alan Greenspan pointed out that, due largely to computerization and related technological innovation, and associated shifts in demand toward information-intensive services, GDP was literally getting lighter (in weight).[8] Moore's Law shows no signs of being repealed, so expect that trend to continue.

What does this mean for the future of money and how it is interwoven in the fabric of economic life? My crystal ball is too fogged up to answer that intriguing question. Consider that six months into the pandemic, the Federal Reserve was scratching its head over how to get inflation back up to its target; now that inflation is near double digits, the Fed is scrambling to bring it down. Not that long ago, the cognoscenti were warning of the "rise of the robots" and AI (artificial intelligence) leading to a "jobless future";[9] now, in the wake of the pandemic, there is an acute labor shortage. The November 2021 Glasgow Climate Pact, a milestone agreement from the COP26 United Nations Climate Change Conference, stands no chance of succeeding without concerted global cooperation; yet, the ink was hardly dry on that when Russia escalated the eight-year war in Eastern Ukraine and major world powers were at each other's throats. There is nothing more hazardous than forecasting the future, let alone the distant future.

One thing is fairly clear, though: money will still keep the world going around.

TECHNICAL HANDOUT: CENTRAL BANK AND BANKING SYSTEM BALANCE SHEET MECHANICS

Consider a simplified central bank balance sheet (ignoring for simplicity its capital and assuming that it holds only government bonds):

Assets	Liabilities
Government bonds (GBCB)	Reserves (R)
	Government deposits (GD)
	Banknotes (BK)

Being an identity, the central bank's balance sheet can be expressed in change terms as:

$$\Delta GBCB = \Delta R + \Delta GD + \Delta BK$$

Assume that $\Delta GBCB = \Delta BK = 0$. Then,
$$\Delta R + \Delta GD = 0, \text{ or } \Delta R = -\Delta GD$$

When the government runs a budget deficit, $\Delta GD < 0$ and it is injecting reserves into the banking system. In colloquial terms, it is "printing money." It is often said that central banks print money; but in this (primitive) case, it is the government (treasury) that is doing so.

One might ask: Where does the government get the money that it injects into the economy? The answer, in this simple setup, is that it just creates it or wills it into existence. Assume that the central bank, which is an arm of the government, allows the government's account to go into overdraft. Then the government could run as big a budget deficit ("print as much money") as it liked: the more GD went down (into negative territory), the more R would go up. If left unchecked, at some point this would lead to inflation, which is why central banks are given "independence." Operationally, the government commits itself not to require the central bank to allow GD to go negative and assigns the decision rights over how many government debt securities (GB) the central bank will hold (GBCB) to the central bank and not to itself.

When a government runs a budget deficit, it typically issues debt securities to the private sector. Now $\Delta R = -\Delta GD$ works in the other direction: GD goes up and reserves go down.

To bring banks into the picture, here is a simplified balance sheet for the banking system:

Assets	Liabilities
Reserves (R)	Deposits (D)
Loans (L)	Equity (E)
Government bonds (GBBK)	

In change terms,

$$\Delta R + \Delta L + \Delta GBBK = \Delta D + \Delta E$$

Assume that $\Delta R = \Delta GBBK = \Delta E = 0$. Then
$$\Delta L = \Delta D$$

This is the fundamental equation of bank credit creation: banks create deposits when they make loans.

What happens when banks take in deposits? The deposits have to come from somewhere: either from deposits at other banks, in which case there is zero net inflow for the banking system as a whole, or from the public when they deposit BK. Focus on the banking system as a whole, rather than on individual banks. Then, assuming that $\Delta L = \Delta GBBK = \Delta E = 0$, it must be that

$$\Delta R = \Delta D$$

When the banking system as a whole takes in deposits, reserves go up. This is clear when we look at the central bank's balance sheet. $\Delta GBCB = \Delta GD = 0$, so

$$\Delta BK = -\Delta R$$

If banknotes go down, reserves must go up (by the same amount).

In fact, there are only three reasons that R can change. Rearranging the central bank balance sheet identity:

$$\Delta R = \Delta GBCB - \Delta GD - \Delta BK$$

Reserves go up when (1) the central bank acquires government bonds (or any asset), (2) when government deposits decline (because the deficit increases), or (3) when the public reduces its demand for banknotes.

Assume that $\Delta GD = \Delta BK = 0$. Then
$$\Delta GBCB = \Delta R$$

This is the fundamental equation of QE: a central bank, in principle without limit, can acquire assets by "printing money" (increasing R). It is not very hard for the central bank to increase R: it just taps a keyboard and the electronic (digital) book entry appears.

When the central bank does QE by buying government bonds held by banks, $\Delta L = \Delta D = \Delta E = 0$, and so

$$\Delta R = -\Delta GBBK$$

The banks receive R in exchange for the bonds they sell to the central bank.

$\Delta GBCB = \Delta GBBK$, so the bonds just go from the banking system's balance sheet to the central bank's.

QE produces lots of R, so it might be thought that banks could "lend out those reserves." The banking system balance-sheet identity appears to suggest that. After all, if $\Delta GBBK = \Delta D = \Delta E = 0$, then it would seem that

$$\Delta R = -\Delta L$$

But, from the central bank's balance sheet, only three things can cause R to change, and L is not one of them! So, the conclusion has to be that if $\Delta GBBK = \Delta D = \Delta E = 0$, then $\Delta R = \Delta L = 0$, too. There is no way for banks to "lend out" their reserves, if the "out" is meant to refer to entities outside of the banking system: households and corporates.

Surely there is some link between reserves and bank lending? Yes, but it is an indirect one. Banks create deposits when they lend, and if borrowers (in aggregate) convert some of those deposits into banknotes, reserves do go down (by that amount: $\Delta R = -\Delta BK$). But that is a far cry from "banks lending out their reserves." One also often hears comments to the effect that banks are "parking" their excess reserves (the reserves created by QE) at the central bank, as if banks in aggregate had any other choice. They don't. Banks don't have any direct control over the three things that influence R, so "park" they must.

If QE doesn't create the R that banks can "lend on," what is the point of it, then? When government debt securities are the asset bought (the usual case), QE is best thought of as a debt refinancing operation of the consolidated government, whereby it retires debt securities (GBBK or GBPB, government bonds held by the public) and refinances them into central bank money (R). R and GB are just two different forms of consolidated government liabilities. QE allows the government to switch between them, in the hope that—R and GB not being perfect substitutes as assets—there is a "portfolio rebalance effect" that alters asset prices and eases financial conditions. At best, this will be a pretty weak effect, which is why QE has been such a weak stimulus tool.

We saw earlier that the government creates reserves when it runs a budget deficit. It also creates bank deposits, which is the bank balance sheet counterpart to the reserves created.

$$\Delta L = \Delta GBBK = \Delta E = 0, \text{ so}$$
$$\Delta R = \Delta D$$

When the government issues bonds, those reserves are extinguished, but whether the deposits are or not depends on who buys the bonds. If banks buy the bonds, they are not; otherwise they are.

Deposit money fundamentally comes from just two places: budget deficits and bank credit creation. This can be seen with a little algebra.

Abstracting from bank equity (E), the two balance sheet identities above can be written, respectively, as:

$$R = GBCB - GD - BK$$

and

$$R = D - L - GBBK$$

which, combining and rearranging, yields

$$D = GBCB + GBBK + L - BK - GD$$

or, given that GB = GBCB + GBBK + GBPB,

$$D = GB + L - GBPB - BK - GD$$

In other words, the stock of bank deposits is equal to total government bonds (which represents cumulative budget deficits plus any bonds placed directly with the central bank, which it still holds, or any budget surplus that has not yet been used to retire outstanding bonds) and total bank lending, minus government bonds held by the public, banknotes, and government deposits at the central bank. Deposits are decreased by the amount that the public holds in government bonds because, when the government sells its bonds to the public, it extinguishes the deposits it created when it ran the associated budget deficit in the first place. Deposits are decreased by the amount of banknotes the public holds because that is where banknotes come from (out of the bank). The last term is subtracted because, to the extent that the government has a positive deposit at the central bank, it must be because (1) it issued bonds to the central bank, which the central bank still holds, or (2) it has run a budget surplus but has not used it to cancel outstanding bonds.

To see how central bank digital currency (CBDC) could enter circulation, we can add it as a component on the liability side of the simplified central bank balance sheet:

$$\Delta CBDC = \Delta GBCB - \Delta R - \Delta GD - \Delta BK$$

Holding the other terms, respectively, constant, we can see that there are four ways that CBDC could enter circulation:

$\Delta CBDC = -\Delta BK$ (assuming $\Delta GBCB = \Delta R = \Delta GD = 0$). The public could exchange banknotes for CBDC.

$\Delta CBDC = -\Delta R$ (assuming $\Delta GBCB = \Delta GD = \Delta BK = 0$). The public could exchange bank deposits for CBDC, the withdrawal of bank deposits causing reserves to fall by the same amount.

ΔCBDC = $-\Delta$GD (assuming ΔGBCB = ΔR = ΔBK = 0). The government could make net payments to the public ("fund its deficit") by having the central bank issue CBDC.

ΔCBDC = ΔGBCB (assuming ΔR = ΔGD = ΔBK = 0). The central bank could acquire government bonds (or other assets) from the public by paying with newly created CBDC.

GLOSSARY OF TERMS

Aggregate demand: The economist's term for all of the final demand for goods and services realized in an economy (after netting out intermediate ones to avoid double counting), as measured by GDP.

Balance sheet: A point-in-time assessment of the value of the assets of an entity and its sources of funding (liabilities and shareholder capital), both sides of which total to the same amount.

Basis point: A unit of interest-rate level or change, representing one-hundredth of one percent, so 50 basis points equals half a percent. Usually abbreviated as "bp."

Bitcoin: The first cryptocurrency, launched on a blockchain in January 2009 by an anonymous character, Satoshi Nakamoto, based on a white paper published online by "him" in October 2008.

Blockchain: A digital database comprising successive blocks of information linked cryptographically.

Budget deficit: How much more the government spends or transfers to the public than it receives in taxes and other charges.

Central bank: The part of the government responsible for issuing banknotes to the public through commercial banks, maintaining deposit accounts for banks to use in settling payments among themselves, managing the government's finances, and operating monetary policy to keep inflation low and stable.

Commercial bank: A bank whose principal job is to make loans to businesses, individuals, and other borrowing entities and to manage customers' deposit accounts.

Consolidated government: The government and the central bank viewed as one operational and accounting unit, with transactions between them netted out.

Credit easing: Lending and other programs of the central bank aimed at supporting financial market functioning and improving the flow of credit in the economy.

Consumer price index (CPI): The cost of a representative collection of consumer goods and services captured in a single number and tracked over time.

Cryptocurrency: A digital currency on a computer network serving as a medium of exchange that uses cryptographic techniques rather than any central authority to maintain and operate it.

Current account balance: The sum of the trade balance and the income balance in the balance of payments or, equivalently, the change in a country's net financial claims on the rest of the world in a given period.

Deflation: A situation (usually a sustained one) of a falling overall price level (a negative inflation rate).

Disinflation: The condition of downward pressure on the inflation rate, or of the inflation rate being positive but below the central bank's target.

Effective lower (interest rate) bound: The level of interest rates below which a central bank judges it is not possible to lower, or is worth lowering, its policy interest rate.

Euro area: The twenty member states of the twenty-seven-member European Union that have adopted the euro as their national currency and whose monetary policy is set by the European Central Bank.

Fiat money: Money that is not "backed" by (that is, exchangeable at a fixed rate for) gold or other commodities, but rather derives its value from government imprimatur and societal acceptance.

Fiscal policy: The use by the government of its spending, income transfer, and taxation policies to try to influence economic activity and the inflation rate.

Foreign exchange intervention: The government, via its central bank, using its own currency to buy foreign currencies, or to sell foreign currencies to buy its own currency, in order to influence the foreign exchange rate of its currency.

Forward guidance: Communication by a central bank about its expected future monetary policy settings aimed at improving the efficacy of monetary policy.

GDP (Gross Domestic Product): The output of goods and services in an economy in a given period measured using market prices or their proxies.

Global Financial Crisis: The financial crisis that the world experienced in the 2007–2009 period, whose most acute phase was triggered by the bankruptcy of Lehman Brothers in September 2008 (also known as the "subprime crisis," referring to the high-risk mortgage loans that were packaged into mortgage-backed securities and held by investors around the world).

Great Recession: The worldwide recession associated with, or triggered by, the Global Financial Crisis of 2007–2009.

Hedge fund: A privately owned investment fund that aims to make above-normal returns by specializing in a particular class of assets or investment style and by leveraging its investments (that is, borrowing a lot to increase its returns).

Inflation: The change in the level of a representative index of prices, sometimes used to mean a rate of change deemed to be too high.

Investment: That part of current economic output that is not consumed but is intended to be used to increase output in the future.

Investment bank: A bank whose principal business is to underwrite, sell, and trade stocks, bonds, and other financial securities issued by businesses and governments, and to broker mergers, acquisitions, and other corporate transactions.

Lender of last resort: The central bank lending to private sector borrowers when they cannot obtain financing from anyone else easily or at all.

Liquidity: Money available immediately to be used to buy things or extinguish debts.

MMT (Modern Monetary Theory): An approach to monetary and fiscal affairs that recognizes at a fundamental level that governments create money when they spend and destroy it when they tax, and therefore cannot run out of money.

Monetary economy: The system that facilitates and tracks economic activity by assigning monetary values to economic output and assets.

Monetary policy: The use by the central bank of its control over interest rates and financial conditions to try to influence economic activity and the inflation rate.

Money supply, the money stock, or monetary aggregates: The amount of money in existence at any point in time or on average in a given period, comprising various subcategories corresponding to varying liquidity characteristics.

Moral hazard: The tendency for an insured party to be less diligent in trying to prevent a risky outcome if they are insured against its consequences.

M1 money supply: In the US, roughly the sum of currency (banknotes and coins), demand deposits, and certain other liquid deposits.

M2 money supply: In the US, roughly M1 plus the sum of time deposits (in amounts less than $100,000) and retail money market fund balances.

Nominal GDP: A money measure of GDP: GDP measured using prices of its various components prevailing in that period.

Programmable money: A digital form of money that contains a mechanism for automated behavior of that money via a computer program, such as varying the interest rate attached to it or restricting the purposes for which it can be used.

Purchasing power: An important aspect of money: the ability to command valuable resources, notably goods and services and real and financial assets.

QE (quantitative easing): A central bank's attempt to ease monetary policy by increasing the size and/or asset composition of its balance sheet, financed by the creation of reserves.

QT (quantitative tightening): The reversal by a central bank of its prior QE.

Real economy: The part of the economy that produces goods and services.

Real GDP: A quantitative measure of GDP: nominal GDP adjusted to remove the effect of inflation.

Reserve currency: A currency, most notably the US dollar, that is widely used in international trade and finance, and that governments and central banks hold as foreign exchange reserves (assets).

Reserves (bank): Deposits of financial institutions with the central bank, classified as part of the monetary base or base money.

Reserves (foreign exchange): Holdings by a government of foreign assets, usually acquired by the government or its central bank as a result of intervening in the foreign exchange market (selling its currency to keep its foreign exchange value down).

Saving: That part of current national income that is neither consumed nor taxed by the government.

Secular stagnation: A macroeconomic situation where desired private sector savings chronically exceed desired private sector investment, such that the putative real equilibrium interest rate is very low or negative.

Sovereign debt: Debt issued by a national government in its own currency or in a foreign currency, usually in the form of bonds or bank borrowings.

Term premium: The compensation investors require for holding government bonds of longer maturity, usually measured in basis points of interest rates.

Too big to fail: The precept that a bank or corporation is so big that its failure will wreak undue havoc on the financial system or economy and so needs to be rescued or "bailed out."

Yield curve: An array of interest rates (yields) on government bonds, from the shortest- to the longest-term maturity.

Yield curve control: A policy whereby the central bank attempts to control longer-term interest rates, as well as the shortest-term one.

Zero lower (interest rate) bound: The (not strictly true) idea that a central bank cannot cut its policy interest rate below zero percent.

ACKNOWLEDGMENTS

I wrote this book over a four-year period as a Senior Fellow and Research Fellow at Harvard Kennedy School's Mossavar-Rahmani Center for Business and Government. I owe a great debt to Lawrence Summers, codirector, for inviting me to the Center and facilitating my stay; to Jason Furman for being my faculty sponsor; and to John Haigh, codirector, for his support and guidance. Special thanks go to Richard Zeckhauser, whose intellectual mentorship is the stuff of legend. I benefited greatly from discussions and interactions with all of them, as well as with faculty and fellows at the Kennedy School: Ignazio Angeloni, Rabah Arezki, Camilia Cavendish, George Chouliarakis, Karen Dynan, Jeffrey Frankel, Jeffrey Fuhrer, the late Robert Glauber, Elizabeth Golberg, Deborah Gordon, Megan Greene, Jo Johnson, Steve Johnson, Jean-Pierre Landau, Phillipe Le Corre, Timothy Massad, William Overholt, Ioana Petrescu, Yair Pines, Richard Porter, Scott Ratzan, Demian Reidel, Christopher Ruhl, Alexandra Schweitzer, Frederic ("Mike") Scherer, Merav Shaviv, Myriam Sidibe, Wake Smith, Sir Paul Tucker, and Antonio Weiss. Thanks go also to Susan Gill, Victoria Groves-Cardillo, Scott Leland, and Daniel Murphy for their administrative support.

I am very grateful to Klaus Schwab for involving me in two World Economic Forum Global Future Councils during this period, one on the New Agenda for Fiscal and Monetary Policy (2020–2022), cochaired by Diana Farrell and Raghuram Rajan, and the other on the New Economic Agenda (2018–2020), cochaired by Mariana Mazzucato and Andrew McAfee. I benefited a lot from interacting with the distinguished members of both Councils.

I developed many of the ideas presented in this book during nearly quarter of a century working as an economist and central bank watcher in financial markets at S&P Global, Nomura Securities, Lehman Brothers, and Baring Asset Management. I owe a great debt to Douglas Peterson, Hideyuki Takahashi, John Llewellyn, Ravi Mattu, and Michael Banton for giving me these opportunities. I learned much from them and from interactions with other colleagues at these institutions, among them Daniel Ahn, Lewis Alexander, Daniel Antman, Samuel "Q" Belk, Laurent Bilke, Beth Ann Bovino, Christian Broda, Marie Cavanaugh, John Chambers, Lisa Clement, Joaquin Cottani, Paul Coughlin, Michael Dicks, David Doyle, Erkan Erturk, David Flynn, Courtney Geduldig, Paul Gruenwald, Ethan Harris, Michael Hume, Russell Jones, Dharmakirti Joshi, Masanobu Kaizu, Ken Kawasaki, John Kingston, Takahide Kiuchi, Moritz Kraemer, Jack Malvey, Catherine Mathis, Sho Matsubara, Michele Meyer, Guillermo Mondino, William Morokoff, Edward Morse, Curt Moulton, Joydeep Mukherji, Jens Nordvig, Ken Okamura, Satyam Panday, Zach Pandl, John Piecuch, Matthew Poggi, David Resler, Lisa Schineller, Jeffrey Shafer, Hiroshi Shiraishi, Jean-Michel Six, Ted Smyth, Jens Sondergaard, Rob Subbaraman, Ed Sweeney, Diane Vazza, and Peter Westaway.

Over the years, I have learned a lot from interactions with numerous interlocutors in the academic, financial markets, media, and policy spheres on the subject matter of this book, among them Tim Adams, Tanweer Akram, Robert Aliber, Edward Altman, Daniel Alpert, Masayoshi Amamiya, Stephen Anthony, the late Masahiko Aoki, Akira Ariyoshi, Masatsugu Asakawa, Ian Banwell, Brian Barnier, the late Christopher Beal, Richard Beason, Moreno Bertoldi, Olivier Blanchard, Alan Blinder, Jan Bos, Thomas Byrne, Kent Calder, Sunjin Choi, Richard Clarida, John Connorton, Alexis Crow, Gerald Curtis, Antonio de Lecea, Vasant Dhar, Tim DiMuzio, Andreas Dombret, Peter Drysdale, Charles DuBois, Bill Emmott, Nick Estes, Robert Feldman, Jacob Frenkel, Glen Fukushima, Andrew Haldane, Lyric Hale and her late husband David Hale, Koichi Hamada, Akinari Horii, Robert Hormats, Takeo Hoshi, Kiyoto Ido, Takatoshi Ito, Kazumasa Iwata, Stephanie Kelton, Lawrence Klestinec, Jesper Koll, Stephen Koukoulus, Haruhiko Kuroda, Noel Lateef, Paul Lebow, Alan Mac-Donald, Krishen Mehta, Bob Miller, Frank Milne, Yoshihiko Miyauchi, Kazuo Momma, Satoru Murase, Junichi Naito, Masazumi Nakayama, Hiroshi Nakaso, Frank Newman, Maarten van Oorschot, Hugh Patrick, Jim Peach, Thierry Porte, Michael Render, Frank-Jürgen Richter, Nicholas Roditi, Brian Rose, Anthony Rowley, Kevin Rudd, Motoatsu Sakurai, Nathan Sheets, Takumi Shibata, Kurt Sieber, Claude Smadja, Yael Smadja, Joseph Stiglitz, Ken Takamiya, Tak Tanikawa, Gillian Tett, Robert Tombs, Georges Ugeux, Kazuo Ueda, Mark Uzan, Ali Velshi, Lucio Vinhas de Souza, Joshua Walker, R "Ray" Wang, Hiroshi Watanabe, Axel Weber, David Weinstein, Stephen Wierhake, Mark Williams, Martin Wolf, L. Randall Wray, Hakuo Yanagisawa, Hiroshi Yoshikawa, and Jeffrey Young.

Rebecca Fannin, Jeffrey Garten, and Matt Miller provided encouragement and introductions, which helped me obtain invaluable advice about the book-publishing process from Flip Brophy, Paul Golob, Jim Levine, Mel Parker, Rafe Sagalyn, and Leah Spiro; I thank them all.

I owe an enormous debt to Robert Dilenschneider for his encouragement, support, and sage guidance over many years, and to his wonderful wife Jan. Above all, I thank Bob for his good offices in introducing me to Matt Holt at BenBella Books. I am deeply grateful to Matt and all the team at BenBella Books, notably Katie Dickman, who provided superb developmental editing and other support; James Fraleigh, who did the copyediting; Brigid Pearson, who designed the cover; Mallory Hyde and Kerri Stebbins, who spearheaded the marketing; and Jessika Rieck, who oversaw design and production. Thanks also to Amy Murphy for the informative and well-crafted index.

There is a family behind every author. I thank my daughters Emiko and Yumiko for their love and support. I owe the biggest debt to my wife Yoshiko for her constant encouragement, support, love, and self-sacrifice. Without her, I would not be the person I am, and this book would not have been.

NOTES

INTRODUCTION

1. Thomas Hobbes, *Leviathan: with Selected Variants from the Latin Edition of 1668*, edited, with introduction and notes, by Edwin Curley (Indianapolis: Hackett Publishing Company, 1994), 76.
2. Although they generally operate as independent agencies within it, central banks today are part of the government. Nonetheless, throughout this book I often follow common usage by referring to "the government and the central bank," as if the latter was not part of the former.
3. W. Stanley Jevons, *Money and the Mechanism of Exchange* (New York: D. Appleton and Company, 1875).
4. Bitcoin and other cryptocurrencies, being new and not carrying the imprimatur of the government, are very unlikely ever to challenge the unit of account status of the US dollar, even if they make limited inroads as a medium of exchange and appeal to some as *risky* stores of value. More on this in chapter nine.
5. Well, not quite: not all economic activity is captured in GDP, or Gross Domestic Product, and not all the activity captured entails market exchanges. For the intricacies, see Diane Coyle, *GDP: A Brief but Affectionate History* (Princeton, NJ: Princeton University Press, 2014).
6. The Federal Reserve targets a slightly different measure, the Personal Consumption Expenditures (PCE) index. In the most recent decade (2013–2022), US inflation as measured by the PCE has averaged about 0.3 percentage points below the CPI measure.
7. See Jeremy J. Siegel, *Stocks for the Long Run: The Definitive Guide to Financial Market Returns and Long-Term Investment Strategies*, 5th ed. (New York: McGraw-Hill, 2014).
8. Yuval Noah Harari, *Sapiens: A Brief History of Mankind* (New York: HarperCollins, 2015), 177.
9. As of August 2008—that is, just before the US banking system nearly imploded that September—total deposits of commercial banks in the US came to $6,871.65 billion, while banks had reserves (including vault cash counted as reserves) and other vault cash of $62.26 billion, equivalent to just 0.9 percent of deposits (calculations using Federal Reserve Bank of St. Louis FRED Economic Data). I use this

date to show how the banking system's balance sheet operated before the Global Financial Crisis and quantitative easing, to be discussed in chapter four.

10. David Graeber, *Debt: The First 5,000 Years* (London: Melville House, 2014).

11. The treasurer of the United States oversees the US Mint, the Bureau of Engraving and Printing, and the United States Bullion Depository at Fort Knox, among other duties.

12. For an interesting historical treatment of how this system started to take shape in the US in the second half of the nineteenth century, see Roger Lowenstein, *Ways and Means: Lincoln and His Cabinet and the Financing of the Civil War* (New York: Penguin Press, 2022).

13. In the US, recessions are officially called by a group of experts, the Business Cycle Dating Committee of the National Bureau of Economic Research, using a range of data, rather than the popular metric of real GDP falling for two or more successive quarters. The NBER marks the Great Recession as beginning in December 2007 and ending in June 2009.

CHAPTER 1: MONEY CREATION

1. John Maynard Keynes, *A Treatise on Money. Volume 1, The Pure Theory of Money* (London: Macmillan and Co., 1930), 6, 31.

2. Terms listed in this book's glossary of terms are bolded the first time they are used after the Introduction.

3. See, for example, Glyn Davies, *A History of Money: From Ancient Times to the Present Day*, 3rd ed. (Cardiff: University of Wales Press, 2002); Niall Ferguson, *The Cash Nexus: Money and Power in the Modern World, 1700–2000* (New York: Basic Books, 2002); Niall Ferguson, *The Ascent of Money: A Financial History of the World* (New York: Penguin, 2008); David Graeber, *Debt: The First 5,000 Years* (London: Melville House, 2014); and Felix Martin, *Money: The Unauthorized Biography* (New York: Knopf, 2013).

4. See L. Randall Wray, *Understanding Modern Money: The Key to Full Employment and Price Stability* (Cheltenham, UK, and Northampton, MA: Edward Elgar, 1998, ch. 3); David Graeber, *Debt: The First 5,000 Years* (London: Melville House, 2014, ch. 2).

5. See M. Keith Chen, Venkat Lakshminarayanan, and Laurie R. Santos, "How Basic Are Behavioral Biases? Evidence from Capuchin Monkey Trading Behavior," *Journal of Political Economy*, 114 no. 3 (2006): 517–37.

6. Reserves are on the right-hand (liability) side of the central bank's balance sheet; foreign exchange reserves, if the central bank (rather than the treasury) holds them, are on the left-hand (asset) side of its balance sheet.

7. There are several other items, the details of which differ by country, such as government deposit accounts (the central bank being the banker to the government), reverse repurchase agreements (used to temporarily "drain" reserves), and the central bank's capital account.

8. These capital requirements have been raised substantially since, and in reaction to, the Global Financial Crisis of 2007–2009.

9. For instance, the Fed used to impose the following minimum reserve requirements on deposits, defined as "net transaction accounts": zero percent up until $16.9 million, 3 percent above that amount but below $127.5 million, and 10 percent above that. In March 2020, the Fed announced that it was cutting all minimum reserve requirements to zero because its large-scale purchases of Treasuries and (government-guaranteed) mortgage-backed securities had created such a large

amount of reserves that the notion of minimum reserve requirements had been rendered moot.

10. The Fed acquired the legal authority to pay interest on reserves in October 2008, during the financial crisis, as part of the Troubled Assets Relief Program legislation.

11. See Stephanie Kelton, *The Deficit Myth: Modern Monetary Theory and the Birth of the People's Economy* (New York: Public Affairs, 2020), particularly ch. 1; Warren Mosler, *Seven Deadly Innocent Frauds of Economic Policy* (Christiansted, St. Croix: Valiance Co., 2010), particularly pp. 13–30; L. Randall Wray, *Understanding Modern Money: The Key to Full Employment and Price Stability* (Cheltenham, UK: Edward Elgar, 1998), particularly ch. 4.

12. Paul Sheard, "Helicopter Money and the Monetary Garden of Eden," S&P Global Ratings RatingsDirect (May 2016).

13. On MMT, see Stephanie Kelton, *The Deficit Myth: Modern Monetary Theory and the Birth of the People's Economy* (New York: Public Affairs, 2020); William Mitchell, L. Randall Wray, and Martin Watts, *Macroeconomics* (London: Red Globe Press, 2019); Warren Mosler, "Soft Currency Economics," (mimeo, 1994); Warren Mosler, *Seven Deadly Innocent Frauds of Economic Policy* (Christiansted, St. Croix: Valiance Co., 2010); L. Randall Wray, *Modern Money Theory: A Primer on Macroeconomics for Sovereign Monetary Systems*, 2nd ed. (Basingstoke: Palgrave Macmillan, 2015).

14. Eric Tymoigne, "Modern Money Theory, and Interrelations Between the Treasury and Central Bank: The Case of the United States," *Journal of Economic Issues* 48, no. 3 (2014): 641–62; Eric Tymoigne, "Government Monetary and Fiscal Operations: Generalising the Endogenous Money Approach," *Cambridge Journal of Economics* 40, no. 5 (2016): 1317–32.

15. The government's account at the central bank is on the asset side of the treasury's balance sheet and on the liability side of the central bank's; because it is on both sides of the consolidated government's balance sheet, it always cancels out.

16. If the government debt securities are bought by the non–banking-system private sector, the effect of the deficit on bank deposits is a wash; but if they are held by banks, deposits are created. See the Technical Handout for details.

17. The second part of this statement needs to be qualified. If we are really tracing a dollar of actual deposits to its "birth," it might be traced to a dollar of government spending, regardless of whether the government is running a budget deficit. A government budget deficit creates a net increase in bank deposits in the banking system (unless the deficit is partly or wholly extinguished by the government issuing bonds), but the deposits that are withdrawn when the government raises revenue are generally not the same deposits that are created when the government pays people for services rendered or as social welfare transfers. However, the fungibility of money makes tracing individual dollars and this finer distinction somewhat moot.

18. The price-to-earnings ratio, or P/E, is a common measure of a company's stock market valuation, and is the ratio of the stock price to earnings-per-share (EPS). Multiplying both the numerator and denominator by the number of shares outstanding (that is, issued and not bought back) makes this the ratio of market capitalization to total earnings but leaves the ratio unchanged.

19. Some countries are starting to experience a decline in their population and their workforces. See Charles Goodhart and Manoj Pradham, *The Great Demographic Reversal: Ageing Societies, Waning Inequality, and an Inflation Revival* (Palgrave Macmillan, 2020). Even with a shrinking population, however, the economy can continue to expand if there is enough offsetting accumulation of capital and technological innovation.

CHAPTER 2: THE POWER OF GOVERNMENT DEBT

1. Frank N. Newman, *Freedom from National Debt* (Minneapolis, MN: Two Harbors Press, 2013), 32.
2. See Warren Mosler, *Seven Deadly Innocent Frauds of Economic Policy* (Christiansted, St. Croix: Valiance Co., 2010), particularly pp. 14–16.
3. See Abba P. Lerner, "Money as a Creature of the State," *American Economic Review* 37, no. 2 (1947): 312–17.
4. I am using the term "generation" here to refer to all the people living at a given point in time, rather than in the sense of the "younger generation" versus the "older generation" at any point in time. In reality, because time flows continuously, generations overlap, which is why in more sophisticated analysis economists talk of "overlapping generations" and construct "overlapping generation models."
5. See Abba P. Lerner, "Functional Finance and the Federal Debt," *Social Research* 10, no. 1 (1943): 38–51.
6. See Alvin H. Hansen, *Full Recovery or Stagnation?* (London: Adam and Charles Black, 1938); Lawrence H. Summers, "The Age of Secular Stagnation: What It Is and What to Do About It," *Foreign Affairs*, March/April 2016, 2–9.
7. Economists have long debated whether the public does or should regard government bonds as net wealth. The strict Ricardian view, after the famous classical economist David Ricardo, is that government bonds are not net wealth because the public expects to be taxed in the future so that the government can repay the bonds, and that the discounted present value of the associated future tax liabilities exactly equals the value of the bonds. The classic article is Robert J. Barro, "Are Government Bonds Net Wealth?," *Journal of Political Economy* 82, no. 6 (1974), 1095–1117.

CHAPTER 3: THE POWER OF CENTRAL BANKS

1. Milton Friedman, *Money Mischief: Episodes in Monetary History* (San Diego: Harcourt Brace & Company, first Harvest edition, 1994), 49.
2. Friedman, *Money Mischief*, 262.
3. Federal Reserve, "Meeting of the Federal Open Market Committee," July 2–3, 1996, https://www.federalreserve.gov/monetarypolicy/files/FOMC19960703meeting.pdf, 51.
4. See Ben S. Bernanke et al., *Inflation Targeting: Lessons from the International Experience* (Princeton, NJ: Princeton University Press, 1999).
5. The number of noncash payments (debit card, credit card, ACH, and check payments) in 2019 was 174.2 billion or about 477 million per day (Federal Reserve System, "The 2019 Federal Reserve Payments Study," December 2019, https://www.federalreserve.gov/newsevents/pressreleases/files/2019-payments-study-20191219.pdf). As of June 30, 2022, there were 4,771 FDIC-insured banks in the US (Federal Deposit Insurance Corporation, "FDIC Statistics at a Glance," June 30, 2022, https://www.fdic.gov/analysis/quarterly-banking-profile/statistics-at-a-glance/2022jun/fdic.pdf).
6. Jeremy Stein, "Overheating in Credit Markets: Origins, Measurement, and Policy Responses," remarks at a research symposium sponsored by the Federal Reserve Bank of St. Louis, Missouri, February 7, 2013, https://www.federalreserve.gov/newsevents/speech/stein20130207a.htm, 17.
7. The Fed targets a slightly different measure of consumer prices than the CPI: the PCE (Personal Consumption Expenditures) index. Over the past twenty-five years, annual CPI inflation has exceeded annual PCE inflation on a monthly basis

by an average of 0.4 percentage points. Annual PCE inflation was 1.3 percent in March 2020, after having averaged 1.5 percent in the preceding twelve months; it averaged 1.2 percent over the next twelve months and started to rise from March 2021, peaking at 7.0 percent in June 2022.

8. See Milton Friedman, "Quantity Theory of Money," in *The New Palgrave: Money*, eds. John Eatwell, Murray Milgate, and Peter Newman, 1st American edition (New York: W. W. Norton & Company, 1989), 10.

CHAPTER 4: THE POWER OF QUANTITATIVE EASING

1. Ben S. Bernanke, "Deflation: Making Sure 'It' Doesn't Happen Here," remarks at the National Economists Club, Washington, DC, November 21, 2002, https://www .federalreserve.gov/boarddocs/speeches/2002/20021121/default.htm.

2. Every central bank operates under a legal or administrative framework, the details of which vary between countries. Central banks are usually restricted to varying degrees in the kind of assets they can acquire or accept as collateral for their lending. The standard and universally preferred asset (because of its liquidity, safety, and "neutrality") is bonds issued by their own government. But most major central banks are able to buy various forms of private sector assets, in some cases conditional on obtaining permission from their government and in other cases of their own accord.

3. See the Technical Handout and Paul Sheard, "Repeat After Me: Banks Cannot and Do Not 'Lend Out' Reserves," Standard & Poor's Ratings Services RatingsDirect, April 13, 2013.

4. The "term premium" refers to the compensation that investors require for having their funds tied up for an extended period (measured in basis points); "duration" refers to the weighted average time to maturity (measured in years) of a bond or portfolio of bonds, or its sensitivity to a change in interest rates (measured in percent changes in price per unit change in yield).

5. Alongside Treasuries, the Fed also bought large quantities of mortgage-backed securities (MBS) as part of its QE (holding $2.74 trillion at the April 2022 peak, compared with peak holdings of Treasuries of $5.77 trillion in June 2022). There is a slight difference with MBS. Unless they default, mortgages eventually are repaid, so, if held to maturity, not only do they disappear from the Fed's balance sheet, they disappear from the system completely as the mortgagor uses bank deposits to extinguish the mortgage.

6. I put "repay" in quotation marks because this is really just a cancelling operation within the consolidated government, the bonds and the government deposits being on both, but opposite sides, of the central bank's and the government's (treasury's) balance sheet, respectively.

7. The reference is to the mythical hotel from the famous 1976 song by the Eagles.

8. As explained in chapter three, if a central bank doing QT did not pay interest on reserves, it would have to drain all (or at least most) of the excess reserves created by its QE *before* it could start to raise its policy interest rate. This is what the BOJ had to do after it announced in March 2006 an end to its five-year QE undertaking; in the BOJ's case, however, because its QE had been so modest in size, compared with the subsequent QE of other central banks and of the BOJ itself, it was able to do this quite quickly, in about four months.

9. Board of Governors of the Federal Reserve System, "Statement Regarding Monetary Policy Implementation and Balance Sheet Normalization," January 30, 2019, https://www.federalreserve.gov/newsevents/pressreleases/monetary20190130c .htm.

CHAPTER 5: THE POWER OF MONEY TO CREATE INEQUALITY—AND WEALTH

1. Thomas Sowell, *Basic Economics: A Common Sense Guide to the Economy*, 5th ed. (New York: Basic Books, 2015), 269.
2. *Forbes*, "The World's Real-Time Billionaires," https://www.forbes.com/real-time-billionaires/#57fe9aa53d78.
3. *Forbes*, "The World's Real-Time Billionaires," https://www.forbes.com/real-time-billionaires/#152665583d78.
4. JP Morgan Chase & Co. 2022 Annual Meeting of Shareholders Proxy Statement, p.6, https://www.jpmorganchase.com/content/dam/jpmc/jpmorgan-chase-and-co/investor-relations/documents/proxy-statement2022.pdf.
5. *Forbes*, "The World's Real-Time Billionaires," https://www.forbes.com/real-time-billionaires/#152665583d78.
6. spotrac, "NBA Player Earnings," https://www.spotrac.com/nba/los-angeles-lakers/lebron-james-2257/; *Forbes*, "The World's Real-Time Billionaires," https://www.forbes.com/real-time-billionaires/#152665583d78.
7. Smiljanic Stasha, "The State of Homelessness in the US—2022," *Policy Advice* (blog), July 30, 2022, https://policyadvice.net/insurance/insights/homelessness-statistics/.
8. Kathryn J. Edin and H. Luke Shaefer, *$2.00 a Day: Living on Almost Nothing in America* (Boston: Houghton Mifflin Harcourt, 2015).
9. Thomas Piketty, *Capital in the Twenty-First Century* (Cambridge, MA: The Belknap Press of Harvard University Press, 2014), 439.
10. See also Malcom Gladwell, *Outliers: The Story of Success* (New York: Little, Brown, 2008); Nassim Nicholas Taleb, *Fooled by Randomness: The Hidden Role of Chance in Life and in the Markets* (New York: Random House, 2005); Sebastian Mallaby, *The Power Law: Venture Capital and the Making of the New Future* (New York: Penguin Press, 2022).
11. See Thomas Sowell, *Discrimination and Disparities* (New York: Basic Books, 2019).
12. Daniel Kahneman, *Thinking, Fast and Slow* (New York: Farrar, Straus and Giroux, 2011).
13. P. J. Lamberson, "Winner-Take-All or Long Tail? A Behavioral Model of Markets with Increasing Returns," *System Dynamics Review* 32, no. 3–4 (2016): 233–60.
14. Robert J. Gordon, *The Rise and Fall of American Growth: The U.S. Standard of Living Since the Civil War* (Princeton, NJ: Princeton University Press, 2016).
15. Andrew Marquardt, "CEO Pay Is Skyrocketing as the Average Worker Struggles to Keep Up with Inflation. Here's Who Got the Biggest Raises," *Fortune*, April 4, 2022, https://fortune.com/2022/04/04/median-ceo-pay-amazon-discovery-raises/.
16. Staff of Representative Keith Ellison, "Rewarding or Hoarding? An Examination of Pay Ratios Revealed by Dodd-Frank," May 2018, https://inequality.org/wp-content/uploads/2019/01/Ellison-Rewarding-Or-Hoarding-Full-Report.pdf.
17. Korn Ferry, "Age and Tenure in the C-suite," https://www.kornferry.com/about-us/press/age-and-tenure-in-the-c-suite.
18. William M. Lafferty, Lisa A. Schmidt, and Donald J. Wolfe Jr., "A Brief Introduction to Fiduciary Duties of Directors Under Delaware Law," *Penn State Law Review* 116, no. 3 (2012): 837–77.
19. Klaus Schwab with Peter Vanham, *Stakeholder Capitalism: A Global Economy that Works for Progress, People and Planet* (Hoboken: John Wiley & Sons, 2021).
20. Business Roundtable, "Statement on the Purpose of a Corporation," August 19, 2019, https://www.businessroundtable.org/business-roundtable-redefines-the-purpose-of-a-corporation-to-promote-an-economy-that-serves-all-americans.

21. Sebastian Mallaby, *More Money Than God: Hedge Funds and the Making of a New Elite* (New York: Penguin, 2010).
22. Rana Foroohar, *Makers and Takers: The Rise of Finance and the Fall of American Business* (New York: Crown Business, 2016).
23. Sofia Karadima, "The Seven Cross-Border M&A Deals That Shaped 2021," Investment Monitor, January 5, 2022, https://www.investmentmonitor.ai/analysis/merger-acquisitions-deals-2021.
24. Microsoft, "Microsoft to Acquire Activision Blizzard to Bring the Joy and Community of Gaming to Everyone, Across Every Device," January 18, 2022, https://news.microsoft.com/2022/01/18/microsoft-to-acquire-activision-blizzard-to-bring-the-joy-and-community-of-gaming-to-everyone-across-every-device/.
25. See Michael E. Hartmann, "How Much Money Is in Nonprofit Endowments in America?," *The Giving Review* (blog), Philanthropy Daily, July 27, 2020, https://www.philanthropydaily.com/how-much-money-is-in-nonprofit-endowments-in-america/.
26. Christopher Leonard, *Kochland: The Secret History of Koch Industries and Corporate Power in America* (New York: Simon & Schuster, 2019).
27. Maria Fernandes, "Jeff Bezos' Highest Earnings Years, Ranked," *The Richest*, November 15, 2019, https://www.therichest.com/lifestyles/jeff-bezo-years-earned-highest/.

CHAPTER 6: THE POWER OF MONEY TO WREAK HAVOC

1. Richard Fuld, "Testimony to Congress on Lehman Bankruptcy," House Oversight and Reform Committee, October 6, 2008, https://www.americanrhetoric.com/speeches/richardfuldlehmanbrosbankruptcytestimony.htm.
2. See Carmen M. Reinhart and Kenneth S. Rogoff, *This Time Is Different: Eight Centuries of Financial Folly* (Princeton, NJ: Princeton University Press, 2009); Robert Z. Aliber, Charles P. Kindleberger, and Robert N. McCauley, *Manias, Panics, and Crashes: A History of Financial Crises* (Houndmills, Basingstoke: Palgrave Macmillan, 8th ed., 2023). First published 1978.
3. Among the many good accounts of what caused the 2007–2009 Global Financial Crisis and how it played out are the following: Alan S. Blinder, *After the Music Stopped: The Financial Crisis, the Response, and the Work Ahead* (New York: Penguin Press, 2013); Andrew Ross Sorkin, *Too Big to Fail: The Inside Story of How Wall Street and Washington Fought to Save the Financial System—and Themselves* (New York: Viking, 2009); Financial Crisis Inquiry Commission, *The Financial Crisis Inquiry Report: Final Report of the National Commission on the Causes of the Financial and Economic Crisis in the United States* (New York: Public Affairs, 2011); Adam Tooze, *Crashed: How a Decade of Financial Crises Changed the World* (New York: Viking, 2018).
4. Paul Tucker, "The Repertoire of Official Sector Interventions in the Financial System: Last Resort Lending, Market-Making, and Capital," remarks at the Bank of Japan 2009 International Conference on the Financial System and Monetary Policy Implementation, Tokyo, May 27 28, 2009, 3.
5. Bank of Japan, "Proposal for a New Scheme to Promote Smooth Corporate Financing by Nurturing the Asset-Backed Securities Market (Summary)," April 8, 2003, https://www.boj.or.jp/en/announcements/release_2003/data/moo0304a.pdf.
6. See David Fettig, "The History of a Powerful Paragraph: Section 13(3) Enacted Fed Business Loans 76 Years Ago," Federal Bank of Minneapolis, June 1, 2008, https://www.minneapolisfed.org/article/2008/the-history-of-a-powerful-paragraph.

7. For details, see Board of Governors of the Federal Reserve System, Office of Inspector General, "The Federal Reserve's Section 13(3) Lending Facilities to Support Overall Market Liquidity: Function, Status, and Risk Management," November 2010, https://oig.federalreserve.gov/reports/FRS_Lending_Facilities_Report_final-11-23-10_web.pdf.

8. An extensive analysis of the 2008 FOMC transcripts is in Paul Sheard, "Step into the Boardroom: The FOMC's 2008 Post-Lehman Transcripts," Standard & Poor's Ratings Services RatingsDirect, March 7, 2014.

9. Meeting of the Federal Open Market Committee on September 16, 2008, 36, https://www.federalreserve.gov/monetarypolicy/files/FOMC20080916meeting.pdf.

10. FOMC Meeting, September 16, 2008, 51.

11. FOMC Meeting, September 16, 2008, 51.

12. The recession triggered by the COVID-19 pandemic was deeper than the one triggered by the Global Financial Crisis, but the recovery was quicker: in the former, US real GDP fell by 10.1 percent in two quarters and recovered its pre-recession level in four quarters, while in the latter real GDP fell by 4.0 percent in four quarters and took six quarters to surpass its pre-recession level.

13. Fannie Mae and Freddie Mac are the names these government-sponsored enterprises commonly go by. Their official names are the Federal National Mortgage Association and the Federal Home Loan Mortgage Corporation, respectively.

14. Ben S. Bernanke, "Current Economic and Financial Conditions," speech at the National Association for Business Economics 50th annual meeting, Washington, DC, October 7, 2008, https://www.federalreserve.gov/newsevents/speech/bernanke20081007a.htm.

15. Meeting of the Federal Open Market Committee on October 28–29, 2008, 149, https://www.federalreserve.gov/monetarypolicy/files/FOMC20081029meeting.pdf.

16. FOMC Meeting, October 28–29, 2008, 150–151.

17. Henry M. Paulson, Jr., *On the Brink: Inside the Race to Stop the Collapse of the Global Financial System* (New York: Business Plus, 2010), 208, 216.

18. The long title of the Dodd-Frank Act, appropriately, was: "An Act to promote the financial stability of the United States by improving accountability and transparency in the financial system, to end 'too big to fail', to protect the American taxpayer by ending bailouts, to protect consumers from abusive financial services practices, and for other purposes."

19. Famous twentieth-century economist Frank Knight drew an important distinction between risk and uncertainty, viewing risk as quantifiable uncertainty. See Frank H. Knight, *Risk, Uncertainty, and Profit* (New York: Harper & Row, 1965).

20. Steven E. Landsburg, *The Armchair Economist: Economics and Everyday Life* (New York: The Free Press, paperback edition, 1993), 9. See also Steven D. Levitt and Stephen J. Dubner, *Freakanomics: A Rogue Economist Explores the Hidden Side of Everything* (New York: HarperCollins, 2005).

21. Jules Ottino-Loffler, "How Much Was the Japanese Imperial Palace Worth?," *Amaral Lab* (blog), August 11, 2016, https://amaral.northwestern.edu/blog/how-much-was-japanese-imperial-palace-worth.

22. "Citigroup Chief Stays Bullish on Buyouts," *Financial Times*, July 9, 2007, https://www.ft.com/content/80e2987a-2e50-11dc-821c-0000779fd2ac.

23. Ezra F. Vogel, *Japan as Number One: Lessons for America* (Cambridge, MA: Harvard University Press, 1979).

24. Paul Sheard, "The Japanese Economy: Where Is It Leading in the Asia Pacific?," in *Japan's Future in East Asia and the Pacific: In Honour of Professor Peter Drysdale*, eds. Mari Pangestu and Ligang Song (Canberra: Asia Pacific Press, 2007), 1–30.

CHAPTER 7: THE FOLLY OF THE EURO

1. Mario Draghi, "Verbatim of the Remarks Made by Mario Draghi," speech at the Global Investment Conference, London, July 26, 2012, https://www.ecb.europa.eu /press/key/date/2012/html/sp120726.en.html.

2. The ECB sets monetary policy for the whole of the euro area, but members of the euro area also retain their own national central banks. The Governing Council of the ECB, which makes the monetary policy decisions, comprises the six members of the ECB's Executive Board and the governors of the national central banks of the twenty euro area countries. In 2014, the ECB assumed responsibility for supervising banks in the EU, under a framework called the Single Supervisory Mechanism. The ECB together with the national central banks and the Single Supervisory Mechanism form what is known as the Eurosystem. Yet another term, the European System of Central Banks, refers to the ECB together with the national central banks of all EU members.

3. The twenty-four signatories to the Maastricht Treaty were all men, as were the heads of states of the twelve countries they represented.

4. Everything about the EU is quite complicated and almost any general statement you make is subject to qualification. Although member states are supposed to adopt the euro, the UK and Denmark joined on the condition that they would not be required to do so.

5. The Westphalian system refers to the system of international relations based on the primacy of, and relations between, sovereign states whereby states have exclusive authority over their own territory. The name derives from the Peace of Westphalia, the name given to two peace treaties signed in 1648 that ended the Thirty Years' War (1618–1648), although many modern scholars dispute this genesis; see Andreas Osiander, "Sovereignty, International Relations, and the Westphalian Myth," *International Organization* 55, no. 2 (2001), 251–78.

6. There is no provision in the EU's governing treaties for a member state that adopts the euro to subsequently abandon the euro and return to its domestic currency, and the exchange rate at which a member state enters the euro is "irrevocably [fixed]" (Article 140(3) of the Treaty on the Functioning of the European Union). However, there is a relatively straightforward procedure for a member state to leave the EU, which, if it had adopted the euro, would presumably mean abandoning the euro, too. The United Kingdom is the only member state to date to leave the EU, but it had not adopted the euro, so there was no need to traverse this tricky monetary and constitutional territory.

7. The renminbi is the Chinese currency. The yuan is the unit of account of the Chinese currency, although the term is often used to refer also to the currency, in much the same way as "the pound," the unit of account in the United Kingdom, is used to mean the British currency, "sterling." In many countries, there is no distinction: in the US, for instance, the dollar refers to both the currency and to the unit of account.

CHAPTER 8: THE POWER OF INTERNATIONAL MONEY

1. Connally's quote is legendary and widely cited, but I have struggled to locate the original source. It is not mentioned in the official US State Department record of the November 22–23 meeting. See Office of the Historian, "191. Editorial Note," Foreign Relations of the United States, 1969–1976, Volume III, Foreign Economic Policy; International Monetary Policy, 1969–1972, https://history.state.gov /historicaldocuments/frus1969-76v03/d191.

   The source seems to be Paul Volcker's recollection of Connally's comment. Volcker does not attribute the comment to Connally speaking at the G-10 meeting, but to his making it "at a later stage," as after August 1971. See Paul A. Volcker and Toyoo Gyohten, *Changing Fortunes: The World's Money and the Threat to American Leadership* (New York: Times Books, 1992), 81.

2. According to the Bank for International Settlement's *Triennial Central Bank Survey of Exchange and Over-the-Counter (OTC) Derivatives Markets in 2019*, https://www .bis.org/statistics/rpfx19.htm (and using world GDP data from the Federal Reserve of St. Louis FRED economic database), the ratio of annual foreign exchange market turnover to world GDP increased from 13.5 times in 2001 to 27.4 times in 2019.

3. See the press release announcing the awarding of the prize to Mundell: https:// www.nobelprize.org/prizes/economic-sciences/1999/press-release/.

4. WorldAtlas, "How Many Currencies Exist in the World?," accessed October 21, 2022, https://www.worldatlas.com/articles/how-many-currencies-are-in-the -world.html.

5. The shares are for the $11.18 trillion in reserves for which the currency breakdown is reported. See International Monetary Fund Currency Composition of Official Foreign Exchange Reserves, https://data.imf.org/?sk=e6a5f467-c14b-4aa8 -9f6d-5a09ec4e62a4.

6. The source for these figures are the respective websites of the monetary authorities, as accessible in the Wikipedia entry, "List of Countries by Foreign-Exchange Reserves": https://en.wikipedia.org/wiki/List_of_countries_by_foreign -exchange_reserves.

7. Carol Bertaut, Bastian von Beschwitz, and Stephen Curcuru, "The International Role of the Dollar," *FEDS Notes*, Board of Governors of the Federal Reserve System, October 6, 2021, https://www.federalreserve.gov/econres/notes/feds-notes /the-international-role-of-the-u-s-dollar-20211006.html.

8. US Department of the Treasury, Bureau of the Fiscal Service, *Treasury Bulletin* September 2022, https://www.fiscal.treasury.gov/files/reports-statements /treasury-bulletin/b2022-3.pdf.

9. By price-quantity space, I mean a graph with price on the vertical axis and quantity on the horizontal axis, the typical way in which economists depict demand and supply curves.

10. Tetsuji Kawamoto, "Helped by Weak Yen, Japan Remains Top Creditor Nation with Record Net Assets," *Reuters*, May 26, 2022, https://www.reuters.com/markets /currencies/japan-remains-top-creditor-nation-net-external-assets-grow-2022 -05-27/.

11. Barry Eichengreen, *Exorbitant Privilege: The Rise and Fall of the Dollar and the Future of the International Monetary System* (Oxford, UK: Oxford University Press, 2011), 4.

12. The idea that the country supplying the reserve currency is fated to run a current account deficit is associated with the economist Robert Triffin and is sometimes called the "Triffin dilemma" or "Triffin paradox."

13. Board of Governors of the Federal Reserve System, "Swap Lines FAQs," March 19, 2020, https://www.federalreserve.gov/newsevents/pressreleases/swap-lines -faqs.htm.

14. C-Span 3, "'Which Foreigners Got the Fed's $500,000,000,000?' Bernanke: 'I Don't Know,'" Representative Alan Grayson, July 21, 2009, YouTube video, 5:11, https://www.youtube.com/watch?v=n0NYBTkE1yQ.

CHAPTER 9: THE DISRUPTIVE POWER OF CRYPTOCURRENCIES

1. Timothy C. May, "The Crypto Anarchist Manifesto," Satoshi Nakamoto Institute, 1988, https://nakamotoinstitute.org/crypto-anarchist-manifesto/.

2. Satoshi Nakamoto, "Bitcoin: A Peer-to-Peer Electronic Cash System," Bitcoin.org, October 31, 2008, https://web.archive.org/web/20140320135003/https://bitcoin .org/bitcoin.pdf.

3. CoinMarketCap, https://coinmarketcap.com/.

4. Francis Elliot and Gary Duncan, "Chancellor Alistair on Verge of Second Bailout for Banks: Billions May Be Needed as Funding Squeeze Tightens," *The Times*, January 3, 2009.

5. Robert Gordon points out how ubiquitous horses were in American cities in the mid- to late nineteenth century: "Towns and cities were entirely dependent on horses for transportation, construction, and distribution. In the geographically compact city of Boston in 1870, 250,000 citizens shared the streets with 50,000 horses." See Robert J. Gordon, *The Rise and Fall of American Growth: The U.S. Standard of Living Since the Civil War* (Princeton, NJ: Princeton University Press, 2016), 48.

6. For a far more detailed exposition, see the excellent book by Eswar S. Prasad, *The Future of Money: How the Digital Revolution Is Transforming Currencies and Finance* (Cambridge, MA: The Belknap Press of Harvard University Press, 2021), particularly chapter six. For another accessible and comprehensive treatment of cryptocurrencies, see Oonagh McDonald, *Cryptocurrencies: Money, Trust and Regulation* (Newcastle upon Tyne, UK: Agenda Publishing, 2021).

7. See Jeffrey E. Garten, *Three Days at Camp David: How a Secret Meeting in 1971 Transformed the Global Economy* (New York: Harper, 2021).

8. See Milton Friedman, *A Program for Monetary Stability* (New York: Fordham University Press, 1960).

9. Nic Carter, "How Much Energy Does Bitcoin Actually Consume?," *Harvard Business Review*, May 5, 2021, https://hbr.org/2021/05/how-much-energy-does -bitcoin-actually-consume.

10. See Irving Fisher, *100% Money* (New York: Adelphi Company, rev. ed., 1936) and Laurence J. Kotlikoff, *Jimmy Stewart Is Dead: Ending the World's Ongoing Financial Plague with Limited Purpose Banking* (Hoboken, NJ: Wiley, 2010).

11. Samuel P. Huntington, *The Clash of Civilizations and the Remaking of World Order* (New York: Simon & Schuster, 1996).

12. See Mitchell Zukoff, *Ponzi's Scheme: The True Story of a Financial Legend* (New York: Random House, 2005).

13. See Lawrence Goodwin, *The Populist Moment: A Short History of the Agrarian Revolt in America* (Oxford, UK: Oxford University Press, 1978).

14. See Anneke Kosse and Illaria Mattei, "Gaining momentum—Results of the 2021 BIS survey on central bank digital currencies," BIS Papers No.125, May 2022.

15. See, for instance, Bank for International Settlements, "Central Bank Digital Currencies: Foundational Principles and Core Features," Report No. 1 in a series of collaborations from a group of central banks (2020); Bank of England, "New Forms of Digital Money: Discussion Paper" (March 2020); Bank of England, "Responses to the Bank of England's March 2020 Discussion Paper on CBDC" (June 2021); Christian Barontini and Henry Holden, "Proceeding with Caution—A Survey on Central Bank Digital Currency," Bank of International Settlements Paper No. 101 (January 2019); Bank of Japan, "The Bank of Japan's Approach to Central Bank Digital Currency" (October 2020); Board of Governors of the Federal Reserve System, "Money and Payments: The U.S. Dollar in the Age of Digital Transformation" (January 2022); European Central Bank, "Report on a Digital Euro" (October 2020); Group of Thirty, "Digital Currencies and Stablecoins: Risks, Opportunities, and Challenges Ahead" (July 2020); Tommaso Mancini-Griffoli, Maria Soledad Martinez Peria, Itai Agur, et al., "Casting Light on Central Bank Digital Currency," IMF Staff Discussion Note (November 2018); President's Working Group on Financial Markets, the Federal Deposit Insurance Corporation, and the Office of the Comptroller of the Currency, "Report on Stablecoins" (November 2021); World Bank Group, "Central Bank Digital Currency: A Payments Perspective" (November 2021).

16. See Central Bank of the Bahamas, "Press Release: Public Update on the Bahamas Digital Currency Rollout," December 31, 2020, https://www.centralbankbahamas .com/viewPDF/documents/2020-12-31-14-45-14-PSDPress-Release-Public-Update -20201231-Final.pdf.

17. See Alexander Lee, "What Is Programmable Money?," *FEDS Notes* (Washington, DC: Board of Governors of the Federal Reserve System), June 23, 2021, https://doi .org/10.17016/2380-7172.2915.

18. On the latter possibilities, see Kenneth S. Rogoff, *The Curse of Cash* (Princeton, NJ: Princeton University Press, 2016).

19. See Shoshana Zuboff, *The Age of Surveillance Capitalism: The Fight for a Human Future at the New Frontier of Power* (New York: Public Affairs, 2019).

CONCLUDING THOUGHTS

1. Lewis Carroll, *The Adventures of Alice in Wonderland & Through the Looking-Glass* (London: Weidenfeld and Nicolson, The Heirloom Library edition, 1949), 175.

2. See, for instance, John Kay, *Other People's Money: The Real Business of Finance* (New York: Public Affairs, 2015); Adair Turner, *Between Debt and the Devil: Money, Credit, and Fixing Global Finance* (Princeton, NJ: Princeton University Press, 2016).

3. For some ideas on how to do this, see Paul Sheard, "Rethinking Macroeconomic Policy Frameworks," in *The 10 Years After: The End of the Familiar . . . Reflections on the Great Financial Economic Crisis*, ed. Reinventing Bretton Woods Committee (Astana, Kazakhstan: Astana International Financial Center, 2018), 177–85; Paul Sheard, "A More Robust Macroeconomic Policy Framework Is Required," in *America in the World 2020*, eds. Noel V. Lateef and Michael R. Austin (New York: Foreign Policy Association, Great Decisions Special Edition, 2020), 45–51; and Paul Sheard, "It's Time to Rethink the Conventional Macroeconomic Policy Framework," *Bretton Woods Committee* (blog), April 29, 2019, https://www.brettonwoods.org/article /its-time-to-rethink-the-conventional-macroeconomic-policy-framework.

4. See Anat Admati and Martin Hellwig, *The Bankers' New Clothes: What's Wrong with Banking and What to Do About It* (Princeton, NJ: Princeton University Press, 2013).

5. See US Department of Treasury, "U.S. Treasury Announces Unprecedented & Extensive Sanctions Against Russia, Imposing Swift and Severe Economic Costs," February 24, 2022, https://home.treasury.gov/news/press-releases/jy0608; US Department of the Treasury, "Treasury Prohibits Transactions with Central Bank of Russia and Imposes Sanctions on Key Sources of Russia's Wealth," February 28, 2022, https://home.treasury.gov/news/press-releases/jy0612; White House Briefing Room, "Joint Statement on Further Restrictive Measures," February 26, 2022, https://www.whitehouse.gov/briefing-room/statements-releases/2022/02/26/joint-statement-on-further-restrictive-economic-measures/; European Commission, "Ukraine: EU Agrees to Exclude Key Russian Banks from SWIFT," https://ec.europa.eu/commission/presscorner/detail/en/ip_22_1484.

6. When comparing the size of one country's economy to that of another, purchasing power parity (PPP) compares their relative costs of living, rather than just using nominal exchange rates to convert (nominal) GDP into a common comparable standard (usually US dollars). Typically, PPP bumps up the size of less developed economies relative to that of more developed ones. If you were a US resident and you spent your US dollars in India, in theory they would buy more comparable goods and services there; if an Indian resident took their rupee and tried to buy the equivalent collection of goods and services in the US, they would come up short. The most famous PPP measure is *The Economist*'s Big Mac Index. Economists usually compare national economies on a PPP basis.

7. For some flavor of this, and where Russia fits in, see the "Joint Statement of the Russian Federation and the People's Republic of China on the International Relations Entering a New Era and the Global Sustainable Development [sic]," http://www.en.kremlin.ru/supplement/5770.

8. See Alan Greenspan, "Technology and Trade," remarks before the Dallas Ambassadors Forum, Dallas, Texas, April 16, 1999, https://www.federalreserve.gov/boarddocs/speeches/1999/19990416.htm.

9. See, for instance, Martin Ford, *Rise of the Robots: Technology and a Jobless Future* (New York: Basic Books, 2015); Carl Benedikt Frey, *The Technology Trap: Capital, Labor, and Power in the Age of Automation* (Princeton, NJ: Princeton University Press, 2019).

INDEX

ABOUT THE AUTHOR

DR. PAUL SHEARD, an Australian American economist, is the former Vice Chairman of S&P Global and a former Senior Fellow and Research Fellow at Harvard Kennedy School. He held chief economist positions at S&P Global, Standard & Poor's Rating Services, Nomura Securities, and Lehman Brothers, and was Japan Strategist and Head of Japanese Investments at Baring Asset Management. He taught at the Australian National University, Osaka University, and Stanford University, and was a Foreign Visiting Scholar at the Bank of Japan. Sheard has been a member of several World Economic Forum expert councils and was appointed by two prime ministers to serve on advisory committees of the Japanese Government. He was a nonexecutive director of ORIX Corporation for seven years, sits on the board of the Foreign Policy Association, and is a member of the Bretton Woods Committee, the Council on Foreign Relations, and the Economic Club of New York. Sheard is the author or editor of several books and numerous academic articles, market newsletters, and op-eds, and his book *The Crisis of Main Bank Capitalism* won the prestigious Suntory-Gakugei Prize in the Economics–Politics Division. Sheard has a Master of Economics and PhD from Australian National University. In 2019, his alma mater, Monash University, conferred on him an honorary Doctor of Laws. He lives on the Upper West Side of Manhattan and likes to walk with his wife in Central Park.